P9-CED-128

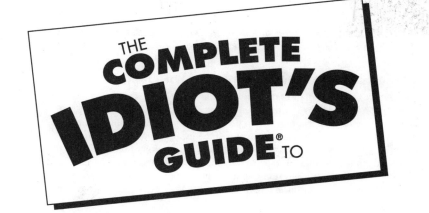

THE
COMPLETE
IDIOT'S GUIDE® TO

Personal Finance in Your 40s and 50s

by Sarah Young Fisher and Susan Shelly

ALPHA

A Pearson Education Company

We extend love and appreciation to our families: Dallas (Chuck), Rob, and Catie Fisher, and Mike, Sara, and Ryan McGovern.

Copyright © 2002 by Sarah Young Fisher and Susan Shelly

All rights reserved. No part of this book shall be reproduced, stored in a retrieval system, or transmitted by any means, electronic, mechanical, photocopying, recording, or otherwise, without written permission from the publisher. No patent liability is assumed with respect to the use of the information contained herein. Although every precaution has been taken in the preparation of this book, the publisher and authors assume no responsibility for errors or omissions. Neither is any liability assumed for damages resulting from the use of information contained herein. For information, address Alpha Books, 201 West 103rd Street, Indianapolis, IN 46290.

THE COMPLETE IDIOT'S GUIDE TO and Design are registered trademarks of Pearson Education, Inc.

International Standard Book Number: 0-02-864273-2
Library of Congress Catalog Card Number: Available upon request.

04   03   02   8   7   6   5   4   3   2   1

Interpretation of the printing code: The rightmost number of the first series of numbers is the year of the book's printing; the rightmost number of the second series of numbers is the number of the book's printing. For example, a printing code of 02-1 shows that the first printing occurred in 2002.

Printed in the United States of America

Note: This publication contains the opinions and ideas of its authors. It is intended to provide helpful and informative material on the subject matter covered. It is sold with the understanding that the authors and publisher are not engaged in rendering professional services in the book. If the reader requires personal assistance or advice, a competent professional should be consulted.

The authors and publisher specifically disclaim any responsibility for any liability, loss, or risk, personal or otherwise, which is incurred as a consequence, directly or indirectly, of the use and application of any of the contents of this book.

Publisher: *Marie Butler-Knight*
Product Manager: *Phil Kitchel*
Managing Editor: *Jennifer Chisholm*
Senior Acquisitions Editor: *Renee Wilmeth*
Development Editor: *Nancy D. Warner*
Senior Production Editor: *Christy Wagner*
Copy Editor: *Cari Luna*
Illustrator: *Jody Schaeffer*
Cover/Book Designer: *Trina Wurst*
Indexer: *Amy Lawrence*
Proofreading: *Svetlana Dominguez*

Contents at a Glance

Contents

Foreword

Not long ago, I dropped my 13-year-old daughter off at a girlfriend's house and met her mother for the first time. A charming woman in her 50s, she introduced me to her son, who was in his early 30s, and then to her infant grandson, who appeared to be on the verge of taking his first steps.

At the time, I thought it a bit unusual that someone could be dealing with a daughter's adolescent angst one moment and coaxing a grandchild to accept the wonders of solid foods the next. But I've come to realize that in many ways, her life patches together the crazy quilt that makes up one's 40s and 50s.

For years, those of us in this age group have heard about the impact our "bulge" in the population has had on everything from real estate values to the health care industry. Yet despite widely reported broad demographic trends and generalizations, the past and current experiences of the baby boom generation defy easy categorization. From the music we listened to as kids to the world events we witnessed, the framework that helped shape us varies. Tail-end boomers born in the late 1950s or early 1960s probably spent their teenage years listening to Stevie Wonder or Eagles albums, while those born in the mid-1940s might have danced to songs of Paul Anka or The Four Seasons. Some can recall the Vietnam War as vividly and passionately as they did when they were soldiers or college students, while others can only remember the era as grade-schoolers viewing grainy black-and-white war footage on TV.

Just as our past experiences differ, those of us in our 40s and 50s are also going through the full spectrum of life stages and financial concerns. One 50-year-old's greatest challenge may be figuring out how to pay for a son or daughter's wedding, while another may be just starting a college fund for his pre-schooler. His slightly older neighbor might be scratching his head about how he'll ever be able to pay for his daughter's dream wedding, just as his company has announced yet another downsizing in which early retirement is being "encouraged." And the woman down the street in her early 40s may be trying to regain her financial footing after a messy divorce.

Even with all these variations, people in their 40s and 50s share some similar financial concerns marked by new and sometimes daunting realities. Chief among them is a shortened time frame for reaching one's goals. In our 20s and 30s, with the luxury of decades to play "catch up," it was possible to put off saving in favor of spending without too much thought. With large expenses either at our doorstep or soon to arrive, procrastinating becomes a much less palatable or viable option.

Each generation faces a unique set of money issues, and those facing us are very different from those of our parents, many of whom came of age during World War II. Sure, colleges were expensive back when we populated campuses from the 1960s and early 1980s. But the cost of higher education has greatly outpaced the rate of inflation over the last 20 years, making it more difficult than ever to foot all or most of the bill for our children as our parents might have done.

And then there's retirement. For our parents' generation, early retirement was more of an option than an ultimatum from an employer. Employees retired when they felt ready, or at age 65, whichever came first, and could rely on a pension plan and Social Security to see them through their golden years.

Today, companies in downsizing mode—a group that encompasses almost all companies at one time or another—frequently sharpen their cutting tools on candidates for early retirement. Sure-thing, fixed pension plans have given way to savings plans that depend heavily on contributions from employees and investment success to provide retirement income. And the "security" of Social Security becomes less and less certain as the number of individuals supporting the fragile, pay-as-you-go system shrinks in relation to the number of people collecting from it. After years of paying taxes into the system, many of us rightly have serious doubts about whether we will ever get anything out of it.

Of course, the financial picture for today's baby boom generation is, in many ways, brighter than it has ever been. Many of us have hit our peak earning years in an economy that, for most of our lifetimes, has seen healthy growth. Two-income families have provided greater financial security and a safety net in the event of job loss. And despite the recent bear market, decades-long bull runs in the securities and real estate markets have allowed many of us to accumulate substantial personal savings, as well as ample equity in residences and vacation homes.

Many of us have rewarded ourselves with attractive homes, fun vacations, late-model cars, or other status symbols we could never afford when we were younger, and which our parents may not have indulged in to the same degree. Does this mean we are wealthier than our parents were at our age? It's hard to say. But judging from outward appearances, we have become much more in tune with the spending side of our personalities.

And there is not necessarily anything wrong with that. Even with all the publicity surrounding Internet-made millionaires barely out of college, statistics show that people with more years under their belts generally have more money in their bank accounts. Why shouldn't we enjoy it?

For many of us coming to terms with (gulp!) middle age, the key is to strike a balance between providing for large, imminent expenses that loom around the corner, such as a child's college education or wedding, with the rightful desire for here-and-now self-fulfillment. The two goals need not be mutually exclusive. With some careful planning, it's possible to enjoy the fruits of our labor in the present while creating financial security for ourselves, our children, and perhaps even our grandchildren in the future.

Marla Brill, author of *Windfall! Managing Unexpected Money So It Doesn't Manage You*

Introduction

Life is busy. Sometimes, we get too caught up in the hustle and bustle of every day to take time to look at the big pictures of our lives.

What do you want to be doing in 10, 15, or 20 years? Do you see yourself still working when you're 60, 65, or even 70? Or perhaps you'll be partially retired. Maybe you envision yourself finally moving into that house in the country you've always wanted, spending your days gardening and reading novels on the front porch.

Whatever your vision is for the rest of your life, now is the time to assure that you can make it happen. Now is the time, if you haven't done so already, to get your finances in good shape. This book will help you do just that. It offers the education and advice you need to successfully navigate the financial arena of middle age.

How This Book Is Organized

The Complete Idiot's Guide to Personal Finance in Your 40s and 50s is written in six parts. Each one addresses a different aspect of finances in middle age.

Part 1, "Taking a Look at the Big Picture," encourages you to step back and have a look at your life—both financial and otherwise. What do you have? What do you need and want? How can you improve your financial situation?

This part of the book also deals with taking care of yourself in ways not directly related to your finances. Middle age can be a stressful time, laden with responsibilities and worries. Taking care of yourself now is really important to assure that you'll be around to enjoy the rewards of good financial planning for a long time.

In **Part 2, "Your Kids and Your Money,"** we look at all the ways your kids consume your money, and why launching them into adulthood costs so darned much. Kids have big wants and needs these days, and, if you're financing them, you've got to be prepared.

If you're currently dealing with the high cost of video games, portable CD players, and mountain bikes, fasten your seat belts. It only gets worse as your little darlings start trading in their bikes for cars and choosing colleges. If you survive the shock of college tuition, give yourself a big pat on the back, but don't relax too much, there may soon be wedding bells ringing.

Kids are expensive; there's no two ways about it. Some methods of supporting kids, however, work better than others, and we'll examine some plans and strategies for getting the most out of your money.

In **Part 3, "Hearth and Home,"** we look at issues relating to where you live, and how you can avoid hitting financial snags as you deal with those issues.

As you get older, your housing needs or wants might change. You might find that your house is way too big, or there's too much lawn to keep up, or not enough kitchen now that the kids have moved out and you're doing more entertaining.

Maybe you're thinking of buying another home, or renovating the one that you have. Perhaps you've even decided to build a brand-new place. Any of these housing options can have a huge impact on your finances.

Part 4, "Life Changes," deals with major transformations that may occur as we get older. When you think about it, just about all changes affect your finances. You lose a job, get divorced, get remarried, start your own business, or experience the loss of a parent. Every one of those situations can directly impact your pocketbook. Knowing how to cope with life's surprises and changes can assure that your financial future remains intact.

Good investments, of course, are very important in financial planning. In **Part 5, "Smart Investing in This Stage of Life,"** you'll review some options for investing at work, and outside of work. We'll have a look at the stock and bond markets, and give you some ideas for investing lump sums, such as an inheritance or bonus. This section also gives advice on finding a good financial advisor. After all, you can't do everything by yourself.

Part 6, "Preparing for the Future," looks down the road a bit, and gives you sound advice about how to arrive there in good financial shape.

Nobody likes to think about preparing a will, but if you haven't already done so, you need to put that task at the top of your to-do list. Estate planning isn't just for old folks, and a will really is the first, and a very important, step in that planning.

This part also offers advice for helping aging parents make decisions concerning their finances, living arrangements, and so forth.

When you've finished the book, we hope that you'll have a clearer picture of your financial achievements so far, and what you need to do now to make sure you're set for a comfortable retirement.

Some Things to Help Out Along the Way

You'll find four types of sidebars in this book. They're meant to steer you away from trouble, amuse you with odd bits of information, clarify terms, or provide tips and advice.

Adding It Up

These are definitions that are meant to help you get a clearer picture of what you're reading in the text.

Don't Go There

These are warnings that are intended to make you stop and think before plunging into dangerous waters.

Money Morsel

These are financial tips and advice, intended to help you improve your current situation and prepare for the future.

Go Figure

These are bits and pieces of information that you can share with friends and family. They contain a lot of information, some practical, and some just for fun.

Acknowledgments

The authors would like to thank the many people who provided time, information, and resources for this book. Especially, we thank our editors—Renee Wilmeth, Nancy Warner, and Christy Wagner—for their advice, guidance, and patience.

A very special thank you goes to Gene Brissie of James Peter Associates, and to Bert Holtje, who we hope is finding time to relax a bit and generally enjoying life.

Trademarks

All terms mentioned in this book that are known to be or are suspected of being trademarks or service marks have been appropriately capitalized. Alpha Books and Pearson Education, Inc., cannot attest to the accuracy of this information. Use of a term in this book should not be regarded as affecting the validity of any trademark or service mark.

Part 1

Taking a Look at the Big Picture

Mid life tends to creep up on you while you're not looking, only to take you completely by surprise one morning when you look into the mirror and can't imagine who's looking back at you.

Once you've acknowledged mid life, or middle age, it's a good idea to step back and take a look at where you are in life. Do you have everything that you need? Is there enough money left for some extras? Are you planning ahead to assure you'll be able to finance big expenses like college and weddings, while not draining your retirement funds?

Chapters 1 through 5 deal with topics that will help you to assess your financial situation, and to improve it if it's not to your liking. You ready? Let's get started.

Chapter 1

So, How's Mid Life Treating You?

In This Chapter

- ◆ Defining mid life and middle age
- ◆ Who knows where the time goes?
- ◆ Nothing ever stays the same
- ◆ Taking charge of your health
- ◆ Did you want ham or cheese on that sandwich?

We hear and talk a lot about mid life. We have mid-life babies, mid-life crises, mid-life issues, and mid-life career changes. But when exactly is this period of time we call mid life? Just when can we expect our mid-life babies, issues, crises, or career changes to come?

Apparently, the definition of mid life depends on who you ask. It's variously defined as the period between 45 and 65 years old, the period between 40 and 60 years old, and even the period between 25 and 75 years old. We would have hated to think when we were 25 that we were already middle-aged. On the other hand, coasting along in middle age until you hit 75 doesn't sound all that bad.

Obviously, the definition of middle age—or the mid-life period—is subjective. And, as we've all certainly realized by the time we reach mid life, age is more of a state of mind than a number. Everybody's all probably met energetic, fun-loving men and women in their 70s who seem years younger than some stuffy, sedentary 50-year-olds.

For the purposes of this book, we're going to assume that middle age—at least as far as your finances are concerned—is the period between when you're 40 and when you're 60. When we talk about personal finances in your 40s and 50s, we're talking about middle-age finances.

We'd all do well to talk—or at least think carefully—about our middle-age personal finances. After all, if we've already hit mid life, can retirement be far ahead? Hopefully, everybody's in pretty good shape with retirement savings, and we'll all have enough to live comfortably and still be able to have some fun right now.

Unfortunately, there are reports out there that indicate many baby boomers—that would be the 76 million of us born between 1946 and 1964—are largely unprepared financially for retirement. The American Savings Education Council's 1999 Retirement Confidence Survey showed that the average amount of assets of 40-somethings is less than $50,000. It should be clear to everyone that $50,000 in savings, even if it's coupled with Social Security payments, isn't enough to assure a comfortable retirement.

The Metropolitan Life Insurance Company reports that the average American spends 18 years in retirement, but fewer than half have put money aside specifically for those years. Those could be 18 very, very long years.

And studies show that most people need at least three quarters as much money to maintain their standard of living during retirement as they required while working. This varies, of course, depending on factors such as health, location, and so forth, but most financial advisors these days are recommending 75 percent or more.

Money Morsel

Social Security is the primary source of income for about 66 percent of elderly Americans. And experts say the rate of dependency is unlikely to drop in the future because of low savings rates among baby boomers.

Social Security benefits for the average retiree are about 40 percent of his or her preretirement earnings. As you can see, there's a large gap between what Social Security provides and what it costs to live in retirement.

That's why it's so important to take a long, hard look at your finances now, while you still have the time to improve your financial situation, if necessary.

How Time Flies

Time is a funny concept. It sometimes seems like just yesterday that you were in college, enjoying the frat life and worrying about whether you'd get that term paper written on time. Or that you'd just landed your first job and were trying to figure out what you would wear and how you would act when your boss came around. You can remember perfectly how you scrimped and saved so you'd have enough money to rent that cute little apartment near your office building.

Time continues, and you remember your wedding day. And the day your first child was born. And the second one. It seems like minutes ago that your daughter was sitting on your lap, absolutely entranced as you read *Sleeping Beauty* for the five-hundredth time. Now she's 19 and starting her second year of college.

No wonder some days we look in the mirror and hardly recognize the middle-aged person who looks back at us. How did *that* happen? Who *is* that person with the graying hair and noticeable laugh lines?

It's hard to comprehend that 25, 30, or 35 years have passed by since those college days. Or that your children, who seemingly just yesterday were looking to you for all the answers, now have all the answers and are grown up and living on their own. Maybe you're a grandparent. You might have moved on from that little, rented apartment to a house, and then a bigger house, and now an even bigger house and a vacation home.

Time passes quickly, that's for sure. We're at what might be the busiest period of our lives—juggling kids, jobs, and aging parents while still trying to find time to walk the dog, work out at the gym, and maintain some semblance of a social life. We often think that there ought to be hours added to every day, just so we can accomplish everything we need to.

> **Go Figure**
>
> The average life expectancy is 76.7 for men and 79.5 for women, according to the National Center for Health Statistics. You'll get an idea of how time flies when you consider where you are on your passage through life.

Dealing with Changes

The bottom line is, we're not kids anymore. And as we move through middle age, our thoughts naturally turn more and more to what's ahead of us. Someone's on-the-Internet definition of middle age is "the period when you start looking at your future in terms of limitations rather than opportunities." We'd like to think that all our futures hold great opportunities, and few limitations.

The fact is, however, that middle age and beyond often presents challenges that our younger years don't. Many of us will be faced with health issues that we wouldn't have given a thought to 20 years ago. Maybe you've had to give up jogging because your knees can't take it anymore. Or your doctor may have suggested that you start exercising because you're 30 pounds overweight and your blood pressure is too high.

A lot of middle-aged folks are helping to care for their aging parents. Anyone who has been there can tell you how incredibly demanding and draining that job can be. At the same time, you may still be taking care of—or at least still worrying about—your kids. And let's face it, kids can cause big worries, especially in the financial department. There's college, cars, weddings, and down payments for homes.

While all of this is going on in your life, you might suddenly face a major career change. Reports show that 142,208 Americans lost their jobs in January 2001. Call it laid off, downsized, terminated, let go, or just plain old fired, that's almost 150,000 people who in one month found themselves without a job. Losing a job when you're 23 might not be that big of a deal. Losing one when you're 52, however, is bound to be a bit more unsettling and traumatic.

How you react to and cope with all these changes of life will, in part, determine what your future will be like. If, at 52 years old, you lose the job you've had for the past 25 years, will you fall apart, moaning about how life (and the American workplace) is unfair and clearly geared toward younger people? Or will you be innovative and figure out how to make your work situation better than it ever was?

Money Morsel

If you're thinking middle age isn't so great, consider this quote by Thomas Arnold, a British author and educator. "Probably the happiest period in life most frequently is in middle age, when the eager passions of youth are cooled, and the infirmities of age not yet begun; as we see that the shadows, which are at morning and evening so large, almost entirely disappear at midday."

If your doctor tells you that you're 30 pounds overweight and your blood pressure is creeping up toward a dangerous level, will you buy yourself a treadmill and start working out every morning? Or will you bury your troubles under a big, thick, juicy steak and baked potato with all the trimmings?

We all must deal with changes as we pass through middle age. Some of them we'll like, others we won't. It's important to remember, though, that the way we handle those changes will impact on our futures and the futures of those around us.

How's Your Health?

You probably gathered from what you've already read, that health gets to be a big deal once you hit mid life. And even if you didn't catch that idea from this chapter, you've no doubt realized it from listening to your friends talk.

A gathering attended primarily by folks in their 40s and 50s can sound more like a visit to a health clinic than a party. Backaches, bad knees, and high cholesterol are high-priority topics of conversation. Comparing the benefits and side effects of various prescription drugs becomes an amusing pastime. Let's face it. Most of us never would have wasted time 20 years ago talking about our aches and pains. Largely because we didn't have aches and pains back then.

The news of what happens to our bodies as we age can be pretty darned discouraging. We gradually lose elastic tissue, resulting in wrinkles and sagging skin. Many of us also have already seen the result of thinning hair.

Between the ages of 30 and 75, our hearts lose 30 percent of their efficiency. As if that's not bad enough, our lungs and kidneys become 40 percent less efficient, and our livers 10 percent less.

If you're not already wearing glasses or contacts, consider yourself lucky. By the time we reach our mid-40s, many of us require reading glasses, thanks to a very common refractive error known as presbyopia. If presbyopia, which also is known as "aging eyes" doesn't get you, myopia (near-sightedness) or hyperopia (farsightedness) just might.

Hearing in many people also becomes less efficient during the 40s and 50s. Most women go through menopause during these years. Bone density decreases. Sleeping habits tend to change. It's enough to make you want to sign up for assisted living, isn't it?

> ### Don't Go There
>
> If you're thinking about buying long-term-care insurance, don't put it off too long. Finding a policy when you're relatively young and healthy is less expensive and a lot easier than waiting until you've already developed health problems. You'll read more about long-term care insurance in Chapter 24, "You're Never Too Young to Plan."

> ### Go Figure
>
> The average person reads at about 16 inches away from his eyes. And it takes just about 40 years for the average person to lose focus ability at 16 inches, due to presbyopia. That means you've got to change the distance at which you read, or get yourself a pair of reading glasses.

All right, enough already. We know we're getting older, and we know that our bodies aren't the same as they were 10 or 20 years ago. That doesn't mean, however, that we should hang up our jogging shoes and head for the showers for good. There are plenty of things we can do during our 40s and 50s to maintain (or help to achieve) good health. Here are a few:

- **Get to your ideal (or near there) weight and stay there.** Being overweight puts extra stress on your heart and other major organs, and contributes to conditions like diabetes, high blood pressure, back problems, and respiratory problems.

- **Quit smoking.** You know that smoking is bad for you. It causes lung cancer and other cancers, is a factor in high blood pressure, strokes and heart problems. Check out "How to Quit: Useful Resources to Quit Smoking" on the Centers for Disease Control and Prevention Web site. You can find it at www.cdc.gov/tobacco/how2quit.htm.

◆ **Exercise.** Exercising helps you to lose weight or maintain a healthy weight. It also can help to regulate cholesterol, strengthen bones, lower your cancer risk, and fight off depression. A bonus for women is that regular exercise can decrease the unpleasant symptoms of menopause. We all know that exercise is good for us, and yet 34 percent of Americans who are 50 or older don't get any. Many more don't get enough. Ask your doctor what kind of exercise would be best for you, then get out there and just do it. Find a buddy if you don't think you'll go it alone.

Money Morsel

Health is more than just being able to get through the day. The World Health Organization describes health as "a state of complete physical, mental, and social well being and not merely the absence of disease or infirmity." There you have it.

Watch what you eat and drink. Cut back on fried and fatty foods (fast-food comes to mind), and limit red meat to twice a week. Eat more fruits and vegetables—most people don't get the five-a-day as recommended for better health. Eat lots of grains and watch out for highly processed foods and overly sugary ones. Keep an eye on how much alcohol you're consuming. If you think you're drinking too much and you can't stop, call the Center for Substance Abuse Treatment at 1-800-662-HELP (1-800-662-4357). Staff will give you information about treatment programs in your area and answer any questions you might have.

Get regular check-ups. Experts recommend a physical every one to three years for people in their 40s and 50s. Ask your doctor what tests and screenings you should have as you age, and how often you need them. Some of those tests include mammograms, prostate cancer screenings, pap smears, cholesterol checks, electrocardiograms, blood pressure checks, stool screenings, rectal exams, and bone density checks. Don't forget eye exams, including glaucoma screenings after age 50.

Take charge of your own health. If you know your blood pressure tends to run high, keep track of it. Don't wait until you see your doctor to have it taken. There are lots of pharmacies and health clubs that have blood pressure monitoring machines, and they're usually free. Know the warning signs of cancer and pay attention if you develop any of them. Read up on vitamin supplements and use them if you think they're necessary. Get enough calcium.

Stay safe. Wear a seat belt. Wear a helmet when biking. Avoid unnecessary risks like using rickety ladders or towels instead of hot pads to remove food from the stove. Wear protective goggles when you're mowing the lawn or using power tools. Practice safe sex. Don't ever drive after you've been drinking, and don't ride with anyone else who's been drinking.

Make time for fun and foster your relationships. The happiest people aren't those who spend 80 hours a week at the office and another 20 catching up with more work at home.

They're not the ones who are constantly plugged in and on call and connected. Happy people know how to kick back and have some fun. They take time—or make time—to spend with the people they love, and they don't take themselves—or life too seriously.

Taking care of yourself during middle age will go a long way in ensuring good health in old age. People who are in good physical condition are more likely to be able to remain living on their own than those who aren't. Being fit and healthy also will keep your insurance premiums at a payable level.

Feeling a Little Bit Stressed?

If you're feeling a little bit stressed (and who isn't these days?) don't worry. A limited amount of stress is actually good for you. It's what makes you productive and active. When stress gets to be too much, however, it can have some really nasty effects on your health. It also can badly strain your relationships and make everyone around you pretty miserable.

All of us get stress from different areas of our lives. Maybe it's your job that's stressing you out. Maybe it's your kids, or your spouse, or your ex, or your dog, or your mom, or the noisy neighbors across the street, or the fact that next Tuesday is your forty-eighth birthday. Let's face it. We live in a pretty stressful world.

A publication from the Clemson University Cooperative Extension Service called "Stress Management—Taking Charge," offers the following suggestions for managing stress:

♦ Manage your physical and psychological well-being so you can resist the harmful effects of stressful events. You can do this by forming good support groups you can turn to when the pressure gets to be too much. You should never keep anger and anxiety bottled up inside of you. Eating well and exercising will keep you healthy and better able to deal with stress. You also should keep a good balance of personal, social, and work-related activities.

> **Go Figure**
>
> Studies on the connection between stress, health, and the proper functioning of the immune system show that stress contributes to 50 percent of all illnesses in the United States.

♦ Monitor your present level of stress so that you can recognize early warning signs of stress and do something about the problems causing it. You could be experiencing stress-related problems without even realizing it. Early warning signs of stress include: exaggerated, out-of-proportion anxiety, excessive moodiness, withdrawal from responsibility, insomnia, feelings of helplessness and dependency, changes in appetite and sex drive, chronic fatigue, and susceptibility to illness. If these symptoms sound familiar, you might be a bit more stressed than you thought.

◆ Maneuver to avoid extremely stressful situations by eliminating the causes of stress and changing your reactions to stressful events. If driving your dad to his therapy appointment every Monday, Wednesday, and Friday at 2 P.M. makes you nuts, takes a chunk out of your day, and puts you behind in your work, try to find a way out of your commitment. Do you have a brother or sister with whom you could alternate weeks? Is there a senior services center that might provide transportation? Recognize the situations that cause your stress, and try to avoid them. If you can't avoid them, recognize that they will be stressful, and handle the stress in the best way that you can. And teach yourself to relax. It's hard to be stressed out when you're relaxed. Practice taking even, measured breaths, and shrug your shoulders up toward your ears and hold. Get away from your desk and take a walk.

Money Morsel

You can check out Clemson's report on handling stress at this Centers for Disease Control and Prevention Web site: www. cdc.gov/niosh/nasd/docs4/ sc98012.html.

Stress may make the world go 'round, but too much of it can stop us in our tracks. If you feel that you have more stress than you can handle, contact a counselor, psychologist, or mental health agency in your area.

Recognizing that you have a problem and getting help before the problem gets out of control is a smart and responsible thing to do. You'll be thankful that you did, and so will your family, friends, and co-workers.

Welcome to the Sandwich Generation

If you're like many baby boomers, you've got two or three kids of your own. And depending on how old you were when they were born, they may be anywhere from toddlers to adults living on their own. We know 50-somethings who are just now making the rounds of elementary school concerts and parent-teacher conferences, and other 50-somethings who are happily playing with their grandkids.

In addition to your kids, regardless of their ages, let's assume that your parents are still living, and that they're elderly. And you're helping to take care of them. Sound familiar? Hello! Welcome to the sandwich generation.

Most of us don't plan to become our parents' caregivers. It begins very suddenly one night, when you get a call from your mother, telling you your dad's had a stroke and is in the hospital. At that point, your life may change drastically.

Suddenly, instead of tending to your kids, your house, your job, your volunteer work, and your social life—you find yourself running back and forth from the hospital, making arrangements for Dad to go a rehabilitation center for therapy, trying to figure out insurance statements, and helping Mom take care of the house while Dad's not there. All of that occurs in addition to your obligations to your own family. Needless to say, being sandwiched between your kids and your parents is not the easiest, or most comfortable, place to be.

If you are a member of the sandwich generation, you're at least in good company. The National Family Caregivers Association (NFCA), based in Kensington, Maryland, estimates that there are 25 million family caregivers in the United States. These caregivers, nearly one quarter of whom are watching over aging parents, provide about two thirds of all home care services. The NFCA estimates the value of these services at $300 billion a year.

More and more baby boomers are caring for aging parents, and making major changes in their own lives as a result. The fastest growing segment of the population today is those who are 85 years or older, including many of our parents. Our parents are living longer, and many of us will be challenged to step up and take our turns as caregivers.

> ### Go Figure
>
> A survey by the National Family Caregivers Association shows that of the 25 million family care-givers in the United States, 81 percent are female, 79 percent are married, and 70 percent are between the ages of 40 and 60. On a scary note, nearly half of all caregivers are thought to suffer from prolonged depression.

If you are, you should know that there's help available. Several good books and Web sites about caring for aging parents are listed in Appendix B, "Resources." You also could contact your local area agency on aging for information about care giving.

One thing to remember is that planning ahead can save you a lot of trouble and heartache if the time ever comes that you need to step in as a caregiver. The best thing you can do is to sit down with your parents today and talk to them. That isn't an easy task, because the topics you need to discuss are difficult. Some of the issues you should discuss with your parents are …

- ◆ Do they have a will and a living will or a health care power of attorney? You might assume that your parents have a will, but don't bet on it. Plenty of people simply never get around to writing one. Living wills and health care powers of attorney are legal documents that express your parents' wishes regarding future medical care and treatment. It also allows them to appoint someone to act on their behalf. Knowing your folks' wishes regarding medical treatment can save you a lot of grief if you need to make decisions for them.

- ◆ What are their preferences for long-term care? Do they want to stay at home for as long as possible, or might they consider a retirement community or assisted living facility? Let them know what options are available to them.

◆ How much income will be available for long-term care and what insurance policies do your parents have? Long-term care is expensive. You don't want to be surprised to find out there's a lot less money available than you thought.

◆ Where are their important documents and records? You should know where your parents keep documents such as their will and living wills, tax returns and receipts for taxes paid, deeds to real estate and titles to vehicles, documents relating to any business ventures they may be involved with, stock certificates, bank materials, and so forth. You also should make sure you have keys to their home and any other buildings they own.

Knowing that you'll be available to help them may be comforting to your parents, but it's likely to be a touchy subject. Admitting that they need help probably isn't easy for them, and the changing roles of parents and children may be difficult.

Breaking the ice and starting a conversation, however, will bring this difficult topic to the surface and begin discussions about how to handle it.

Mid life is not without challenges, to be sure. There are, however, plenty of opportunities as well, both for now and the future. Take a deep breath, and think about all the good aspects of your life. And now, let's get started on some of those middle-age financial issues.

The Least You Need to Know

◆ There are lots of definitions for middle age, but it means for sure that we're not kids anymore.

◆ Time flies, and nothing stays the same, so you've got to be able to cope with the changes life brings.

◆ Paying attention to your health now can help you avoid a lot of problems when you reach your 60s, 70s, and 80s.

◆ A reasonable amount of stress may help you to be productive, but too much can have serious consequences on your health and relationships.

◆ If you're caring for elderly parents as well as your kids and all your other obligations, know that there's help available for you.

Figuring Out Where You Are in Life

In This Chapter

- ◆ Need and want are very different
- ◆ Recognizing your financial needs
- ◆ Taking care of the most important needs first
- ◆ Considering things that you want
- ◆ Conducting periodic financial reality checks

It's easy to look around at your friends and neighbors and notice that they seem to have more than you do. Maybe they have bigger houses with nicer furnishings—perhaps even swimming pools or tennis courts. There's a new car parked in the driveway, while you're trying to figure out if your old sedan will make it through another winter.

Of course, you and your husband did take that great ski vacation last winter to celebrate your twentieth wedding anniversary. And you've managed to get two of your three kids through college without going broke.

Once in a while we need to stop and take a good, long look at exactly where we are in our lives. We need to tally up the pluses and minuses—financial and otherwise. We'll be talking more about assets and liabilities in Chapters 3, "On the Plus Side," and 4, "On the Minus Side." In this chapter, we'd like to focus on the difference between need and want, and how important it is to know the difference.

Maybe you really do need a new car. But you don't need a $42,000 Lincoln Navigator, even if there is one parked in your neighbor's driveway. A bigger house would be nice, but with the kids getting near the point when they'll be moving out, do you really need—or want—it? Do you really want the extra responsibilities and costs that accompany expensive cars and large homes?

It's easy to confuse wants and needs, especially in this affluent society where we're continually told we need more and more.

Knowing What You Need

A need—a real need—is something we require in order to live. We need food, water, shelter, and clothing. A want, however, is something much different than a need.

Although we say that really need to buy a treadmill before winter sets in, we no more really *need* a treadmill than we need a mosquito bite. We'd like to have a treadmill before winter sets in so we can avoid accumulating the extra 5 or 10 pounds again this holiday season. And, when we think about it, we actually could achieve that goal without a treadmill if we took to walking outside, cross-country skiing, shoveling snow, or passing up the brie and truffles at the holiday parties.

We need the real needs in life, although there are lots of ways to shave down costs of food, clothing, and housing. If we learn to control and limit our needs, our chances of having enough money to get what we need during the years of retirement improve dramatically.

Don't Go There

It's easy to overspend on "needs," such as food and clothing. We need to eat, but we don't need to eat steak and lobster every week. Try to cut these expenses when you can so you'll have enough money to fund other needs, such as emergency accounts and insurance policies.

If everyone knew they would die when they were 62 years old, it would be easier to know what you could spend today. There would be less concern about having enough money for the future, because there would be less future. Fortunately, though, most of us will live to be older than 62, and hopefully will be healthy and active long past that age. Because of that, we will need to have enough money so that we're not waiting by the mailbox each month for the Social Security check to come in so we can go to the grocery store.

Besides our basic human needs of food, water, shelter, and clothing, people in their 40s and 50s have some basic financial needs. By the time you've reached financial middle age, you should have—that is, you need—certain tools to assure your financial health both now and in the future.

Emergency Fund

We live in an uncertain world. Those of us who hadn't considered that fact previously got a loud and decisive wake-up call on September 11, 2001, when hijacking terrorists killed thousands of civilians, destroyed the hundred-plus-story towers of the World Trade Center in New York, and badly damaged the Pentagon building.

That event sent an already skittish stock market into chaos, causing great uncertainty, fear, and problems for millions of investors. Maybe you sometimes wake up at night, wondering what the state of your retirement fund will be when you get around to retiring. Internet companies come and go, their huge profits of one quarter plummeting to huge losses in the next. Even established, well-heeled firms are not immune to the shifts and dips of the economy, especially in these uncertain and troublesome times.

Because of all this uncertainty, an emergency fund should be near the top on your list of mid-life financial needs. Unfortunately, funding a source of emergency money is difficult for many who are trying to find enough cash for vacation, summer camp for the kids, and throwing that forty-fifth wedding anniversary party for their parents.

 **Money Morsel**

Most financial advisors suggest that you have between three and six months' income saved in an emergency fund.

You'll be extremely happy, however, to have an emergency fund available in the event that life throws you a curve ball. You lose your job; it happens all the time. You're in a car accident and have to supplement your health insurances for the expenses it doesn't pick up. Your car dies and you need a new one. Your elderly mother needs some financial help while she's in an assisted living facility recovering from a stroke.

Some people need an emergency fund to tap into because their income is unsteady. If you're in a business where you earn a lot of money some of the time, and next to nothing at other times, you should have an emergency fund you can use during the lean periods.

Many people have gotten into big debt trouble because they encountered financial hardship and didn't have an emergency fund. Let's face it. You need money to live. If your income suddenly stops and you have no emergency money to fall back on, what are you going to do? Pull out your good old Visa and MasterCard, what else?

Sure, you could live perfectly well on your credit cards for several months, depending on your limits. Nearly, everyone from your doctor to your grocery store clerk will be happy to take your plastic instead of cash, and your credit card issuer will be delighted.

The party ends, however, when after three months you're still out of work and your credit card bill is up somewhere around $12,000. Then what?

Establishing an emergency fund should be a priority in your financial plan. You can use a money market fund (more about those in the next section of this chapter), so your money is accessible and liquid.

The Right Accounts

Saving up three to six months' income for an emergency fund is a significant undertaking. And, you'll want to make sure that you invest your emergency fund—and all your money, for that matter, in the best possible accounts. Hopefully, we all understand that some accounts are better than others for maximizing your money.

The 1990s was a banner decade for the stock market. We sat back and watched it climb higher and higher and higher—knowing all the while that the high times couldn't possibly last forever. They didn't. The market dropped dramatically in 2000, hopefully sending the clear message to everyone that it's important to diversify your investments. It's really important, especially considering the present uncertainty of the stock market after the terrorist attacks in September 2001, to have some money in funds that aren't subject to the whims of the stock market.

A client keeps his new car fund in an equity fund, also called a stock fund. This is a mutual fund that limits its investments to shares of common stock. The risk factor of these funds varies, depending on the type of stocks in which the funds invest. The fund had done well until 2000, when it tanked with a 19 percent drop. Goodbye Lexus, hello Honda.

Money such as what you have in an emergency fund, a new car fund, or new house fund, should be invested in a money market fund. A money market fund is a mutual fund with a nonfluctuating $1 investment value per share. That means that you buy a share at $1, and sell the share later at $1. Like a savings account, if you put $800 into a money market fund, you'll get $800 out—plus the interest.

Money market funds are good, safe choices for short-term investing. Your original investment is fairly secure, while you earn competitive interest rates. Money market funds aren't the most exciting investment vehicles, but they assure that your money will be there when you need it. That's why they're desirable accounts for money such as an emergency fund, which needs to be kept at a constant value.

Money market accounts usually pay more interest than savings or checking accounts at the local bank. And most money market funds permit some check writing, though they may set a minor check minimum—$500. Some money market funds are now insured, so be sure to check with your bank or credit union.

Money Morsel _____

Certificates of deposit (CDs) typically pay higher interest than bank accounts, and some pay more than money market accounts. The problem with using CDs to store your emergency fund account is that, if you need the money and have to withdraw it from the CD before the specified investment time ends, you'll be penalized—perhaps severely. If there's a hefty penalty, it's possible that you could end up with less money than you had invested.

There are various types of money market funds. Some are invested in only U.S. Treasury obligations and are not subject to local income tax liability. Some are invested in municipal bonds and similar investments, so they are known as tax-free investments. If you purchase a tax-free mutual fund that participates only in investments within your state, the fund is called a triple tax-free fund. That means it is not subject to federal, state, or local income tax. If you're in one of the higher tax brackets, this kind of money market fund might be something you'll want to consider.

Insurance

You don't often hear somebody say that they want insurance. "Boy, I wish I could double up on my homeowner's insurance," is a phrase that certainly would cause you to look twice at the person speaking. Insurance, unfortunately, is something we buy because we need it—not because we want it.

We need insurance to protect ourselves from the environment, from others, and from ourselves. Insurance is a way to reduce risk by sharing financial losses within a group of people. There are many types of risks, both financial and nonfinancial. These risks include the following:

- ◆ Disability or death
- ◆ Property loss
- ◆ Personal liability
- ◆ Risk from failure of others, such as a breach of contract
- ◆ Speculative risks, such as the stock market

When considering these risks, you must decide if the protection you receive is worth the cost of the insurance you buy.

Many types of insurance are required. If you have a mortgage, your lender requires you to have homeowner's insurance. Most states require auto insurance.

Money Morsel

An insurance deductible is an amount you'll be required to pay in the event that you file a claim. Your insurance company will pay the remaining expenses, after your deductible. The higher the deductible you have, the lower your premium should be.

In addition to these required insurances, you must decide what type of coverage you need for your family, and what you're able to spend on them. Riders, options, and basic insurance all come at a cost so you need to review the price and the coverage as part of your total financial picture.

You may need to provide your own insurance for some risks by putting aside funds on your own. You might want to set aside money for dental bills or a nursing home stay, for instance.

Let's look at some of the kinds of insurance that are important to you and your family.

Disability Insurance

Disability insurance kicks in if you're unable to work for an extended period of time due to illness or injury. This type of insurance is imperative if your family depends on your income to keep a house, maintain its current standard of living, and so forth.

Don't depend on health insurance in the event that you're out of work due to being disabled. Your health insurance will cover (hopefully) your medical bills, but it won't cover the loss of your salary.

Most disability insurance policies don't cover the full amount of a salary, but kick in about 60 percent. Hopefully, you'll have an emergency fund to supplement the gap between your income and the insurance. There are various types of disability insurance, and some factors you should be sure to consider when comparing them.

An own-occupation policy pays benefits if you're unable to perform your normal work. Other policies will only kick in if you're unable to do the job for which you're reasonably trained. Many infirmities permit you to work, but not at the type of job you held prior to your infirmity.

Own-occupation policies are the most expensive type of disability insurance, because it's more likely that the insurance company will have to pay you. It may not be worth the extra cost unless you're earning big bucks in a specialized job and would need to take a pay cut if you were forced to change jobs.

When looking at disability insurance plans, keep the following information in mind.

- **Guaranteed renewable.** This means that your policy can't be cancelled if you get sick. If your policy requires you to have a physical every so often, you risk losing your coverage just when you need it.

- ◆ **Waiting period.** This is the period of time between when you get disabled and when the plan starts paying. The longer the waiting period, the less the policy should cost. The minimum on most policies is thirty days, and the maximum can be up to two years. A good compromise would be 90 days to 6 months.

- ◆ **Cost-of-living adjustments.** This feature automatically boosts your benefits, either by a specified amount or depending on the rate of inflation.

- ◆ **Future insurability.** This feature allows you to buy additional coverage down the road. It's good if you have a job in which you expect to be earning much more in several years than you are presently.

There is a greater probability of being disabled than of dying by the time you're 65. Disability insurance is coverage that is often overlooked but very, very important.

Homeowner's Insurance

Your home probably is the biggest investment you'll ever make, and you need an adequate *homeowner's insurance* policy to protect it and what's in it.

You'll be required to have homeowner's insurance before you get a mortgage. The trick is to get a policy that offers the best protection for your home and its contents.

It's worth taking a look at your current policy to see exactly what it covers. Most homeowner's policies have personal property coverage, as well as liability coverage. Thus, if your house burns down, all your furniture will be replaced under the personal property coverage. Make certain you have enough to cover what you own.

It's important to realize that most standard insurance policies don't cover special property. To insure items such as sterling silver, jewelry, and artwork, you'll need to get an insurance rider at an additional cost.

In addition to protecting your house and property, homeowner's coverage also provides liability coverage in case somebody falls down your front steps and breaks an ankle. We'll spend a lot more time on homeowner's insurance in Part 3, "Hearth and Home." For now, just understand that it's a need.

Adding It Up

Homeowner's insurance covers your home and its contents against perils, which are the insurance industry's term for anything bad that could happen to your house. Perils may include fire, damage caused by falling objects (think trees), an explosion in your heater, riots, vandalism, and hurricanes.

Auto Insurance

If you own and drive a car, you need insurance to protect yourself from injury in the event of an accident. Auto insurance is expensive, and nearly every state requires drivers to have it. Even if it's not required, however, you can't afford to go without it.

Auto insurance includes different types of coverage, but the one that nearly all states require is liability. Liability covers bodily injury and property damage for you and others, if you're at fault in an accident. Most states require that you carry a minimum amount of bodily injury coverage—usually $25,000 per person, and $50,000 per accident.

Personal Catastrophic Casualty Policy (PCAT)

Your auto and homeowner's policies provide liability coverage up to a certain amount. What happens, however, if someone sues you for more than the limitations of your policy?

> **Go Figure**
>
> Many insurance companies provide maximum liability coverage under your homeowner's policy of $500,000. If your neighbor falls down your steps and sues you for $750,000, you're likely to be in for some sleepless nights.

We live in an extremely litigious society. If you have a pool, a trampoline in your yard, or a dog with a nasty temper, you may need liability coverage that is more than that provided on your homeowner's and auto policies.

A PCAT policy comes in $1 million increments. If you've got sizeable assets, it's good to think about getting one. A PCAT policy supplements other policies that you have and is not overly expensive (usually about $150 a year). Such a policy should cover damages from accidents at your home and automobile accidents.

Life Insurance

Nobody likes to think about needing life insurance. If you're a source of income for your family, however, it really is necessary. If you're single, you probably don't need much life insurance. If you're married or in a relationship, but don't have children, you should have life insurance if your spouse or partner would have to make a drastic change in financial lifestyle if you were no longer around. If you have kids, you need life insurance.

Life insurance should be purchased according to income replacement need and should be five to eight times the amount of your current salary. There are two types of life insurance policies: term and cash value.

- ◆ **Term life insurance.** This type of policy pays a predetermined amount of money to your beneficiaries if you die during the term in which you're insured. All you have to do, of course, is keep paying your annual premium. The trick is that the premium increases as you get older, and may eventually become prohibitive. Term insurance is invaluable for your family if you die prematurely. It can be a source of college money, cover the cost of a mortgage, and generally provide financial security. This type of policy is intended to be used for a limited time period and is generally for younger persons. Most people can't afford to keep the coverage as they get older because the cost increases so much.

- ◆ **Cash value life insurance.** If the cost of your term life insurance policy has been creeping up, it might be time to consider trading it in for a cash value policy. Under a cash value life insurance plan, part of the premium is used to provide death bene-fits, and the rest is used to earn interest. It's both a protection plan and a savings plan that can actually provide some income in your later years. There currently are two types of cash value insurance. One invests your money in an assortment of mutual funds, while the other invests it in something similar to a certificate of deposit, with a fixed interest rate. Ask your insurance agent for more details about cash value life insurance policies.

Money Morsel

If your kids are out of college and pretty well settled on their own, a term life plan might not make as much sense for you as it used to. This might be a good time to think about exchanging your term life policy for a cash value plan.

Knowing What You Want

The financial necessities we've discussed—an emergency fund, the right accounts, good insurance policies—all can be the step between being comfortable and feeling secure, and fearing that you may lose everything that you've worked for. Once you're secure that you've got all your needs covered, you can begin to think about the things you want.

Maybe you want to build a great portfolio (we spend all of Part 5, "Smart Investing in This Stage of Life," talking about investments), or perhaps you've been dreaming of a fabulous vacation to the Australian Outback. A little vacation home might be nice, or maybe now's a good time to think about upgrading your car. Let's have a look at some of the wants you can think about after your needs have been met.

A Tropical Paradise for Two

Maybe you've put off vacations for a while, opting instead to use that money to buy and furnish your home, braces for the kids, a new car here and there, and so forth. Your vacations may have been pretty much restricted to a day or two at the beach, or a quick get-away to a nearby city.

Finally, though, you're able to think about a real vacation. Maybe you'll take your family to Disney World for a week, or you and your spouse will finally visit the Eiffel Tower. It's great to be able to plan to do something you've wanted for a long time, but take a minute to weigh the cost of a great vacation against the security you want to have in retirement.

Money Morsel

Check out Travelocity.com for comparisons of prices of plane fares, hotel accommodations, car rentals, and even complete vacation packages. It's on the Internet at www.travelocity.com.

We're not saying that you shouldn't see the Eiffel Tower—no way. The opportunity for travel is enriching and broadening. We're saying, however, that maybe you don't need to sail to Europe on the *Queen Elizabeth II* and stay in the most luxurious Parisian hotel.

Great trips are wonderful, but they're a luxury. Just make sure you don't go footloose and fancy free at the expense of your mortgage and retirement fund. And watch that you don't run up outrageous credit card bills that you'll end up paying until it's time for your next vacation.

A Cozy Little Cabin

Maybe you're at the point now where your mortgage payment is very manageable, or you've even got it paid off. If so, you might be considering buying a vacation home.

A vacation home can be anything from a hunting cabin in the mountains without running water or electricity to a luxury condo on Maui. What you get depends on what you want, and what you can afford. Some folks love roughing it in the woods, while to others, the only vacation spot worth considering comes complete with all the comforts of home and a beautiful beach.

A vacation home can be a good investment and a means of getting a break at income tax time (more about that in Chapter 12, "A Home Away from Home"), but again, it's definitely a want—not a need. If you've paid off your home or have a very manageable mortgage, you have the funds needed for your children's college educations, your car payments are under control, and you don't have any other outrageous bills, a second home may be within your reach.

A BMW of Your Very Own

If you've never had a brand-new car, or at least one that you really liked, you might be thinking now about the perfect machine.

Maybe you're ready to say good-bye to the stodgy station wagon or van you always needed to haul around your kids, their friends, and all their gear. Maybe the sedate sedan you've been cruising in just doesn't do it for you anymore. Perhaps you're looking for something with a little more style.

Luxury cars are expensive, there's no question about it, and frankly, unless you've got more cash than you know what to do with, we just can't see spending $30,000 or $40,000 on a car. If you're in a comfortable financial position at this stage, however, and you've always wanted a BMW, go ahead and give one a test drive.

This may be the point in your life when leasing a vehicle makes more sense than buying it. You don't need a big down payment to lease, and you normally can afford to lease a car that you couldn't comfortably afford to own outright.

Leasing is the practice of paying a specified amount of money over a specified time for the use of a product. It's similar to renting, although some types of leases allow you to buy the vehicle at the end of the contract.

An open-end lease permits you to buy the vehicle for its residual value at the end of your agreement. The residual value is what a car is worth at the end of a lease agreement, and the amount you'd pay to buy the vehicle at that time. A closed-end lease agreement states that you simply turn in your vehicle and walk away.

There are some good reason to lease a car, and also some good reasons not to. We'll talk more about leasing in Chapter 7, "Trading In the Bikes for Cars," when we discuss buying a car for your teenager.

There are many more wants in which you could indulge yourself if you're financially able to do so. You could buy a boat, hire a decorator to do your house, or refurbish your kitchen. It's not wrong to want things, or to buy the things that you want. Just make sure you take care of the needs first.

Understanding the Difference Between Want and Need

We've spent a significant amount of time discussing necessities versus wants. Hopefully, you have a clear understanding of your financial needs, and what you might be able to afford past those needs.

Just as it is for our children, the cookie jar is tempting. There are lots and lots of goodies out there, and advertisers tell us that we should have them all.

Credit cards and bank credit can be a tempting means of providing us with the toys we think we need. If we recognize the difference between wanting and needing, however, we may be better able to resist the temptations of overspending and running up debt. Middle age is a great time to look ahead, financially. The trick is to balance the present with the future, so you'll be able to enjoy yourself now as well as after you retire.

Get Real

It's imperative at this stage of your life to do a quarterly reality check. Are you struggling to make ends meet? Are you paying the minimums on your credit cards while wondering if you'll be able to pay them off the next time around? Or are you saving every penny you can, gloating about how comfy your retirement years will be?

Most of us are somewhere in between, and that's good. You need to recognize what you have, what you need, and what you can afford to want. Hopefully, you recognize that wanting something doesn't mean you've got to have it immediately—or even have it at all.

If you know your limitations and stay within your means, you'll be much better off financially in the long run and a lot happier in the years to come.

The Least You Need to Know

- There's a big difference between what you need and what you want, and it's important to know the difference.
- Everyone should have an emergency fund containing between three and six months' income.
- Having the necessary insurances will assure that you're covered and give you peace of mind and security.
- Once you've got all your financial needs taken care of, you can think about some of the things you want, such as vacations or a new car.
- It's important to do periodic financial checks so you know what you can afford—and what you can't.

Chapter 3

On the Plus Side

In This Chapter

- ◆ Considering your assets
- ◆ Your home as an asset
- ◆ Salaries, savings, and investments
- ◆ The vehicle that you drive
- ◆ Valuing nonmaterial assets

Many of us probably look back occasionally with incredible fondness at our youth. We think of how carefree we were, with no house to take care of, no children to worry about, no elderly parents requiring our time.

Sure, you had a job and some other obligations, but those were nothing like the responsibilities you have today. As you look back through those rose-colored glasses, however, try to recall some of the less desirable aspects of your younger years.

Most of us probably had incredible anxiety over things like whether the guy or girl you were going out with Friday night would like you, and how the evening would turn out. Or whether your boss would notice the report he asked for was a day or two late. Would you be able to afford a new muffler for your car? Would you have enough money to go away for the weekend, or did you have to save it all in order to pay the rent next week?

When you really think about it, you'll probably conclude that being young and just starting out had some drawbacks as well as some advantages.

Hopefully, you're more financially comfortable today than you were 20 or 30 years ago even if you're not quite at where you had hoped you would be by now. In this chapter, we're going to consider your assets—both the material kind and the really important assets like family and good friends. Let's take a look on the plus side. You just might end up feeling better than you thought you would after reading this.

Your House

If you own a home, you've got a great investment, and you're in some good company. Almost 72 million Americans owned their own homes in the latter part of 2000, according to the U.S. Department of Housing and Urban Development.

Whether you've lived in your home for 25 years or two months, it no doubt is very important to you. We go to extraordinary lengths to make our homes and yards attractive, and we invest a lot of ourselves—not to mention our money—in our homes. Why?

To most people, a house is much more than a building in which they live, or an investment that they hope to resell for more than what they paid.

Your house is the place where you raise your kids, and maybe care for your grandkids, too. It's where you entertain your friends and family. Your house is filled with (or will be) memories of birthday parties, dinners with friends, and nights by the fireplace.

You decorate your house on special holidays, and watch to make sure the roof isn't leaking or the paint peeling too badly from the window sash. Your house is your escape from the big, noisy, and busy world. It's the place you can go and take your shoes off, and just relax.

In addition to all that, your home probably is the most expensive investment you've ever made. Whether you paid $80,000 or $300,000 for your home, it probably represents a good portion of your overall assets. If you've been in your home for a while and have a lot of equity, the property is a good source of financial security. Equity, you'll remember, is the difference between the current market value of the home, and what you still owe on the mortgage.

> **Go Figure**
>
> Almost 68 percent of Americans own their own homes—a record high. There must be something about home ownership that we like!

You can borrow money against the equity in your home. Or you can downsize after your kids have moved out and invest the money you make from the sale of the bigger house in your retirement fund.

If you find when you're older that you're strapped for cash, you can even take out a home equity conversion loan on your home, also known as a reverse mortgage.

These are arrangements in which a lender pays the homeowner (that would be you) a monthly payment with the idea that the lender will be repaid after the property is sold. It's the opposite of a traditional mortgage, in which the person living in the home pays a monthly rate with the goal of eventually owning the property.

There are several types of reverse mortgages, including those that are federally insured, those that are uninsured, and one called a reverse annuity mortgage. Each type includes advantages and disadvantages. A reverse mortgage, which is available in most states through a bank or agency, is probably not something you would consider for now. Reverse mortgages aren't available to folks in their 40s and 50s, but you can keep this information in mind for later, or in case it becomes necessary for your parent.

Maybe you're at the point where you're starting to think about moving. Maybe you're tired of spending all weekend keeping up with your yard work and are thinking of moving to a place with less upkeep. Or maybe you're looking for a home that would be suitable in case Dad has to move in with you. Maybe your house is just too big, now that the kids have moved out.

All of Part 3, "Hearth and Home," is devoted to housing issues, so we won't spend time discussing them now. If you are thinking about moving, however, you've made a wise choice to start looking at your options early, instead of waiting until you're forced to make a move. It's always better to move because you want to than because you have to.

> **Money Morsel**
>
> Just for fun, go to www.realtor.com, and click on the area that says "average home price." Enter your zip code when the box comes onto the screen, and you'll get, in addition to the average home price, all kinds of great information about your own zip code area. You can check out the crime rate, average age and income of residents, and a lot more.

Income

Regardless of what your income is, you probably wish it was more. The most frequent job-related complaints don't involve bosses or working conditions—they're all about salary. Living these days costs a lot of money, there's no question about it. We swear that groceries cost more every time we go to the store. Gas prices are enough to make you want to take a train. Dinner for two can easily top $60 or $70. Even a movie for two without the popcorn can run you $15 or $20. If you're still looking down the road at paying college costs while trying to save up for retirement at the same time, chances are you sometimes feel a little squeezed in the financial department.

Maybe you're lucky and have a fabulous job with a great salary. They're out there, after all. In 1999, John T. Chambers, the president of Silicon Valley–based Cisco Systems received total compensation (cash, bonuses, his gain on stock options, and other forms of compensation) of $121,701,629. That's—no kidding—more than $120,000,000.

Money Morsel

For information about every job you can imagine, including average salaries, required training, job outlooks, and so forth, check out the 2000–2001 edition of the Occupational Outlook Handbook from the Bureau of Labor Statistics. You can find it online at stats.bls.gov/ocohome.htm.

Don't feel too inferior, though. Chambers, who was 50 at the time, was the highest-paid of all Silicon Valley executives that year. Poor Timothy Cook, the senior vice president at Apple Computer, was the 100th highest paid. He made only $4,260,818 in total compensation. Cook was 39 at the time.

In all likelihood, your salary doesn't come anywhere close to what either Chambers or Cook earned in 1999. Hopefully, though, you're making enough to live comfortably while still able to save some money for later in life. Regardless of what your salary is, it's probably your main source of income and a very important asset. It's what you count on, week after week, and month after month. It buys your groceries, pays your mortgage or rent, and keeps your lights, phone, and cable turned on.

Without your salary coming in, life could get pretty uncomfortable. You'd probably be forced to very quickly alter your lifestyle and rethink your priorities. You should have an emergency fund available that would cover your living costs for three to six months in the event that you lose your job, get sick and can't work, or face other emergency circumstances.

If you're really dissatisfied with the salary you're earning and you're convinced that you've performed your job at least adequately, consider asking your boss for a raise. Check out comparable salaries in similar companies. Look in the classified employment ads to get an idea of salaries for jobs like yours. If you do decide to ask for a raise, keep these pointers in mind.

- ◆ Approach your boss with confidence. He probably doesn't enjoy talking about money any more than you do.

- ◆ Have some data ready. Show him some salaries of comparable jobs at other companies that are higher than yours.

- ◆ Remind your boss of your strong points and times that you've gone above and beyond the call of duty.

- ◆ Listen respectfully to her responses, but don't give up too easily if you really think you deserve a raise.

- ◆ Be polite, even if your boss says no to your request, and start planning how you can improve your pitch for the next time around.

If you're a good employee and you're staying in a job for which you're badly underpaid out of loyalty, or inertia, or because you're scared to make a move, know that you're not doing yourself or your family any favors. There is a high demand for experienced, dependable employees right now. If you're not getting the salary you deserve, you should look around at what else is available.

Money Morsel _____

If you're looking for a job, remember that the Age Discrimination in Employment Act of 1967 was written for people who are 40 or older. It's to protect us from employment discrimination based on age, both as employees and job applicants. If you feel that you've faced discrimination because of your age, contact the U.S. Equal Employment Opportunity Commission. Check to see if there's an office in your area. If there isn't, call 1-800-669-4000.

If your salary doesn't seem like it's enough, maybe you ought to look at bit more closely at how you're spending it. We'll talk about budgeting in Chapter 5, "Getting It All Together," but for now, just give a little thought about where your salary—one of your chief assets—goes.

Savings and Investments

If you've been watching and planning your finances up to this point, you should have some money in savings accounts and other investments. Most people automatically think of the stock market in terms of investing, but you could have multiple investments without owning one stock.

There are many types of investments—stocks being just one of them. If you've been contributing to a 401(k) plan at work, that's a very good investment, and one you'll be really happy to have when you retire. Other retirement-based investments you might own include individual retirement accounts, Roth IRAs, SEP IRAs, Keoghs, and annuities.

In addition to retirement accounts, which we really hope you've got a good start on, you may have other investments as well. These could include stocks and bonds, mutual funds, money market accounts, and certificates of deposit. You may have money invested in real estate, personal property, or collectibles.

You should have some money available in savings accounts, although it's not a good idea to keep too much money there. Most financial planners will advise you to keep enough in your savings account to help you with your bills and ensure adequate cash flow. If a major bill is due on Tuesday, and pay day isn't until Friday, you can use the money in your savings account to cover the bill, then pay yourself back when you get paid. You probably shouldn't keep more than about $3,000 in a savings account.

All these accounts and other investments are important assets that you should carefully monitor.

Vehicles

We Americans sure do love our vehicles, don't we? Ever since Henry Ford rolled out that first Model T in the early part of the twentieth century, we've been in love with automobiles.

We write songs about them, collect replicas of them, spend hours washing them, and compare the ones we've got to what somebody else has. Cars and their variations—trucks, vans, and sport utility vehicles—are by no means unique to America, but many people in other countries have trouble understanding our fascination with them. They also harbor some resentment over our gas-guzzling vehicles and how they eat up so much more than our share of that limited natural resource—oil.

All that aside, your car, truck, SUV, or whatever assemblage of vehicles you own, must be included with your assets. If you're financially savvy, you're not likely to get sucked into the vehicle game that requires you to have two designer-edition SUVs in the driveway and a flashy little Boxter in the garage to drive on weekends. All that status comes at a high price. Unless you've got more money than you know what to do with, we're hoping that you've got a couple of Fords parked in the driveway and the rest of that SUV/Boxter money invested in your retirement funds.

Your Family

We all know that families can be exasperating. Your spouse or significant other sometimes irritates the heck out of you. Your kids, stepkids, his kids, her kids—whoever they belong to—talk back to you and get huffy when you try to pass along the smallest bit of advice. Your mom still think she can tell you how to live your life, and your stepdad has an annoying habit of showing up on Saturdays and hanging around for hours. A bit of sibling rivalry remains between you and your brothers and sisters. Your aunts and uncles still embarrass you at family get-togethers, and your cousins think that it's fine to tease you the way they used to when you all were kids. Family …

What is a family, anyway? These days, there are more definitions for family than there are for middle age. One thing we know is that the definition of family has changed significantly in the past 40 or 50 years. Gone are the days when the only "real" families were those with two parents who lived together with their children. We came across a definition on the Internet that we like. It says simply, "The family is who they say they are."

Nowadays, families are anything from two parents and kids to same-sex couples. There are single parents raising their kids, and families where two sets of kids live with a parent and stepparent. There are grandparents raising grandkids, foster parents raising kids, and people who share housing out of necessity.

However you define your family, and as trying as your family members may sometimes be, think for a minute how empty your life would be without them. Family and real friends—the people who stick by us through everything—are the greatest assets and should be those that we guard most closely.

A Place in Your Community

By the time you reach middle age, many people have found their place within the community where they live. You've probably made some friends—good friends—in your community. Maybe you serve on a municipal or school board, volunteer at the local library, or coach your son's Little League team. Perhaps you're active within your church or synagogue and have connected there with other community members. Or, you might direct a theater group or run a community music school.

Most people enjoy getting involved with the people and activities around them. Not everyone, however, has the opportunity to be a part of a community, and some people simply don't choose to be.

Those who have to move frequently because of their jobs or for other reasons may never get a chance to connect with the people around them. People in poor health may find it difficult to be involved in their communities. And, those folks who work 60 hours a week and 12 more on weekends are not the most likely candidates for community-minded citizen awards. Some people simply prefer to keep to themselves and not get involved with their communities any more than is absolutely necessary.

 Don't Go There

Don't expect your kids to be community-minded citizens if you're not. Some parents want their children be involved in community events while they ignore what's going on around them. Kids learn first by example.

Being an active part of your community can be a real asset. The best way to get to know people and to pursue your own areas of interest is to get involved. Some advantages of being active in your community include the following:

◆ Provides opportunity to meet people and make new friends. This is especially important if you've recently moved to a new community.

◆ Keeps you informed about what's going on and gives you a chance to be part of decision making. If you're involved, you're more likely to know what's happening in your community. We're not saying you should get involved so that you get the latest gossip, but you will be more informed if you're active, and will have a voice when decisions are made.

◆ Gives you a greater sense of purpose. We all need to feel that we give something back, and contributing to your community is a great way to do so.

◆ Gives you opportunity to pursue your interests. If you're an avid conservationist, start an environmental group in your community. If you love dance, organize a community dance center.

◆ Keeps your community strong. Communities need people to make them work and run effectively. People working together toward a common goal form the basis for strong, healthy communities.

If you don't think of your community and the opportunity you have for involvement there as assets, give the concept a little thought. Your community is really an extension of your family and your home. It's the place where you make your life.

Hopefully, your assets are many, and you're grateful for them. Remember when you tally up your balance sheet of life that your assets include a lot more than your home and portfolio.

The Least You Need to Know

◆ One of the advantages of middle age is that you've had time to build up some assets—both material and nonmaterial.

◆ Your house probably is your most expensive asset, and one that can serve you well in the future.

◆ There are various types of investments, all of which come in on the plus side of your ledger.

◆ Vehicles can be assets, but they also can be a drain on your finances.

◆ The most important assets aren't money, houses, or cars; they're your family, friends, and community.

Chapter 4

On the Minus Side

In This Chapter

- Adding up your liabilities
- Mortgages and refinancing
- Dealing with credit card debt
- Getting the best deal on a car loan
- Cutting daily expenses
- Minimizing the financial ouch of divorce

You've got your home, your salary, some savings and investments, a couple of vehicles, and the not-so-tangible assets such as your family, friends, and your place within your community.

Sounds like you're doing just fine.

Of course, life isn't all assets. Chances are you have some liabilities as well. Hopefully, the numbers you tally up on the minus side of your balance sheet aren't out of control, and you're managing nicely.

In this chapter, we'll take a look at some of the common liabilities most of us deal with, such as mortgages, credit card debt, car payments, and routine living expenses. Some of us have extra expenses we need to take care of such as payments to an ex-spouse or child support.

While bills and payments are parts of life, it's important to keep them in balance with your assets. If you routinely run up more credit card debt than you can pay off, you're headed for serious trouble.

Your Mortgage

It's ironic in a way, that while your home is one of your primary assets, the mortgage on that home factors high on your list of liabilities.

It's a fact of life that most homeowners need to borrow funds to pay for their homes, and then spend a good chunk of their lives paying the money back, along with a hefty dose of interest.

Mortgage interest, however, has a huge advantage over car loan or credit card interest. As you probably know, the interest you pay on your mortgage is tax deductible. Every April, you get to note on your tax return the amount of mortgage interest you've paid that year. Deducting the interest payment can significantly lower the amount of money you've got to hand over to Uncle Sam. Financial planners net this figure (interest paid less the tax savings), knowing that being able to deduct mortgage interest lowers the cost of borrowing for the house.

At this point of your life, you may or may not have a mortgage. If you've lived in the same house since you got married when you were 24, you very well may have paid off your mortgage by this time. Many of us, though, are still paying—either on our first home, or because we've moved to a more expensive home and needed to borrow to cover costs.

If you no longer are paying a mortgage, you've hopefully found some other helpful tax deductions. And you can skip over the rest of this section.

Those who are still struggling with house payments, however, may wonder from time to time whether you've got the best type of mortgage you can. Maybe you've thought about refinancing your mortgage for a lower interest rate. Some folks refinance every time the interest rate drops even the slightest amount. Others regard refinancing as too much trouble, or not worth the money you have to pay to do it.

> **Go Figure**
>
> A lower interest rate isn't the only reason people refinance their homes. Many people refinance to accommodate debt consolidation, or to pay for remodeling, college bills, and so forth.

Deciding whether it's worth refinancing your home can be a challenge, for sure. You refinance in order to save money, but how do you know when the interest rates have dropped enough to make it worthwhile? If the drop has been significant, you might be able to refinance into a lower-cost loan, which can put extra dollars in your pocket.

Be aware, however, that just because a loan offers a lower interest rate, does not mean that you'll save money. To refinance a mortgage or equity loan, you'll have to pay title insurance; loan fees, such as a broker's commission and appraisal fee; and points (a fee imposed by the lender that equals a percentage of the loan amount) all over again. These costs can take a big bite out of any savings you'll realize from reduced interest rates and lower monthly payments.

If you're thinking of refinancing, you'll need to find out how much it will cost to do so, and then figure out how long it will take you to recoup those costs. A representative from the lending institution you're using should be able to help you determine that.

When negotiating a refinancing deal, you'll have to decide whether you'll pay the fees up front, or include them in the amount of your loan. There is a type of loan called a no-cost loan, which allows you to waive the up-front costs and have them included in amount of your loan. The interest rate on your loan will increase one-eighth of one percent for every *point* you opt not to pay at the time you refinance.

If you choose a no-cost loan and pay no points or other loan expenses up front, you can typically expect to pay between half and five eighths of 1 percent higher than you would for the same loan on which you'd paid the expenses up front.

If you plan to stay in the home for more than five years, it's a good idea to pay as much of the loan costs up front as possible so that you can lock in a lower interest rate. Here's why.

Let's say you get a $200,000 loan at 6.7 percent. You pay $5,000 in total loan costs and points. Your friend, however, borrows the same amount of money, but opts to pay no costs up front. His interest rate, as a result, is set at 7.4 percent.

At the end of 10 years, you will have paid about $128,900 in interest, compared to $139,400 for

Adding It Up

Points are expensive and can be a problem if you have to pay them up front. Equal to one percent of the total amount of the loan, one point on a $100,000 loan is $1,000. Three points are worth $3,000, and so forth.

your friend. You'll have saved $10,000 in interest, from which you'll need to subtract the $5,000 you paid for fees at the start of the loan. Still, over 10 years you've saved $5,000.

Another reason you might consider refinancing is to change the length of your mortgage. Many people refinance a 30-year mortgage to get a 15-year mortgage as their financial situation changes.

Or if you have a *fixed-rate* mortgage, you may be interested in refinancing to get an *adjustable-rate* loan with a lower interest rate.

Fixed-rate mortgages usually carry higher rates than adjustable-rate loans. They make sense for homeowners who plan on holding a mortgage for a longer term (at least seven years), and who don't like the rate fluctuations that occur with an adjustable mortgage.

Adding It Up

A **fixed-rate** mortgage is one where the interest rate remains constant over the life of the loan. An **adjustable-rate** mortgage is one where the rate normally stays the same for a specified amount of time, and then may fluctuate.

Money Morsel

Get all the information you need about mortgages at Mortgage.com. You can find it on the Internet at www.mortgage.com.

When interest rates drop, as they've been doing recently, many borrowers rush to dump their adjustable-rate loans for the certainty of fixed-rate mortgages. If you expect to move or refinance over the next five to seven years, however, an adjustable-rate mortgage probably will result in fewer costs.

There also is a type of mortgage known as a two-step, or hybrid adjustable loan. This has a fixed rate during the first three, five, seven, or ten years (depending on your agreement), and then converts to a standard adjustable or fixed mortgage. These loans offer the comfort of a fixed-rate loan during the initial period and have a lower rate than the average 30-year fixed rate.

There are many types of mortgages available, as discussed further in Chapter 13, "Paying for a New Home or Second Home." If you're interested in refinancing to get a better rate, a different type of mortgage, or to change the length of your loan, keep the following tips in mind.

♦ Don't get a loan with a repayment penalty. This provision typically charges you a fee if you repay more than 20 percent of your loan during the first 5 years.

♦ Get the lock-in in writing. Some lenders will lock the interest rate on the mortgage for a fee. Some lock-ins allow borrowers to benefit from a drop in interest rates while protecting them from increases.

♦ Shop around. Compare the fees and terms of at least four lenders. Look at the rates and the total cost of refinancing from each lender.

♦ Don't allow every potential lender to run a credit check on you. You can't blame potential lenders for wanting to be sure that you're credit worthy, but repeated requests for *credit reports* can send up red flags at the credit agency and actually lower your credit score. Allow the first lender you contact to run a credit report on the condition that you receive a copy. Provide the report to other lenders as you shop around.

Many mortgage refinancing companies are replacing 30-year loans with 15-year mortgages. A shorter-term mortgage usually offers slightly lower interest rates, which will save a lot of interest over the life of the loan. This means, however, that your monthly payments will be a little higher. Shorter-term loans are a good idea for people who want to pay off their mortgage in time for retirement.

Biweekly mortgage payments allow you to make 26 mortgage payments a year, which is equal to 13 monthly payments instead of the usual 12. This is a disciplined approach to paying off your mortgage early. Ask your lender about the possibility of changing a monthly mortgage to a biweekly schedule. There may be a minimal fee, but the extra payment every year will make a difference.

> **Adding It Up**
>
> Your **credit report** is a compilation of information, including your name, Social Security number, date of birth, address from the time you got your first credit card, all places of employment, and how you pay your bills. Your report is stored at a credit agency. You're entitled to see your credit report and can do so by contacting a credit agency.

As you can see, there are many factors to think about if you're considering refinancing your mortgage. It's a good idea to meet with a representative of a lending company for more information if you're thinking about changing the terms of your current loan.

Credit Card Debt

Much attention has been given lately to America's obsession with credit cards and spending. A book in 2000 by Dr. Robert D. Manning, a leading expert on the credit card industry, revealed that Americans collectively owe a staggering $600 billion in credit card debt.

Manning's book, *Credit Card Nation: The Consequences of America's Addiction to Credit*, is critical of the credit card industry, which is quick to issue cards to just about anyone, regardless of the person's financial situation. The book attracted attention from the national media and got many people thinking a bit more carefully about their own relationships with their plastic.

More than 60 million households in the United States are carrying balances on their credit cards.

> **Go Figure**
>
> The credit card industry experienced a 26 percent annual growth rate over the past 10 years. In addition, the credit card industry's advertising budget doubled between 1994 and 1998, increasing from $425 million to $870 million.

That means they're not paying off the bills each month and racking up serious interest charges on the money they still owe.

Credit card debt is a big problem in America and a huge liability to many, many people. If you have serious credit card debt, it's very important to address the problem and figure out a way to reduce or eliminate the debt.

Credit Card Nightmares

Let's say that you always paid off your credit card bill every month. You get the bill, take out your checkbook, and write a check for the full amount. You don't even know what the interest rate is, because you never incur any interest.

Suddenly, a series of events wreaks havoc with your financial situation. Your husband loses his job. You need major dental work—and it's not covered by insurance. Your father gets very ill, and you spend huge amounts of money flying back and forth across the country to spend time with him. You're depending more and more heavily on your credit cards, and now you're unable to pay off the balance in full when the bill arrives.

Only after you can no longer pay off your balance do you learn that your interest rate is 17 percent, and you're paying $28 a month in interest on a $2,000 balance.

Still, you keep using your credit cards to buy what you need, because there just isn't enough money to pay cash for everything. Your balance keeps getting higher and higher, and although you're paying a little bit each month, the interest fees keep mounting. Soon you owe thousands and thousands of dollars and have no idea of where the money to pay it back will come from.

This scenario is not at all unusual. Credit card debt has caused nightmares for millions of people, some of whom have been distraught enough over their debt to kill themselves. In addition, the number of American households filing for personal bankruptcy protection each year is on the rise.

So what to do if your credit card debt is out of control? Read on.

Don't Go There

Don't think that if you make the minimum payment on each of your credit cards each month, you're doing well at repaying debt. By paying only the minimum each month, you're still wracking up big interest fees, especially if you're carrying a high balance.

Paying Off Your Debt

If you default on your credit card bill—that is, you just stop paying anything for a period of time—your credit card company normally will sell your debt to a collection agency. If this happens, watch out, because the collection agency will add its fees onto your bill. Before you know it, your $3,000 credit card debt has ballooned to $5,000, and you're in even worse shape than before.

If you're in trouble with credit card debt, the first thing you should do is get a copy of your credit report from one of the three big, nationwide credit agencies. You can do this online, or by requesting a copy in writing. There's a charge of about $8.50 for a report, depending on the state in which you live.

Each of these agencies probably has the same information concerning your credit history. They get it from banks, finance companies, credit card suppliers, department stores, mail order companies, and various other places with which you've had dealings. Smaller, regional credit bureaus supplement the information.

The big three when it comes to credit agencies are as follows:

◆ Equifax Credit Services, PO Box 740241, Atlanta, GA 30374; toll-free: 1-800-685-1111; www.equifax.com

◆ Trans Union, PO Box 2000, Chester, PA 19022; toll-free: 1-800-888-4213; www.transunion.com

◆ Experian, PO Box 2002, Allen, TX 75013; toll free: 1-888-397-3742; www.experian.com

Once you get a copy of your credit report, examine it carefully for errors, and note when your credit troubles began.

When you fully understand your credit history, try to negotiate a repayment program with all creditors. Some credit card companies and other creditors will work with you to establish a payment schedule that you can meet. Let them know that you acknowledge your debt and will work in good faith to pay it off. Once a payment plan has been established, be sure to stick to it.

Repaying loans on which you've defaulted won't undo a damaged credit history, but it may help you to be able to get credit in the future.

If your credit has been severely damaged and you're unable to pay back your debt, you should talk to a nonprofit credit advisor. A listing for such as person can be found in the yellow pages of your phone book under credit and debt counseling. A credit advisor may be able to help you consolidate your debt and find a lower-interest loan that you could use to pay off higher-interest credit card debt. Be ready to cut expenses elsewhere until your credit card debt is repaid.

Money Morsel

If you're in trouble with credit card debt, the first thing you should do is cut up all your cards. The last thing you want is to run up more debt. If you really need a card in case of an emergency, give it to someone else to hold for you until it's necessary—really necessary—to use.

Finding a Better Deal

If you haven't read over the terms of your credit card agreement lately, take a little time to look at it. What interest rate does your credit card company charge? Ten percent? Twelve? Eighteen? Twenty?

What sort of advantages does your card provide? If you're not earning any "rewards" from your card, such as flyer miles, you might want to take a look at what's out there. Many credit cards give you points for every dollar spent, then let you use your points to get free flights, clothing, dinners out, books, CDs, and so forth.

Be careful, though, if you don't pay off your bill every month. Cards that offer rewards may come with much higher interest rates than standard cards.

If you're paying an annual fee on your credit card, either look for a card that doesn't charge the fee, or ask your credit card provider to waive it. There's intense competition among credit card companies, and many will do whatever's necessary to keep you on board.

Money Morsel

For information and comparisons on many different credit cards, check out CardRatings.com. You can compare interest rates, application procedures, and rewards. It's on the Internet at www.cardratings.com.

And, watch for late fees on your card. Most providers charge at least $20 if your payment comes in even a day after the due date. If your payment is late once, call and ask to have the fee waived.

Remember that there are hundreds of credit card deals out there, and many, many companies that would love to have your business. Compare the terms of various credit cards, and select one that sounds right for you.

Car Payments

Most of us need to have a car. And, we know that cars are expensive. As a result, many people in their 40s and 50s are still dealing with car payments, which can take a big chunk out of your monthly income.

If you're still doing car payments, you've hopefully negotiated the best deal possible. The following are some tips to keep in mind when looking for an auto loan.

◆ Don't finance your vehicle through the dealership. Dealer financing normally costs at least a percentage point or two more than a loan from a bank or credit union.

◆ Try to get a pre-approved loan from a bank or credit union before you go new car shopping. This puts you in a position of knowing exactly how much money you have and what you're able to spend. And, the car dealer will know you're serious about buying and do what he can to get your business.

- Pay as much up front for the car as possible.

- Use rebates to increase your down payment, not to get a more expensive car.

- Take the shortest loan term you can manage. Never pay back a car loan over five years if you can do it in two or three.

- Consider getting a home equity loan to pay for your car. Car loan interest isn't tax deductible, but the interest on a home equity loan is.

- Pay off the loan early, if possible. Some lenders will penalize you for paying back early, so be sure to look for a deal that doesn't.

Money Morsel

Don't put yourself in debt for a vehicle that you don't need. A $45,000 sport utility vehicle might look great in your driveway and make you feel good when you drive it, but a car that costs half that much will still get you where you're going and cause a lot less damage to your pocketbook.

If you need a new car, you might consider leasing, rather than buying. A third of all new-car customers are leasing today, compared to only 15 percent 5 years ago. More information about leasing a car is included in Chapter 7, "Trading In the Bikes for Cars."

Expenses, Expenses, Expenses

Groceries; clothing; electric, water, phone, and cable bills; tolls; and gas for the car. Daily expenses add up alarmingly fast and seem to increase continuously. And, if you're like many people, you're not even sure where your money goes.

Walk around with $100 in your pocket sometime, and try to account for where you spent it when it's gone. Chances are you'll be amazed at how fast the money disappeared, and not all that sure about how you actually spent it. If you're trying to control or cut back on daily expenses, however, it's imperative you know exactly where your money is going.

The topic of budgets is covered in Chapter 5, "Getting It All Together," so we won't go into too much detail here. Know that in order to control expenses, however, you first must set financial goals. Once you've done that, you can determine how much money you have to spend, and then decide where you'll make cuts, if necessary.

Some expenses are unavoidable. You've got to pay your mortgage, meet your car payment if you have one and take care of household expenses such as water and electricity. Keep the following tips in mind, however, for saving dollars on everyday expenses.

- Limit your visits to restaurants. Even the cost of dinner at the local diner adds up if you eat there four nights a week. You really can eat at home for much less than you'll pay in a restaurant.

◆ Purchase prepared meals at the grocery store rather than eating in a restaurant. You still won't have to cook, but the meal will cost less than in a restaurant.

◆ Use gas cards that give you a discount or a rebate. An Exxon-Mobil card gives you a 3 percent rebate on all gas at Exxon or Mobil stations. The Shell MasterCard takes 5 percent off your gas purchase.

◆ Don't use a higher-grade gasoline than your car requires. Check your owner's manual to verify the lowest grade of octane your car can handle.

◆ Drop or reduce the comprehensive and collision coverage on an older car. Some insurance experts suggest scaling back as soon as the premiums climb higher than 10 percent of the car's market value.

◆ Shop around for your homeowner's, auto, and liability insurance. The cost of identical policies vary from company to company. Also, raising the deductible on your policies can result in significant savings over time.

◆ Cut back on cable. How often do you really watch the golf channel? Or TV at all, for that matter? Cable bills are expensive, so if you're not using all that you're paying for, consider scaling back.

◆ Compare alternative utility providers. Consumers in some states are free to choose their own suppliers, and prices vary. Check out www.lowermybills.com to assess your current electric and gas bills and find out if there's a better deal.

◆ Comparison shop your phone bills. You can do this at www.ABTolls.com, an alternative rate-comparison site that compares long distance by factoring in all those fees and basic charges to calculate your true rate per minute.

◆ Get rid of telephone extras such as caller ID. Depending on your rates, you may be able to save at least $10 a month by eliminating services such as caller ID and call waiting.

◆ Install a programmable thermostat, and go on a budget and/or prepayment plan to lower your monthly heating bills.

◆ Call your long-distance phone carrier and comparison-shop. Ask a representative to review your current usage and tell you if there's a better plan available for your needs.

◆ Use frequent buyer cards if you shop at the same stores all the time. These cards offer discounts after you spend a specified amount of money.

◆ Bargain shop for major purchases. No one likes going to six stores to comparison shop for a refrigerator, but your savings could be significant.

These are just a few suggestions for saving money on everyday expenses. Just remember that every penny you save can be put aside for more significant costs, such as college, weddings, and retirement.

And Then There's Your Ex

Divorce can be devastating to your financial situation, there's no question about it. We spend a good portion of Chapter 19, "Other Changes to Think About," on the financial implications of divorce, so we won't go into much detail here.

Know, however, that there are ways to make divorce less financially detrimental for both parties. The catch is that you've both got to be willing to cooperate to make it happen.

If you've had an ugly divorce, it might be difficult to work with your ex on anything—including your financial situation. If you keep in mind, though, that you may benefit from cooperating, you'll probably find it easier to do so.

We probably can think of divorce situations that ended in financial hardship for one or both partners. The husband and wife may have fought bitterly throughout the process, hiring lawyers, private investigators, and other professionals without any regard to the cost. Or, perhaps they couldn't agree on any financial, custody, or property matter, dragging out the proceedings and running up huge bills in the process.

Divorce proceedings can occur in an orderly manner, and much of the need for professionals can be eliminated if both partners are willing to cooperate. If you're in a divorce situation, it's important to understand that the cost of legal proceedings can chew up a big chunk of your financial assets.

And once divorced, you could end up paying alimony and child support that will further impact upon your financial situation. Divorce often is inevitable, and we'd never urge you to stay in a bad marriage for the sake of your finances. Resolving to settle a divorce as amicably and cleanly as possible, however, can impact positively on your net worth—and that of your ex.

Once you've determined all your assets, along with your liabilities, you can start getting a handle on your net worth. Your net worth, covered in detail in the next chapter, is the indicator of your overall financial situation.

The Least You Need to Know

- You may be able to refinance your mortgage in order to get lower interest rates or other benefits that could lower your costs.
- If credit card debt is a problem, you'll need to take strong and immediate steps to reduce it.
- Looking around for the best car loan you can find, or considering leasing a car instead of buying, may save you significant dollars.

◆ Daily expenses can be financial killers, but there are ways to reduce them.

◆ If you're willing to cooperate with your ex, you may be able to minimize the financial pain of a divorce.

Chapter 5

Getting It All Together

In This Chapter

- ◆ Assessing your net worth
- ◆ Knowing if you need a budget
- ◆ Cutting back on expenses
- ◆ Planning ahead financially
- ◆ Keeping it all organized

We've spent this first part of the book considering where you are at this point of your life. We've looked at your life situation, your health, and the very fact that you—or any of us—aren't as young as we used to be.

On the financial side of life, we've discussed what you need at this stage, what you might be wanting (remember that little BMW?) and how to know whether you can afford those tempting, but not necessary, luxuries.

And we've checked out your assets and talked about what you might owe. Hopefully, you're not over your head in debt. If you are, the best thing you can do is get somebody to help you come up with a plan to reduce it. Debt, especially the high-interest credit card kind, can be a financial killer.

Having discussed all these topics, it's time to tally them all up and determine your net worth. Maybe you've already got a good handle on your net worth, but many people never take the time to figure it out. Once you fully understand your net worth, you can take a good, hard look at it and decide if you're satisfied. If you're not, we'll give you some suggestions about how you can improve it. This chapter also contains a couple of worksheets to help you get a better handle on your situation.

What Is Net Worth?

Your *net worth*, simply, is your financial situation. It's what you get when you tally up your assets (the financial kind, that is) and subtract from them your liabilities.

You may have a net worth of $2 million (wouldn't *that* be nice!), $200,000, $20,000, or $2,000. It's whatever you figure out you have once you've subtracted the total of your liabilities from the total of your assets.

Adding It Up

Your **net worth** is the difference between your financial assets and financial liabilities.

You'll need to consider all those assets we talked about Chapter 3, "On the Plus Side"—your house, income, savings and investments, and vehicles—and any others. On the minus side, you'll need to refer back to Chapter 4, "On the Minus Side," and consider all those nasty things like car payments, credit card debt, mortgages, and monthly bills.

Figuring It Out

The trick to figuring out your net worth is to be specific and thorough. You've got to know exactly what your assets are and the entire array of expenses.

So gather up your bank statements, tax returns, and whatever other documents might provide information about your finances. Once you have, you can take a few minutes to fill out this net worth worksheet.

Personal Financial Statement of Net Worth–as of the ____ Day of _____

Assets	Amount $
Cash (Schedule A)	_____
Stocks and Bonds (Schedule B)	_____
Accounts and Notes Receivable:	
Due from relatives and friends	_____
Due from others—good	_____
Doubtful	_____
Real Estate Owned (Schedule C)	_____

Assets	Amount $
Mortgages Owned	_____
Cash Surrender Value Life Insurance (Schedule D)	_____
Other Assets (Itemize):	
_____	_____
_____	_____
_____	_____
TOTAL $	_____
Amount of Assets Pledged $	_____

****

Liabilities	Amount $
Notes Payable Banks (Schedule A)	_____
Notes Payable to Relatives	_____
Notes Payable to Others	_____
Accounts Payable	_____
Federal and State Income Taxes Payable	_____
Other Accrued Taxes and Interest	_____
Mortgages Payable (Schedule C)	_____
Installment Contracts Payable	_____
Loans against Life Insurance (Schedule D)	_____
Other Liabilities (itemize):	
_____	_____
_____	_____
_____	_____
TOTAL $	_____
Amount of Liabilities Secured $	_____

****

Annual Income: Salary	$_____
Fees or Commissions	$_____
Other	$_____
Business or Occupation	_____
Name of Employer	_____

continues

Personal Financial Statement of Net Worth—as of the ___ Day of _____

(continued)

Assets	Amount $
Are you a partner or officer in any other business or venture?	_____
Age:	_____
Marital Status: Single/Married/ Widow(er)/Divorced	
Spouse's Name	_____
Number of Dependents	_____
Are there any unsatisfied judgments or legal actions pending against you?	_____
Have you ever gone through bankruptcy or made a general assignment?	_____
As of the date of this financial statement, I had not pledged, assigned, hypothecated, or transferred the title to pay of my assets, except as noted on this form or on a supporting schedule, nor has any such action been taken since that date, except as follows (give details):	_____
Contingent Liabilities: As endorser or co-maker	_____
On receivables discounted or sold	_____
As guarantor	_____
On leases, mortgages or contracts	_____
Unsettled claims	_____
Other (itemize)	_____

Schedule A—Cash Balances and Bank Loans

Statement Date

Name of Bank	Cash Balance	Amount Owing	Method of Borrowing
_____	_____	_____	_____
_____	_____	_____	_____
_____	_____	_____	_____
_____	_____	_____	_____
Cash on hand	_____	_____	_____
Totals as per statement	_____	_____	_____

Schedule B—Stocks and Bonds

Shares or Bonds	Name of Security	In Name Of	Present Market Value	If pledged State to Whom
_____	_____	_____	_____	_____
_____	_____	_____	_____	_____
_____	_____	_____	_____	_____
_____	_____	_____	_____	_____
_____	_____	_____	_____	_____

Schedule C—Real Estate Owned

Location, Type of Property and Date Acquired	Title in Name of	Cost	Recent Appraised Value	Mortgage Amount/When Due
_____	_____	_____	_____	____ / _____
_____	_____	_____	_____	____ / _____
_____	_____	_____	_____	____ / _____
_____	_____	_____	_____	____ / _____

Are there any other liens against any of the above property?

Are there any mortgage payments, interest, or taxes in arrears?

Schedule D—Life Insurance

Face Amount	Name of Company	Beneficiary	Type of Policy	Cash Value	Loans Against Policy
_____	_____	_____	_____	_____	_____
_____	_____	_____	_____	_____	_____
_____	_____	_____	_____	_____	_____
_____	_____	_____	_____	_____	_____

Are any of the above policies assigned except for loans as shown?

Hopefully, you're pleasantly surprised at what you're worth. If not, you've got some financial work ahead of you.

Maybe You Need a Budget

Despite what most people think, "budget" is not a dirty word. Granted, it's not as great a word as "vacation" or "windfall," but there are much worse things in life than living with a budget. A budget is a schedule of income and expenses, usually broken into monthly intervals and typically covering a one-year period.

If your net worth is not where you'd like it to be, you've got a choice. You can increase your assets, or you can decrease your liabilities.

You could get another job, but it's nice to be able to sleep now and then. Or you could start playing the lottery and sit back to wait until you hit it big. Of course, chances are you *won't* hit it big, and the money you've spent on tickets will make your net worth even less appealing than it is now.

> **Go Figure**
>
> We don't know if this statistic reflects the national average, but in 2000 in Harvey County, Kansas, residents bought $1,779,868 worth of lottery tickets. There are only 33,000 residents of Harvey County, which means that every man, woman, and child spent $54 on lottery tickets.

If increasing your assets is not feasible at this point, you'll need to cut back on your expenses. And that's where a budget comes in. Before you begin hyperventilating, understand that a budget doesn't have to dictate every penny you spend. You don't need to account for every pack of gum or cup of coffee you buy. A budget simply is a tool to help you get a better sense of where you're spending your money, and in which areas you could spend less. A budget is a good thing.

A Sample Budget Worksheet

We've included a sample budget worksheet that can serve as a guide for your own budget. Don't assume, however, that this sample is a universal budget. We all have different expenses. Be sure to take some time to customize the worksheet to reflect your own spending.

Sample Budget Worksheet

Item	Estimated	Amount/Worth
Housing	$	$
Mortgage/rent		
Utilities		
Phone		
Cable		

Item	Estimated	Amount/Worth
Internet service		
Furniture		
Appliances		
Maintenance		
Real estate taxes		
Total:		
Transportation	$	$
Fuel		
Maintenance		
Lease		
License/taxes		
Public transportation		
Insurance		
Total:		
Taxes	$	$
Federal		
State		
Local		
Social Security		
Luxury		
Total:		
Debt	$	$
Credit card		
Car loans		
Personal loans		
Line of credit		
Total:		
Entertainment	$	$
Vacation		
Movies, concerts, and theater		
Hobbies (golf, tennis fees, etc.)		
Pets		
Magazines and books		
Videos and music CDs/tapes		

continues

Sample Budget Worksheet   (continued)

Item	Estimated	Amount/Worth
Restaurants		
Total:		
Personal	$	$
Food		
Gifts		
Clothes/shoes		
Jewelry		
Dry cleaning		
Hair/makeup		
Health club		
Other		
Total:		
Health Care	$	$
Co-payments		
Drugs		
Uncovered services		
Total:		
Insurance	$	$
Car		
Home		
Disability		
Life		
Health		
Total:		
Children	$	$
College savings		
Day care/baby-sitting		
Clothes		
Uncovered medical/dental expenses		
Lessons/activities/classes		
Camps		
Other		
Total:		

Item	Estimated	Amount/Worth
Caregiving	$	$
Nursing care		
Elder care services		
Adult day care		
Other		
Total:		
Charity	$	$
Donations		
Total:		
Grand Total:		

Once you've completed this worksheet, taking into account that your areas of expense may vary, you'll have a clear picture of how much you're spending.

Cutting Back When Necessary

In the interests of improving your bottom line, it may be necessary to cut back on your spending. As a quick review, there are different types of expenses.

- **Routine expenses.** These are the ones that get you at regular intervals. You can count on routine expenses. These include the mortgage, insurance, taxes, groceries, your health club fee, and your utility bills.

- **Nonroutine expenses.** Your car breaks down and you've suddenly got to come up with $425. Your 22-year-old has a once-in-a-lifetime chance to spend a semester in France, and she needs $1,575 right away to reserve her spot. Your wife gets a promotion at work and you spend $200 celebrating at the best restaurant in town. These are nonroutine expenses. They don't come at regular intervals, and that makes them harder to plan for.

- **Fixed expenses.** If expenses are for the same amount every payment period, they're called fixed expenses. Your mortgage, insurance, and health club fee are all fixed expenses.

- **Variable expenses.** You probably don't spend the same amount in the grocery store every week. And some months you pay out twice as much for dinners in restaurants as

Money Morsel

Expenses can fall into more than one category. A routine expense, for instance, may be fixed or variable. If you lease a car and pay the same amount every month, that's a routine, fixed expense.

other months. These are variable expenses. You know that you'll have them, but the amount that they'll cost you varies.

- **Nondiscretionary expenses.** These are the ones that you can't get around. You've got to pay them. They include insurance, your mortgage, utilities, food, and so forth.

- **Discretionary expenses.** You need to buy food, but you don't need to spend $45 a month to belong to a health club. You could, after all, take up jogging. You need to pay your insurance bill, but you don't need to spend $2,000 on a vacation. The health club, vacations, movies, restaurants (all the fun things), and so forth are discretionary expenses.

Don't Go There

When looking to reduce expenses, begin with moderate cuts. Don't decide, for instance, that you're going to reduce your food bill by 50 percent all at one time. Start at 10 percent, and see how that goes. Trying to cut back too drastically at one time may cause you to get discouraged and give up trying to save.

Money Morsel

If you need some ideas for how to save, pick up a copy of *1,001 Ways to Cut Your Expenses.* Written by Jonathan D. Pond, it was published in 1992 by Dell Books and is available on Amazon.com.

If you're like most people, it's easier to cut spending on variable expenses than nonvariable. If your mortgage is $1,500 a month, you have no choice but to pay $1,500 a month if you plan to continue living in your house. If you're spending $400 a month on food, however, there probably are ways you could reduce that bill.

Use manufacturer's coupons, or buy generic or store brands instead of name brands. Trade in the Chilean sea bass for flounder, and find some good recipes for rice and beans or pasta. Buy only what you'll use that week, even if a particular item is on sale.

Other variable expenses that usually aren't too difficult to reduce include discretionary expenses such as vacations and entertainment. That's not to say you should give up your trips, movies, and dinners out all together. After all, you've probably been working hard for 20 or 30 years now, and you certainly deserve some fun. If your net worth isn't what you'd like it to be, however, you might consider trading the cruise vacation for a week in a little cabin on a lake. Or your ski vacation in Aspen might be reduced to a couple of days at your local slopes.

Some fixed expenses you may be able to reduce or eliminate include ones such as the monthly gym fee, the $150 or so that you spend in restaurants each month, and the $70 tab you run up on your hair and nails at the beauty shop every six weeks. You might reduce your car lease payment by trading in the Lexus for a Honda.

Once you really think about it, you'll probably come up with many ways to cut your expenses. Look over the budget worksheet and see which areas seem to be the best candidates for cutting back. Come up with a plan on how you'll save, and put your plan into action.

Software to Help You Budget

How you keep your budget is a personal choice. Some people like to keep track of their spending on paper, while others prefer to do it on the computer. If you prefer a keyboard to a pencil, there are dozens of software programs especially designed to help with home budgets. Some good ones are listed here:

- Balance Point
- Organizitall Budgeting System
- Home Finances (an Excel spreadsheet)
- Money Counts Personal
- Quicken for Windows
- Microsoft Money

A good software program might make it easier for you to set up a budget, but the only way to make your budget work for you is to control spending.

If you've been used to buying what you want whenever you want it, cutting back on or eliminating expenses might be quite difficult. Try to get yourself into a savings mindset, where figuring out how you'll reduce or eliminate expenses is something you do every time you pull out your wallet, checkbook, or credit card.

Ask yourself if you really need to buy whatever it is you're about to pay for. Obviously, if it's your mortgage bill, you'll need to write the check. If it's a new pair of shoes or a blouse, however, you might be able to tuck your checkbook back into your pocket and head home without the shoes or blouse, but with that much more money in your account.

And don't give up on your budget. You spending habits aren't the same every month, so you'll need to keep track of your expenses for several years to really get a clear picture of your spending over the long term.

Planning for What You'll Need

While you're assessing your net worth and maybe setting up a budget plan for your family finances, take a good, hard look at expenses coming down the road.

Failing to plan in advance for upcoming expenses can really derail your finances. Many people plan for big costs like college or a wedding, but fail to think about how they'll pay for the plane tickets they'll need to have in order to travel to their goddaughter's wedding next spring.

Don't Go There

If you're working with a budget, you may become fixed on your current spending and not pay enough attention to future expenses. Ignoring expenses down the road can lead to unpleasant surprises, so be sure to plan ahead.

Think long term and short term, and come up with a list of known expenses. If you're planning to move or buy a vacation home in five years, include those costs on your list. If you want to take your husband on a special vacation for his fiftieth birthday, write it down. If your son needs airfare to travel back and forth between home and college, don't forget to include that cost.

Looking at what your expenses will be in the future makes it easier to know what you can spend now, and how much you need to be saving.

Keeping Your Finances on Track

Whether or not you decide to use a budget, it's important to keep track of your finances. Many people have little idea of how much money they have or how much they spend.

If you're not going to use a budget, you can at least give some careful thought to how and where you spend your money. You might be surprised to realize how much you spend a week on incidentals like having the car washed, the coffee and bagel you buy on your way to the office each morning, dry-cleaning bills, postage stamps, and so forth.

Attaining a good understanding of your net worth, knowing where your money goes, and planning for upcoming expenses will help to assure that you'll maintain control of your financial situation.

The Least You Need to Know

◆ Your net worth is the difference between all your financial assets and all your financial liabilities.

◆ If you don't have a clear picture of your expenses, a budget can help you to know exactly where you spend your money.

◆ It may be necessary to cut back on your expenses in order to improve your net worth.

◆ Planning ahead for future expenses can help you avoid some unpleasant financial surprises.

◆ Having a good overview of your finances can help you maintain control over how much you spend and what you're able to save.

Your Kids and Your Money

Raising kids, and all that comes with it, is an expensive proposition. And, they seem to require more and more money as they get older.

They trade in their Big Wheels for roller blades, the roller blades for expensive mountain bikes, and then the bikes for cars. And we, as parents, are expected to finance all this. Or are we?

Sure, we all want to help our kids as much as we can. Giving them everything they want, however, is not always the smartest, or most responsible, way to go. Chapters 6 through 10 discuss methods of paying for big expenses, such as college and weddings, as well as some limits parents might think about imposing.

Chapter **6**

The Big, Expensive Parent Trap

In This Chapter

- ◆ Understanding why kids want so much
- ◆ Teaching the difference between want and need
- ◆ Looking past their own circle
- ◆ Helping them understand personal finances
- ◆ Letting them earn their own money
- ◆ Helping out is fine sometimes

Kids cost money, there's no two ways about it. And, the older they get, the more expensive they seem to be. They exchange their Big Wheels for mountain bikes, and after that for cars. They trade in their Legos for PlayStations and those frightfully expensive video games. Backyard baseball becomes organized ball requiring registration fees, uniforms, and fundraisers. J.C. Penney jeans are replaced with Gap, Old Navy, and Aeropostale.

And yet, you can avoid at least some of this expensive parent trap if you plan ahead and decide just how you'll relate to your kids about money. Most kids, until they start to earn their own money, and sometimes long after that, don't have a good sense of the difference between want and need. If they want something, they're convinced that they need it. And they probably, in their minds, need it today.

Kids are bombarded from the time they're babies with tremendous pressure to acquire, and they learn to want a lot of stuff very early on. They learn from television commercials that their favorite cartoon characters can come home with them on T-shirts, in books, and on videos. All Mom and Dad have to do is buy them. They know what kind of cereal is cool to eat, which professional sports team jerseys they should buy, and which action figure soon will be available in the kids' meal at their favorite fast-food restaurant.

As parents, it's your job to help kids understand the value of money and the difference between wanting an item and needing it. In this chapter, we'll look at how you can do that, and also how you can set an example of financial responsibility for your kids.

Cell Phones, Jeeps, and PlayStation 2s

Today's teenagers are the richest generation of teens in American history and they're spending money at record levels. A recent report on the PBS television program *That Money Show*, revealed that teens will spend close to $155 billion in 2001. Much of that amount is money that parents give their children.

That affluence makes them prime targets for marketers and advertisers, who are happy to make their products as desirable to teenagers as possible. Phones and CD players come in 10 colors, two include sparkles. It's the rare teen that doesn't know which brands are cool to wear and which are not. There's a lot of tempting stuff out there, and teens are anxious to get their hands on it.

Teens and young adults aren't afraid to say what they want, either. What parent hasn't heard the refrain, "but Mom (or Dad), I really need it!" dozens of times?

Money Morsel

To get an idea of the advertising pressure teens are under, pick up a copy of a teenager's magazine sometime. The ads run the gamut for everything from acne medicine to cell phones, and they give teens the clear message to buy, buy, buy.

There's been a huge influx of toys and gadgets into our society in the past 20 years. Twenty years ago, personal computers at home were pretty rare. Now many households have more than one computer, each equipped with Internet access and a drawer full of games. Kids "need" their own computers to help them with school projects and to chat with their friends.

They "need" cell phones so they can keep in touch with each other (and sometimes with you), they "need" a vehicle (preferably new instead of used) as soon as they're able to drive, and they "need" roomfuls of other items that are made to seem so appealing to teens.

Kids, teens, and young adults have more money to spend than ever before, there's more available for them to buy, and they're constantly bombarded with messages that buying is good. Is it any wonder that young people "need" so much?

But Mom, All My Friends Have One

While kids and teens are under tremendous pressure to acquire all those tempting toys and gadgets available, parents are under equally tremendous pressure to buy for them. Studies show that kids are typically exposed to 360,000 ads by the time they graduate from high school.

Many parents find it difficult to say "no" to their children. It's easier to give in and get them what they ask for than have to explain why the child won't get what she wants. This seems to be especially true of parents who don't deny themselves anything. Some parents buy into the notion that their 15-year-old needs his own cell phone because they don't want their neighbor's kid to have something their child does not. The parents' "gotta keep up with the Joneses" attitude spills right over to his kids and the Jones' kids.

As parents, we know that buying kids everything they want is not a good idea. And it's our job to help our kids understand why that's so.

Living in an Affluent Society

We live in the most affluent society in the world. We're the world's richest people. Our kids spend more pocket money in a year than half a billion of the world's poorest people earn in income.

The problem is, kids who are raised in affluence often don't recognize what they have. They take for granted three meals a day and snacks in between, a good-size house, two cars in the driveway, two or three TVs and VCRs in the house, their own CD players, telephones in their bedrooms, and money in their pockets.

It's difficult to fully appreciate what you have when you only know to compare your wealth with the wealth of those in your immediate circle. And so, when a 13-year-old comes home from her friend's very large house, in which Rachael's bedroom is complete with a complex stereo system, television and VCR, phone with a private number, a walk-in closet filled with clothing, and a computer equipped with Internet access, the 13-year-old is less than satisfied for a time with her smaller bedroom that contains far fewer accessories.

A friend's 12-year-old daughter was disappointed the first time she slept over at her girl-friend's house and discovered that she and Amanda would be sleeping in separate rooms. Karen was expected to sleep in the guest room of Amanda's suite.

As a society, we've grown used to having more. Residential space per American increased from 312 square feet in 1950 to 742 square feet in 1993, according to a report by the Worldwatch Institute.

Affluence is fine, but children must be taught that it's a great privilege and a large measure of good fortune that they live in such an affluent society.

Helping Them Appreciate What They've Got

It's hard for kids to fully appreciate what they have. Sure, they catch a glimpse of a TV show about an impoverished country when they're flipping through the channels. Or they might read an account of a community that was ravaged by a flood, earthquake, mudslide, or tornado.

We, or teachers at their schools or places of worship, can tell them about sweatshops and child labor and starving children. And while our children may feel sympathy for those situations, they can't ever appreciate the anguish of a mother who's watching her child starve to death and is powerless to do anything about it. They can't imagine what it would be like to lose everything you own, including members of your family, in a devastating earthquake or flood.

Money Morsel

Two thirds of all people in the world have a standard of living that's just 20 percent of the U.S. average. We should tell our kids that they, as an average American, are five times better off financially than two out of every three people in the world.

We should do what we can, though, to help our children—regardless of their age—understand how fortunate they are on a global level. We also should show them examples in their own community or surrounding area of people who aren't as well off as they are.

We know a minister who takes groups of pre-teens and teenagers to a homeless shelter in the middle of Philadelphia. He and the kids serve meals to homeless men and then spend the night in an area of the shelter in which the men sleep. Every kid who goes comes back with a story, and a better idea of how people who are less fortunate than they are live.

A neighbor volunteers in a city soup kitchen in our area and takes her three children along to help serve. Our children save the clothing they've outgrown and deliver it to a Salvation Army shelter for women and children. The shelter is much, much different from Rachael's luxurious room or Amanda's bedroom suite, and my daughter comes home and is happy for a while with her own room and possessions.

Social Responsibility

Money and *social responsibility* are directly related to some people, while others see no correlation. People of great wealth—Bill Gates types—are pressured to be socially responsible and share some of what they have. The Bill and Melinda Gates Foundation is endowed with 17 billion dollars to support philanthropic efforts in the areas of global health and learning.

We don't think we need to have our children go to great extremes to be socially responsible. We do think, though, that they should be aware of the concept of social responsibility and encouraged to develop it in their own time.

Adding It Up

There are many definitions of **social responsibility,** but we think that it's understanding your place in the world, doing what you can to help others, and respecting and protecting your environment.

You can do that by setting an example of being socially responsible yourself. Tell your children why you take used clothing to the Goodwill Center, where low-income families can buy it inexpensively, instead of tossing it in the trash can. Explain to them why you give up a Sunday afternoon to participate in a walk to raise money for hungry people around the world. Keep a jar on the kitchen counter and have everybody throw in loose change. When the jar is filled, contribute the money to your local food pantry.

You don't have to go to great lengths to be socially responsible. But, teaching your kids at an early age to appreciate what they have and to share when they can will instill in them the concept of social responsibility while giving them a sense of their good fortune for their place in the world.

Teaching Kids About Money

Most financial experts agree that parents should start teaching kids about money at an early age. Most also agree that parents aren't doing enough to help their children understand issues relating to money.

The Joint Council on Economic Education surveyed a group of high-school students and found that the great majority of them had very little understanding about money-related issues, including profit and loss as they apply to business, investment opportunities, and credit.

Some experts feel that parents avoid teaching children about money because they're uncomfortable with the very topic. While money should be a tool we use in daily living, it often becomes a thorny and emotional issue. Anne Ziff, a family therapist

Don't Go There

Watch out that you don't overwhelm younger children with too much financial information at one time. Start slowly when teaching your kids or grandkids about finances and get into more complex matters as they get older. Too much too soon can discourage children from wanting to learn about finances at all.

Money Morsel

The current prevailing philosophy concerning allowance seems to be that kids should get an allowance that is not tied to doing chores. Chores should be presented as an obligation of all family members in order to keep the household functioning smoothly.

in Westport, Connecticut, gives her view on why many parents do not successfully teach their children about money.

"The money scene in many households is horrendous," Ziff says. "What should be cool, calm communication becomes complex emotional anxiety and also a source of manipulation. Parents are often at opposite poles, and children get mixed messages instead of good financial experience."

It's never too early for Money 101, and the lessons should begin at home. Most schools do an inadequate job with financial education if indeed they include it at all. Kids should start learning about money as soon as they're old enough to understand the concept that money gets us what we need and want. Most kids, experts feel, are ready to begin learning at about age three.

Parents should use clear examples to teach their children about money concepts. Some of those concepts include the following:

♦ Earning money

♦ Saving money

♦ Borrowing money

♦ Spending money

♦ Budgeting money

♦ Checking accounts and checkbooks

♦ Credit cards and credit card debt

Parents can start teaching kids about checking accounts and checkbooks, for example, by explaining how they write checks each month to pay the bills. When children are older, they could help to balance the checkbook. If your kids already are older and you're not satisfied with their level of financial know-how, there are books and Web sites that can help. Some of them are listed in Appendix B, "Resources."

Although there's constant and ongoing dispute concerning the role of allowance in teaching kids about money, most financial experts agree that giving an allowance is better than not giving one. Whether or not you tie it to chores is up to you, but you should keep the following allowance tips in mind:

◆ Be clear about how much the child will get for allowance. This is directly tied in with the next tip.

◆ Be clear about what she'll be responsible for buying for herself. To figure out how much allowance she should get, decide what she'll need to buy with the money, and total up how much those items cost. For instance, if you're already giving her $7 every week to go to the movies, count that money as part of her allowance, and make it clear that she'll pay her own way from now on. Go through the same process with everything that you decide she'll pay for herself, and total up the cost of those expenses to figure out how much allowance you'll give her.

Money Morsel

Although it's good to let your child make her own decisions about how she'll spend her allowance, make sure to give her some up-front guidance about spending and how she can get the most from her money. Point out, for instance, that a less expensive shampoo and conditioner will work just as well on her hair as the more expensive ones.

◆ Once you both understand what she's responsible for buying on her own, stand back and let her make her own decisions about what she'll do with her allowance. If she overspends on a sweater and doesn't have money for the movies, she may learn a valuable lesson about planning her spending.

◆ Set up rules in advance about borrowing. If she encounters an unexpected expense and needs more money before her next allowance, use the situation as an opportunity to teach her about borrowing and interest. You don't have to charge much interest, but let her know that it costs money to borrow money.

◆ Pay on time. If you don't hand over the allowance when it's due, you're telling your kid that it's okay to be late with your financial obligations.

If your kids are older and you want them to know more about money matters such as investing, take them along with you when you visit your financial advisor or accountant. Ask them to join in your dinner discussion about the latest news on Wall Street, or the 401(k) that's just been instituted at your place of employment. Or encourage them to start or join an *investment club*.

More than half a million Americans have already joined these clubs, in which members contribute a certain amount of money each month. The money is pooled, and then invested in stocks approved by

Adding It Up

An **investment club** is a group of people with similar interests and outlooks, who research the investment pros and cons of various stocks, then use their pooled resources to buy those stocks that members feel will give them the best returns. Check out *The Complete Idiot's Guide to Starting an Investment Club* for lots of good information.

the members. Investment clubs have formed in some schools, and others are set up and operated over the Internet.

If you're financially savvy about money, chances are your children will be, too. Teaching them early on to be financially responsible will save you—and them—a lot of headaches and trouble down the road.

Letting Them Earn Their Own

The older your kids get, the more money they'll want and need. If you've reached your allowance limit, and your kids are constantly griping that they don't have enough money, show them a copy of the classified section's employment ads.

More and more teenagers are working, and holding a part-time job while juggling other responsibilities is a good way to prepare them for the real world.

While working a part-time job can be a good experience for a teen, there are some points that both parents and the potential employee should keep in mind.

◆ The job shouldn't consume so much time that it makes it impossible for the child to fulfill other responsibilities, such as homework or band practice. And, make sure your teen still has enough time to just be a kid.

Don't Go There

The National Consumers League says the five worst jobs for teens are delivery and other jobs that include driving; working alone in cash-based businesses such as convenience stores; construction, including work in high places and contact with electrical power; traveling youth crews that sell candy, magazine subscriptions, etc. in strange neighborhoods; and jobs in which employers pay "under the table."

◆ Some jobs are better than others. Make sure the job your teen gets is appropriate for her age and experience. For example, your 16-year-old should not be working the counter of a restaurant that has a cocktail lounge in another part of the building, or the late-night shift by herself in a convenience store. Some jobs, such as roofing, driving a motor vehicle, meat packing, and excavating are prohibited by the Fair Labor Standards Act for all youth under the age of 18.

◆ Decide with your child how much of his earnings he can have to spend and how much will be put into savings. Encourage him to contribute at least a small amount to a charity or another good cause.

◆ If your child earns more than $4,400 a year, she'll need to file a federal income tax return.

◆ Don't discount traditional jobs for teenagers such as baby-sitting, mowing lawns, washing cars, and shoveling snow. These types of jobs offer a little more flexibility and can be done for people that you and your teenager know.

Summer jobs serve a good purpose in addition to just giving your kid some spending money. Let's face it, working in a fast food place or mowing lawns when it's 90 degrees probably isn't something your child will want to do forever. Summer jobs such as these can be good reminders about how important it is to get a good education, and eventually, a more rewarding type of job.

You're Not a Fairy Godmother

If your 16-year-old comes to you the day after she gets her driver's license and tells you she wants a new car, what do you do? Believe it or not, a substantial number of parents will drive her to the car lot and tell her to pick out her favorite color.

We are of the firm opinion that giving your child money every time she asks, or buying her expensive gifts like a car or computer, is doing her no favors. Unless you're going to support her throughout your life, and have the means to leave her enough money to maintain her lifestyle when you're gone, you're setting her up for a very big fall.

Kids want a lot. The best way to teach them how the world works is to have them pay, or help pay, for the things they want. Giving kids everything they desire fosters in them a feeling of entitlement, without a sense of responsibility.

Teach them instead that even a little bit of money saved each week will eventually add up to enough to buy a PlayStation game or new in-line skates. And remember that your job as a parent is to provide a good home, a stable environment, and all the love you can. Nowhere in the book of parenting does it say you must indulge your child with every object that catches his fancy.

Helping Out with Big Expenses

Having just said all that, we think it's perfectly all right to help your kids out with big expenses. If your 13-year-old has cut lawns all summer, saved every penny he made, and still comes up $60 short for the bike he wants to buy, by all means give him the $60 and tell him you're proud of him for earning the rest of it.

If your 17-year-old has saved her baby-sitting money from the time she was 12 because she's been planning to buy a car, it's fine to throw in the last couple of hundred dollars or to offer to pay her first year of auto insurance.

And if your responsible, hard-working 24-year-old has found a little house that he and his wife just love, but needs a few thousand dollars for the down payment, go ahead and help him out. You can give him money as a gift, or work out a schedule to have him pay you back.

There are times when it's completely appropriate to give your child money to help buy something she wants. If you've taught her well, she'll only ask occasionally, and only when it's important.

Our job as parents is to help our kids grow up to be responsible adults. Teaching them the value of money when they're young, and the concepts of money management and sharing some of what they have, will help to assure that goal.

The Least You Need to Know

- Kids have more money today than ever before, and they're prime targets for marketers and advertisers.
- Children generally do not have a good feeling for the difference between want and need, and must be taught to recognize it.
- If kids aren't aware that most people in the world have far less than they do, they may not be able to fully appreciate what they have.
- Parents should start teaching their kids the simple facts about money at a very young age, then deal with more complex money matters as the children get older.
- It's not your job as a parent to give your kids everything they ask for.
- Helping kids to pay for big expenses is fine, as long as they've done their share.

Trading In the Bikes for Cars

In This Chapter

- ◆ Teens get cars and parents get anxious
- ◆ Judging if your teen is ready to own a car
- ◆ Deciding who will buy the vehicle
- ◆ How to pay for a car
- ◆ Determining what kind of car to buy
- ◆ Dealing with ongoing costs of owning a car

Although you'd swear it was just yesterday that your Becky was 10 and still wearing braces on her teeth and her hair in pigtails, today she's 16 and talking nonstop about learning to drive a car.

For years Becky and her friends rode their bikes through the neighborhood, venturing out further and further as they got older and braver. Eventually, they could ride those bikes across town to get to the video store with the best selection of movies or the ice-cream shop with the most flavors.

While you encouraged Becky's independence on her bike, thinking about her operating a car probably seems a bit frightening. Driving a car, after all, is a lot different from riding a bicycle on the sidewalk with a couple of friends.

Where will she and her friends venture out to in a car? Across town? To the other side of the county? The country? Will she remember to wear her seatbelt every time she drives, and remind her friends to buckle up, too? Will she drive responsibly? What if she's in an accident? What if she's hurt, or even killed?

Most parents experience a significant level of anxiety as their children trade in their bikes for automobiles. And with good reason. About 7,000 teens are killed each year in car accidents. What parents don't have qualms as they watch their child climb in behind the wheel and drive off alone for the first time?

The anxiety level also may cross over to your pocketbook. If you agree that Becky may have a car, should you buy it for her? Maybe you'll loan her money, or give her a certain amount to use toward a vehicle. Who will pay for the car insurance?

Once you've decided if you'll open your wallet to fund the car thing, you'll face another set of issues. Should Becky get a brand-new car with the latest safety features and a warranty, or will a little used car be suitable for the driving she'll do? And you should take some time to think about rules you'll apply to the car and Becky's driving.

Those are some of the topics we'll hash out in this chapter, which is intended to take a bit of that anxiety out of the car issue.

When Your Kid Wants a Car

There's a great probability that, sooner or later, your teenager is going to want to have his own car. The question is, will you agree to let him have one?

Let's dispel the notion right up front that every teenager needs to have his or her own car. Plenty of kids do just fine without a Jetta of their own. They walk. They keep riding their trusty bikes. They skateboard. They take a bus. They bum rides from their friends (and that's another issue), or from you.

Tom and Ray Magliozzi, the brothers who host National Public Radio's *Car Talk*, polled 5,000 listeners a couple of years ago on whether or not a 16-year-old should have his own car. Sixty-seven percent of those listeners answered with a resounding "no."

We all know, however, that plenty of kids do own cars. Check out any suburban or rural high school parking lot. Chances are that it's filled with students' cars. When contemplating whether or not your child should have one, consider these points:

◆ Does your teen *need* a car, or just want one because all her friends are getting them? If she goes straight from school to her job at the assisted living center every day, and right on to her dance lesson after work, then it may make good sense for her to have a car. If her primary motivation to getting one is to load up her friends and cruise around on Saturday nights, however, she doesn't need a car.

◆ Is your teenager responsible enough to have his own car? We'll discuss this at length in the next section.

◆ Will letting your son or daughter get a car make your life significantly easier? If your child's school is 20 minutes from your house and you're making two round trips a day, you're spending a lot of time as a kid chauffeur. Letting her drive herself to school could take a lot of pressure off your schedule.

◆ Is there money available to buy a car? Even used cars can be expensive. If buying a vehicle is a strain on your finances and your teen doesn't have money to pay for a car, postpone the purchase until she can buy it herself, or your financial position improves.

Money Morsel

Remember that buying the car is only the first expense. Fueling, maintaining, and insuring a car is expensive business, too.

Carefully considering these questions, and discussing them with your teenager will get you started in deciding whether or not he should have his own car. Be sure to read the next section carefully before deciding whether he's responsible enough to own a vehicle.

Knowing If He or She Is Ready

We all know that kids mature at different rates. For that reason, deciding whether or not your child can handle the responsibility of having his own car is a judgment call.

Some kids make it easy to decide. They're either obviously mature and responsible or obviously immature and irresponsible. If your kid is typical, though, he's probably basically trustworthy and sensible, but subject to frightening lapses in judgment.

Car accidents are the leading cause of death among teenagers in the United States, accounting for 36 percent of all deaths of persons aged 15 to 19 years. Obviously, you don't want your child to become a statistic.

Remember that teenagers often change quickly. If you have doubts over whether your son or daughter is responsible enough to own a car at age 16, wait for a year. Tell her that if she continues to mature and exhibit responsible behavior during the next year, you'll re-address the car thing when she's 17. Meanwhile, you can make sure she gets

Don't Go There

Parents should be aware of car surfing, an incredibly dangerous game that resulted in about 500 deaths between 1995 and 2000. Car surfers stand on the hood of a moving car. The person driving the car slams on the brakes, causing the surfer to fly off the hood. Most of those killed car surfing are between 16 and 24 years old.

plenty of driver training, and you can let her use your car and observe her level of responsibility.

You also should observe her friends' behavior concerning autos and driving. If you ever observe, or hear about any of them driving irresponsibly, address the issue immediately. Think about limiting the number of people she can ride with in one car. It's a known fact that accidents happen more frequently when a lot of kids are in the vehicle. Some states have passed laws limiting the number of teenagers in one car without an adult present.

While we're on the subject of safety, consider these safety tips from the Insurance Institute for Highway Safety:

- Give beginning drivers as much supervised driving time as possible.
- Teens should wait six months before driving with other teenage passengers.
- Don't assume your teen drives the same way when you're not around as she does under your supervision.
- Restrict unsupervised nighttime driving.
- Select safe cars. Large cars with safety bags are extra safety features to consider when purchasing a car your teen will drive.

You know your child better than anyone, and you'll have to decide whether or not he's mature and responsible enough to have a car. If you decide that he's not, don't feel bad about denying him. Explain your reasoning and tell him you'll reconsider the matter in six months. Keeping your teenager safe is more important than keeping him completely satisfied.

Ann Landers, the syndicated answers lady, recently included in one of her columns a suggested driving contract between you and your child. The reason for the contract is twofold. It serves as a reminder that driving a car is a serious responsibility, and it addresses potential driving situations before they occur. The contract, Landers says, should include the following stipulations.

- If your child gets a traffic ticket, she's responsible for paying the cost of the ticket, as well as the difference in the insurance premium for as long as the premium increase is in effect.
- At no time will your child ever drink and drive, or carry any alcohol in the car.
- Your child must agree to pay for any damage he causes to the car that is not covered by insurance.
- He will never have more people in the car than there are seat belts, and he will not begin driving until all passengers have buckled up.
- She will keep the car clean, refill the gas tank, check the oil, and so forth.

We think that this, or a contract between you and your child that you come up with on your own, is a great idea. Be sure that your child understands the consequences of not living up to the agreement, and be sure that the consequences are serious enough to get his attention.

Who Should Buy the Car?

Once you've cast a nay or yea on whether or not your teen gets a car, you're faced with the question of who buys the vehicle.

Should you buy it? Should your child buy it? Or should you share the cost? If you buy the car, should it be an outright gift, or do you expect your teen to make payments to you? Will the car be in your name or his? What costs relating to the vehicle will he be responsible for?

We feel strongly that it's not a good idea to buy your child a car with no financial strings attached. Bearing or sharing the cost of the vehicle will give your teen more ownership and (theoretically, at least) make him more responsible for taking care of the car.

If you're going to help your teen buy a car, be very clear about the arrangement. Tell him exactly how much you'll contribute, and make it clear that he's responsible for the remaining costs. If you're loaning him money for a car, work out a schedule for him to repay you and make sure he sticks to it, just as he would have to do if he had a car loan.

 Money Morsel

If you and your teenager are in the market for a vehicle, have her check out "Car Buying Information for Teenagers," an online excerpt from *The Teenagers Guide to the Real World,* by Marshall Brain. Located at www.bygpub.com/books/ tg2rw/cars.htm, the article contains links to all sorts of useful car sites.

If he's buying the car himself and will need to finance it, it's a good idea to help him with that process so you make sure he doesn't get into a bad loan situation. You're likely to have to sign or co-sign for the loan if your child is under 18, so you'll want to get the best deal possible.

If you're helping your teen to get a loan or you decide to buy the vehicle for him and are going to finance it, keep the following tips in mind. Remember, though, that you're likely to negotiate a better deal if you're able to pay for the car up front.

◆ Use a loan from a bank or credit union instead of the car dealership. Dealer financing usually costs at least a percentage point or two more than a bank.

◆ Make the biggest down payment you can comfortably afford. This lowers your interest rate and cuts the amount you're financing, saving money in the long run.

- If the car you're buying comes with a rebate offer, use the rebate money as part of the down payment.

- Get the shortest-term loan you can afford. Explain to your teen how a car loan works, and consider having her contribute some of her Burger King salary to help out with the monthly payments.

- Think about getting a home equity loan instead of a car loan if you're going to finance a car for your teen. Interest on a car loan is not tax-deductible, but interest on a home equity loan is.

- If your child comes into extra money at a birthday, high school graduation, or other occasion, encourage him to apply the money to the car loan and get it paid off early, if possible.

Money Morsel

If you decide to buy or lease a car for your teenager, be sure to include him in the process. This will help to prepare him for the time when he'll be buying a car on his own.

- Look for a simple interest loan instead of an installment loan. A simple interest loan lets you pay interest only on the money you still owe. A front-end installment loan, on the other hand, requires that you pay interest on the entire loan, even after you've repaid a portion of it. If you borrow $5,000 and pay back $2,500, you'd still be paying interest on the full amount, even though you only owe half.

What About a Lease?

If you lease your own car and are happy with the arrangement, you might consider leasing a vehicle for your teen. As you probably know, there are two schools of thought on leasing versus buying. Some people swear that leasing is the only way to go, while others would rather take a bus than lease a car.

Basically, when you lease a vehicle, you're paying for the estimated depreciation that occurs to the car while you're driving it. You pay only for the part of the car's value that you use—plus interest.

There are pros and cons to leasing a car, and some special considerations to keep in mind if you're thinking of leasing a car for your teenager.

Advantages to leasing a car include:

- You probably can lease a more expensive car than you can buy. Since you're getting this car for your teenager, however, that shouldn't be an issue. Your kid doesn't need to drive a Lexus.

◆ Many leases don't require a down payment, or require only a minimal down payment. This makes leasing very appealing to many people.

◆ You don't have to worry about selling or trading in the car when the lease ends.

◆ You can lease a small new car for almost the same price you would be paying for a used car, and you'll need only a small down payment. You won't own the car at the end of the lease, but this may enable you to get your teenager a more reliable car for the money.

Disadvantages to leasing a car include:

◆ It's almost always more expensive in the long run to lease a car than it is to buy one. Leasing is usually more expensive than financing, too.

◆ When the lease ends, your kid will no longer have a car. Actually, you can consider this either an advantage or a disadvantage. If you lease a car for your teen with the understanding that when the lease ends and the car is returned, she's responsible for getting her next car, that's pretty good incentive for her to start saving her money. If you'll just end up buying her another car when the lease ends, however, you're back to square one.

◆ Most lease agreements impose mileage restrictions, and charge a penalty if you exceed the limit. If your kid is driving six hours each way to visit his girlfriend every weekend and every chance in between, chances are he'll exceed the limit and end up costing even more money than you're already paying out.

◆ You might end up paying disposition charges when the lease ends. These charges cover the dealer's cost of auctioning the car.

Don't Go There

If you suspect your teen isn't going to take good care of a vehicle, don't lease one for her. Your dealer will be very unhappy if you try to turn in a leased car that's been trashed. And you will pay dearly for it.

Once you've decided whether your child should have a car and who's going to pay for the vehicle, you'll need to think about what kind to buy.

New Jetta or a Junker?

Ask your 17-year-old what kind of car she wants, and chances are that she'll have some pretty strong opinions on the topic. Even many 10- and 11-year-olds know what kind of car they hope to have when they're old enough to drive.

Back in the early 1970s, when we were beginning drivers, kids didn't drive brand-new cars. In fact, most kids didn't have their own cars. We borrowed Mom's or Dad's car, or Dad would buy one little car that you got to share with your brothers and sisters. Nobody expected to get a new car as soon as they were able to pass their driver's test.

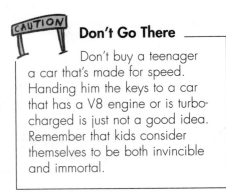

Don't Go There

Don't buy a teenager a car that's made for speed. Handing him the keys to a car that has a V8 engine or is turbocharged is just not a good idea. Remember that kids consider themselves to be both invincible and immortal.

Drive by your local high school some day and take a look at what's sitting in the parking lot. Sport utility vehicles, flashy pickups, BMWs, spanking-new Volkswagon Bugs. Gone are the days when kids were grateful for any old junker that appeared in their driveway. Many teenagers are very status-conscious, and they are painfully aware of what their affluent peers have.

Your job is to convince your teenager that there's nothing wrong with driving a good, dependable, used car, even if it's not the prettiest vehicle in the high school parking lot. There's no need, in our opinion, to dash out and buy a beginning driver a brand-new car.

Regardless of what type of car you're considering, its safety factors should be your primary concern.

- Air bags. Remember that cars manufactured before 1992 were not required to have air bags on the driver's side. Some do, others don't. If you're thinking about an older car, make sure it's air bag equipped, preferably on the driver's and passenger's sides.

- Watch out for SUVs. Sport utility vehicles give the illusion of safety because they're so big, but remember that they're way more likely to roll over than cars. For a report on the likelihood of rollovers for various types of cars, SUVs, and light trucks, go on the Internet to the National Highway Traffic Safety Administration's site at www.nhtsa.dot.gov. SUVs also can be unwieldy to drive and difficult to maneuver in a situation such as if you're trying to avoid an accident.

- Don't go too small. A tiny car won't offer the protection of a larger one in the event of a crash. Don't be tempted to trade in safety for better gas mileage. Crash test scores also can be found on the National Highway Traffic Safety Administration's Web site.

- Make sure your teen has adequate training and experience before you allow her to begin driving on her own. Most highway safety experts feel that it's too easy to get a driver's license in the United States and that the requirements should be stricter.

Once you've considered safety issues concerning your child's vehicle, look to reliability. The last thing you want to happen is to have your 16-year-old stranded on a dark road some night because her car has broken down. If you're going with a used car, try to be sure that it's certified, which means it's been inspected and tested to make sure everything is in working order. It's a good idea to have a private mechanic check out a car before you buy it, especially if you're buying from an individual. Dealers who sell used cars are subject to the *Federal Trade Commission's Used Car Rule*, but individuals are not.

A used-car dealer should be willing to let you test drive the car, and under the Used Car Rule must provide information about the major mechanical and electrical systems, including what problems you should be on the lookout for. Be sure to ask for the car's maintenance and repair records, and get any promises the dealer makes in writing.

For many people, the cost of a car is one of their key considerations. The trick is to get the best car you can for the money you have, or the money that your teenager has. If your friends or acquaintances have purchased used cars for teens, find out where they got them and whether or not they're satisfied with their purchase.

Adding It Up

The **Federal Trade Commission's Used Car Rule** requires dealers to provide certain types of information about a car to potential buyers. Information that must be revealed includes whether the car comes with a warranty, what percentage of repair costs the dealer will pay, and so forth.

Also, check out Edmunds.com for used new and used car prices and information. You'll find it on the Internet at www.edmunds.com. The site also includes an affordability calculator to help you or your teenager figure out exactly what kind of vehicle you can afford.

Safety, reliability, and expense are the three main factors you'll consider when buying a used car. Of course, your teenager will no doubt consider some factors of her own, such as the make of the car the color, and its peer acceptability.

The Cost of Keeping a Car

Those of us who own cars understand that buying one is just the beginning of the strain that a vehicle can place on your pocketbook. Most teenagers understand that it takes significant money to buy a car, but are uninformed about the continuing costs.

Keeping a car is expensive business. You've got to buy gas and pay to have the car maintained. Gas prices on the East Coast currently are hovering somewhere around between $1.30 and $1.60 a gallon, depending on the grade. Our shaky world political situation at the moment; however, makes it impossible to predict what gas prices will be like in the future.

An oil change, depending on where you live, can cost anywhere between $25 and $50, and then there are all the little costs such as washing the car, inspection fees, parking fees, tolls, and so forth. And then there are registration fees, costs to have your driver's license renewed, and the big one—auto insurance.

When your teenager starts driving, he'll either have to buy his own auto insurance or you'll have to add him to your policy. Most insurers will require your teen to be added to your policy or to have his own policy as soon as he gets his learner's permit. However, because a licensed driver is required to be in the car with a learner, some insurers don't consider a learner to be a significant risk, and will charge only a minimal amount to add

> ### Go Figure
>
> Insurance companies figure that drivers between 16 and 24 are most at risk for accidents. Insurance rates for that age group reflect the industry's feelings.

him to your policy. Other insurers, however, will up your rates significantly as soon as your teen gets the permit. Insurance companies consider teens to be high-risk customers, because they're inexperienced and make more frequent mistakes than those who have been driving for longer. Unfortunately, statistics show that while teens make up 10 percent of the general population, they're responsible for 14 percent of all motor vehicle deaths.

While it's common practice for parents to add their kids onto their policies, it isn't always the least expensive way to insure your child. If you've got two or three expensive cars in the garage and your kid is going to drive one of them, it's going to cost a hefty sum to add him onto your policy because expensive cars cost a lot of money to fix. If your kid is driving a used car that didn't cost an arm and a leg, however, and you buy him only basic insurance coverage, it may be less expensive to get him his own policy than to add him onto yours. On the other hand, if you have discounts on your policy, such as safe driver or multi-vehicle, adding your teen to your policy might be the way to go. You'll need to sit down with your agent to determine the best plan for you and your teen.

Ask your agent to run the policy costs of adding your child to your current policy and the cost of having him insured under his own policy. Many insurers will require your child to be included on your policy for a certain amount of time after he's started driving. That can be fine, but if your teen has an accident or commits a traffic violation, your policy will reflect that. And an accident or violation may prevent your teen from being able to get his own policy.

When considering what to do about your teen's car insurance, consider all the options and ask a lot of questions.

An important consideration to keep in mind if your teen is included on your policy, is the designation of the car he'll be driving. You sure don't want to designate your brand-new Volvo as the car he'll be driving when you can just as easily designate the eight-year-old Honda Civic. The rates will be increased on the car your teen will be driving, and you don't want to have to pay even more to insure a new car than you'll already be charged.

Also keep in mind that, just as with your own auto insurance, insurance rates for teens vary depending on where you live. Insuring a teen driver in Los Angeles, for instance, can cost many times more than insuring a teen with the same vehicle in a rural area of Kansas.

Explain to your child that owning a car is expensive business, and that the costs do not end the day the car is purchased. Teach her the value of taking care of her car, and make sure she understands what needs to be done in the way of maintenance and daily care. And, be sure that he or she knows exactly what to do in the event of an emergency. Come up with a plan in case of trouble like a flat tire or engine trouble.

Money Morsel

Remember that many insurance companies offer lower rates to teens who have completed a high school driver's education course, who earn good grades in school, or who meet other requirements. You may save up to 10 percent of the additional premium for a new driver, so be sure to ask your agent what's available.

Teens and cars can be a worrisome mix, and paying for the vehicle is just one of those worries. If your kid has a car, do what you can to educate him in every applicable area—from finances to safety. Then sit back and try not to worry too much. Remember that most teens make it through to adulthood relatively unscathed, and your teen most likely will, too.

The Least You Need to Know

- ◆ Seeing your teenager get in a car and drive off can be a great source of anxiety but is something most of us will go through.
- ◆ Only you can judge whether or not your child is responsible and mature enough to own a car.
- ◆ Making your teen at least partially responsible for paying for a car gives him a good sense of ownership and appreciation.
- ◆ When deciding what kind of car to buy, you'll need to consider safety, dependability, and expense.
- ◆ Make sure your teen understands the cost of owning a car doesn't stop once the actual purchase is completed.
- ◆ Teach your child well, and then trust that she'll use good judgement.

Chapter 8

Paying for College

In This Chapter

- Knowing the differences in college costs
- Traditional and not-so-traditional college accounts
- Locating an affordable school
- Finding out if you qualify for financial aid
- Using your home to pay for college

If your son or daughter is getting ready to go off to college, you're probably experiencing an array of feelings on many different levels. You're no doubt happy for your child, but a little anxious and worried, as well.

She's really going away—maybe far away—and you might not see her again for months. You wonder if she'll be okay without you. Will she get along with her roommate? Will she eat right? Will she be able to keep up with all the work involved? Will she be happy?

After you finish considering your child's well being as it relates to college, the next thing to enter your mind may well be the cost. College is expensive, that's for sure.

Hopefully, you've been stashing away money that's earmarked for college costs for years. Unfortunately, however, some people are unable to save much, and many of us don't save as much as we should. That might mean that we'll need to get creative when it comes time to send our kids to college. College costs are a major financial issue for many, many families, so don't feel like you're on your own here. In this chapter, we'll look at different possibilities for paying for your kids' educations, and how you might be able to get some help with those costs.

The Cost of Higher Education

Yearly costs at Harvard University in Cambridge, Massachusetts, have topped $34,000 a year, while students at Georgetown University in Washington, D.C., pay about $33,000. An education at the University of Pennsylvania in Philadelphia costs approximately $32,000 a year, Tulane University in New Orleans is about $31,000, and students at Rice University in Houston hand over about $23,000 a year. Of course, not all colleges and universities cost as much as these prestigious institutions, but college these days is an expensive venture.

Go Figure
Tuition at Utica College in Utica, New York, cost $4,014 for the 1980–1981 school year. The cost for the 1999–2000 year was $16,150. This kind of increase is not unusual on a national basis.

The cost of college has significantly outpaced inflation since the early 1970s. Nationally, the cost of college tuition has quadrupled since 1980.

As you can imagine, and may well know firsthand, paying for a college education (not to mention two or three of them) can be a tremendous strain on a family's finances. The problem is that we realize how important college is to our kids' futures. Many of us consider college to be a necessity, not a luxury or an option.

Census Bureau data points out a clear link between education level and finances. Both male and female college graduates earn significantly more than high school graduates, and it's been shown that income rises faster among people who have higher education.

So how does the average family find the cash to send its kids to college, and still meet all its other expenses? If you've become extremely discouraged from reading the first part of this chapter, cheer up. Not all colleges are nudging at the $30,000 a year or over mark. There are still some educational bargains out there.

Community colleges come at a much lower cost—averaging roughly $3,000 a year. State-owned colleges and universities generally are affordable for state residents. And many schools offer financial aid to deserving students.

Even if you find a bargain, however, you'll face significant expenses. In addition to tuition, room, and meals, there are costs for books, fees, and transportation. Add to that the cost of phone cards, a microwave, computer, and one of those little refrigerators for the dorm room, and you've got yourself a bill that may look to you like the national debt.

So how do we go about paying for college? Let's have a look.

Starting Early to Save for College

If we all started to save for college the day our children were born, we'd probably be in pretty good shape by the time that baby reached 18 or 19 years old.

Unfortunately, most of us don't do that. Life and daily bills get in the way, meaning that all too often, the college fund is the last account on the deposit list each month.

If you're not convinced that it's important to start saving early for college, consider these figures from the T. Rowe Price investment firm. These numbers are the amounts parents need to save per month and per year at 10 percent return in order to have $100,000 saved when it's time for college.

- Parents who start saving money when their child is born need to save $161 a month, or $1,938 a year.
- Parents who start saving when their child is eight will have to save $447 a month, or $5,364 a year.
- Parents who start saving when their child is 13 will need to save $1,140 a month, or $13,681 a year.

Unless you hit the lottery when your kid's 15, it's easier for most people to pay a manageable amount over a long period of time than a huge chunk each month for a shorter time.

If your children are still young and you've decided you'd like to start saving for college early on, you've got some choices as to how to do so.

You could invest money in a uniform gifts to minors account, an educational IRA, 529 plans, EE bonds, or just accumulate money in your name that's designated for your child's college expenses. All of these methods have some pros and cons.

> **Go Figure**
>
> Parents who invest $100 a month for 18 years at a modest 6 percent total return would have $39,000 when their child is ready for his freshman year at college.

Traditional College Accounts

Putting money aside in an account in your name that's designated as a college fund for your child is what financial advisers call a traditional college account. The money in that account is yours, which means you can use it in case of a real emergency.

If your child for some reason doesn't go to college, you simply use the money for something else. All income and capital gains from the account are yours, and must be reported on your annual income tax returns. This means that there isn't any compounding on the funds, and you won't earn interest on your interest. If your precious decides that he'd prefer to work on a shrimp boat in Louisiana instead of head off for college, however, all the money in the account is yours. This means of saving doesn't have any tax benefits, which has made it less popular as other, more tax-friendly methods of saving for college have been introduced.

Another tactic for funding a college education is to use proceeds from appreciated stock. Grandma, or whoever it is that owns the stock, can give it to the student, who can then sell it and apply it toward his first semester's tuition. He'll still have to pay capital gains on the stock, but they'll be based on the child's tax bracket, which is much lower than Grandma's.

Money Morsel

Many colleges and universities offer payment plans and incentives to try to entice future students to their campuses. If you're interested in a particular school, see if there's a payment program you can get into early on.

You also can pay money directly to an educational institution for the cost of your child's education. There isn't any limitation to the amount you can give, except it must be earmarked for tuition. The funds must be paid directly to the college, not channeled through the student. Be sure to tell Grandma that she shouldn't pay any tuition funds to the college until she sees a bill, though. If she hands over tuition money to Cornell, for instance, and then your child decides to tour Europe instead, the money can't be returned. It becomes a charitable gift to the college.

Other Options for College Savings

Traditional methods of saving for college are still popular, but there are some newer and more creative methods of saving, as well.

You really should sit down with a financial advisor, who will assess your financial situation and recommend a plan that best suits your situation.

So you know what the advisor is talking about, some information about other options for saving for college is given in the following sections.

EE Bonds

A method of saving for college that's gaining in popularity is utilizing EE Bonds. These bonds are special because the interest accrues on them from the time the bonds are purchased until they are cashed, with the proceeds used toward college exempt from federal income tax liability. This is a beneficial tool, but you should know that it's not available to everyone.

A person over the age of 24 must purchase the bonds in the name of the parents of the child for whom the money is earmarked—not in the child's name. And the bonds must be held for at least five years before they can be used for college costs. That means you can't go out and buy them when your child is 17 and expect to use them to pay for college costs.

When you cash in the bonds to pay for educational expenses, the entire interest amount is tax free, provided your joint household income is less than $79,650. The amount is pro-rated up to a maximum of $109,650 of family income, and, once you're over $109,650, the accrued interest is taxed.

EE bonds can be a nice supplement to your college savings, but not a practical means of funding an entire college education. If your child doesn't go to college, the bonds remain in your name.

> **Money Morsel**
>
> In order to cash in on the income tax exemption of EE bonds, they can only be used for educational expenses for you, your spouse, or your dependent children. The bonds can be used to pay for tuition, room and board, and books.

Uniform Gifts to Minors Act (UGMA) Accounts

These are older style accounts that are set up to lower the income tax liability that individuals pay for funds in their children's names. Funds set aside for college, or given as gifts to your children, are placed into an account in the child's name under the Uniform Gifts to Minors Act. The funds belong to the child. Since the child is a minor, however, the funds must have a custodian—usually a parent. The funds accumulate and are invested, with the child earning investment income. The nice thing about these kinds of accounts is that the first $750 of investment income the child earns is not taxed, and the next $750 is taxed at the lowest tax bracket. After that, the rate increases and is paid at the parents' tax rate. After age 14, the rate is always taxed at the rate of the child's tax bracket.

A possible downside of these funds is that the money belongs to your child. If Rob decides to buy a motorcycle and ride through Europe instead of going to college, as long as he's no longer a minor, you can't stop him from taking his "college" money with him. It's a good idea to only invest enough in these types of funds to get the income tax advantage, and put the rest of your child's college money somewhere else.

> **Don't Go There**
>
> Life insurance is not a good investment for a college account. Neither are limited partnerships or tax deferred annuities. These are long-term investments that aren't suitable for college savings. If your financial advisor recommends any of these investment tools, run and find another advisor.

The custodian of a UGMA account can set it up as a savings account in the local bank, and change it to a brokerage account as the account grows. You can even buy stocks or bonds with the money, but not unless you know what you're doing.

Gift tax limitations dictate that a maximum of $10,000 a year can be placed in a UGMA account. That amount can be doubled if a couple is gifting.

Education IRAs

The recent tax law change will increase the annual limit on contributions to an education IRA from the current $500 per year to $2,000 per year. Thank goodness! It was hardly worth the hassle of setting up one of these accounts for a measly $500 a year. With a $2,000 limit, however, you can reach, or get close to your college goal if you start saving as soon as your child is born.

As with all IRAs, the income and capital growth are deferred within an education IRA until the funds are withdrawn for college.

Education IRAs have income limits for the parents, but you can change the beneficiary designation to another child if your first child decides not to go to college. One of the problems with education IRAs is that you can only use the funds for your children, so if none of your children go to college, the funds become taxable to the last named beneficiary when they reach 30 years of age. Unfortunately, you can't roll the unused education IRA over into a personal IRA, the accumulated capital gain and income are taxed to the beneficiary.

Tax Credits for Parents of College Students

There are two tax credits that may be available to you during the time that your children are in college. As with so much of the income tax code, these tax credits are not cut and dried, but depend on your annual income and some other stipulations.

As you know, there are tax deductions and then there are tax credits. The difference is where they can be used on your tax return. A deduction is listed on Schedule A of your income tax return, and if your deductions are large enough to exceed your standard deduction, you can subtract the deductible sum from your adjusted gross income. After you've subtracted out your exemptions, this figure is called your taxable income and used to calculate your tax.

A tax credit is usually better because you don't have to itemize your deductions to use the credit. You can file your return using a standard deduction and still use a credit. Once you've calculated your tax, a credit is subtracted from this tax to lower what you owe the IRS.

The HOPE (Higher Opportunities for Performance in Education) credit has been available since 1998. It's a tax credit for qualified tuition and related expenses during a student's first two years of college. The student must attend college or other post-high school courses at least half time.

The credit is for 100 percent of the first $1,000 of qualified expenses paid during the year, plus 50 percent of the next $2,000, for a maximum of $3,000.

A Lifetime Learning Credit is a credit for expenses that don't qualify for the HOPE credit. The Lifetime Learning Credit is available for any school year for courses aimed at acquiring or improving job skills. The credit may be for undergraduate, graduate, or professional degree courses.

The Lifetime Learning Credit is equal to 2 percent of expenses up to $5,000, for a maximum credit of $1,000 per year. After the year 2003, the credit will rise to 20 percent of $10,000, for a maximum credit of $5,000 per year.

The Lifetime Learning Credit is for you, your spouse, and your children or other dependents. It's intended to be used for tuition and related fees—not room and board, commuting, or other expenses. And, of course, there are income limits.

What the IRS giveth, the IRS taketh away. The credit begins to phase out with adjusted gross income over $80,000 per year and is completely gone if your income is more than $100,000 per year (for married filers, the figures are halved for single filers). We're not talking about $80,000 in taxable income, we're talking adjusted gross income—the total of all your income, with some adjustments.

Qualified State Tuition Plans

There are two types of qualified state tuition plans, both of which are 529 plans. That means they fall under section 529 of the tax code, which permits investing for college in a *tax-deferred* vehicle. One type of qualified state plan is known as a Prepaid Tuition Plan or Tuition Assistance Plan. The other is simply called a 529 Plan.

The 529 Plan was revised in 1997 and again in 2001. This plan is the newest way to save for a child's college education. Basically, it's an account that's set aside for a child's education, and is tax deferred until it's used. The money, however, can't

Money Morsel

If you qualify (by attending a college or post-high school at least half time), you could use the HOPE credit for your child's freshman and sophomore years, and the Lifetime Learning Credit for her junior and senior years.

Adding It Up

Tax-deferred income is earned, but not taxed until the income is used. **Tax-free** income is never taxed.

be accessed by the child. If Rob buys that motorcycle and takes off for Europe, he can't grab the money from the account on the way out.

A 529 Plan is even more appealing under the most recent Tax Act, which will in 2002 make all earnings within a 529 Plan *tax free*, not just tax deferred. And, up to $50,000 can be contributed to a 529 Plan each year by an individual, or up to $100,000 by a couple. Contributions to these plans are considered gifts. The person setting up the account and depositing money is called a contributor, and remains in control of the money. If the child for whom the money is intended does not go to college, the money can be passed along to another beneficiary (within the large family unit—nieces and nephews rather than just brothers and sisters like an education IRA), or retained by the contributor.

At that point, if the contributor retained the money, it would become taxable, and there would be a 10 percent penalty. The penalty is meant to be a deterrent to people using a 529 Plan as a convenient way to stash away tax-free money, never intending to use it to pay for college.

The Prepaid Tuition Plan is intended to fund tuition expenses only. Money in these plans can't be used to prepay room, board, books, fees, and so forth. It's strictly for tuition. That means you'll probably need to have another college investment vehicle, as well.

The governments of various states normally set up these Prepaid Tuition Plans, which are guaranteed against losses in the stock market. You probably will need to be a resident of the state in which you set up a plan.

A Prepaid Tuition Plan guarantees that your tuition credits will pay for your child's tuition. No matter what happens to tuition costs, your purchase "locks in" the cost of future tuition. The plan can be used for tuition at any accredited, public or private college or technical school in the United States.

This plan may keep you eligible for financial aid, since it only covers the cost of tuition. You'll still need to come up with the money for room and board.

The funds you contribute to a Prepaid Tuition Plan are used to buy tuition credits that equal credit hours paid at different types of institutions. You'll need more credits for a four-year college or university, for instance, than you would for an area community college. You'll need to purchase more credits if your child is interested in a university, while you'll need to purchase less if your child is interested in a community college.

If your child doesn't use all the tuition credits you've purchased, you may be able to get a refund.

Figuring Out What You Can Afford

The staff of many colleges will advise you to identify the schools in which you and your child are interested, and then worry about how you'll pay for it. They encourage you to consider their schools by telling you there is financial aid available. We hear them, but there's a basic problem with that philosophy.

If the cost of a particular school is so great, it may be that even after financial aid you won't be able to afford it.

The cost for one year of tuition, room, and board at Lehigh University in Bethlehem, Pennsylvania, is $32,000. That doesn't include books, or expenses such as transportation, phone, and so forth. If your child receives $16,000 a year in financial aid, you'd be thrilled, right? That is, until you realized you'd still have to shell out $16,000 a year, plus expenses.

Money Morsel

To get an idea of the financial aid for which you might qualify, check out www.FinAid.org. You then can compare the aid package to the total costs for the school in which you're interested.

At the end of four years, you'd have paid more than $64,000, and that's only for your first child. If a school offers a financial aid package for your son or daughter, make sure the college is within the framework of what you can afford, even with the package.

Regardless of how much money you've managed to put aside, you'll still need to take a good, hard look at what expenses will be involved with the college you choose. If you've saved $80,000 and are feeling great about it, consider that you could spend that money in two years if your child goes to one of the most prestigious schools, and encounters heavy additional expenses.

We'd all like for our kids to go to a great college, but chances are, if your child is motivated, he or she will do well in a state school or a less expensive private school. Most kids don't go to Yale or Harvard, and they turn out to be just fine.

And there's nothing that says your child shouldn't, or can't contribute to her college fund. Many, many students work while they're attending college, either for extra money or to help with the costs of tuition, books, and so forth.

Decide how much you can pay for your child's college before she applies to a particular school. That way, you'll have an idea if the school is affordable, with or without a financial aid package. College is a matter that affects the finances of an entire family, and all sides of the issue should be considered.

Besides tuition, fees, room and board, your child will have other expenses while at school. Decide before she leaves in late August what you'll pay for, and what costs she'll be responsible for. Fraternities and sororities are wonderful social experiences, but if you and your child are accumulating tens of thousand of dollars in debt, maybe another $1,000 per term or year in frat fees might not be necessary.

Some schools lower the cost of room and board if a student houses in a fraternity or sorority house, but even if your child stays in the dorm, frats cost money.

Be prepared to discuss spring break. Will your child come home for the break or will he fly directly on to the Florida beaches? If so, who will pay for the flight and other costs, such as a motel, meals, and beer? Most parents leave paying for the fun stuff up to their kids.

Finding Financial Aid

Once you've worked through the financial aid worksheet on the finaid.org Web site, or determined in another way that you should qualify for some financial aid, you'll need to complete a College Scholarship Service (CSS) PROFILE. You do this during your child's senior year of high school.

PROFILE is a program through the financial aid division of the College Board, a national, nonprofit association of schools and school systems, colleges and universities, and educational organizations. The College Board uses the information you supply to help it award nonfederal student aid funds. It forwards your information to the colleges in which you are interested, so that staff there can determine whether there's aid available for you.

Money Morsel

You can get a copy of the Free Application for Federal Student Aid by logging on to the FAFSA Web site at www.fafsa.com.

To apply for federal financial aid—which includes federal grants, loans, and work-study money—you'll need a form known as the Free Application for Federal Student Aid (FAFSA). There are some basic requirements for these federal programs. The requirements are as follows:

- Must be a U.S. citizen or eligible noncitizen
- Must be registered with Selective Service (if required)
- Must attend a college that participates in the government programs listed below
- Must be working toward a degree or certificate
- Must be making satisfactory academic progress
- Cannot owe a refund on a federal grant or be in default on a federal educational loan
- Must have financial need as determined in part by the form

The following programs are included under federal financial aid:

- Federal Pell Grants
- Federal Supplemental Educational Opportunity Grants (FSEOG)

- ◆ Federal Subsidized and Unsubsidized Stafford Loans
- ◆ Stafford/Ford Federal Direct Subsidized and Unsubsidized Loans
- ◆ Federal Perkins Loans
- ◆ Federal Work Study (FWS)
- ◆ Title VII and Public Health Act Programs

Don't Go There _____

Be careful that you don't get a financial aid advisor who is out to sell you a loan on which he'll receive a commission. Ask how the advisor is paid, and ask for recommendations from several families with comparable financial situations. Check to see if those families are satisfied.

Basically, grants are aid that you don't have to repay. Loans must be repaid. A work-study program pays students for campus jobs.

Because filling out these federal application forms can be complicated, you may want to consider using a financial aid advisor. These advisors are available in most areas; you can check your phone book to locate one.

There also are books and online information to help you apply effectively for financial aid. Once you know what your financial situation will be, you can begin looking realistically at different schools.

Other Ways to Finance College

If your college savings are slim, and your son or daughter doesn't qualify for enough scholarships or financial aid to cover the cost of an education, don't despair. There may be another way for you to come up with money for Bobby's tuition.

Over the years, you've probably built up equity in your home. Equity is part of your net worth, and it can be used to help pay for your children's education. You can utilize this equity by taking a second mortgage or obtaining a line of credit.

A second mortgage is an additional loan to your primary mortgage, and it increases the amount that you'll need to repay. Not all financial institutions offer second mortgages.

A line of credit is approval for a designated loan, up to a pre-approved limit. Your home is used as collateral against that loan.

You can use as little or much of the approved amount of the loan as you need. If you get a line of credit for $25,000, for instance, and find that you end up needing only $18,000, you don't need to use the entire amount. The funds are available and usually accessed by writing a check for a portion of the limit. Interest charged is usually variable, with repayment calculated on the amount of the loan, and the current interest rate.

An equity loan is a fixed-rate loan for a designated amount. It uses your home as collateral. Fixed-equity loans are usually issued for between five and seven years.

You should consider these factors when deciding which type of home equity loan makes the most sense for you:

♦ Interest on a second mortgage, home equity line of credit (HELOC), or home equity loan can be tax deductible if the collateral is your first or second home.

♦ A second mortgage is paid to you in a lump sum. You may not need it all for one year of college, which means you'll need to invest the rest of it in a money market fund or another type of account until you need it all.

♦ The repayment schedule on a second mortgage is usually fairly long, which means you don't have to repay a great amount each month. On the other hand, it prolongs the period during which you'll be paying on your house.

♦ The interest rates on second mortgages and equity loans are usually *fixed*, while lines of credit have *variable* interest rates (usually higher than first mortgage interest rates).

♦ A line of credit has no set repayment schedule, and you can re-borrow the funds up to the pre-approved limit, as long as you meet the monthly payments.

If you don't own a home, or haven't built up sufficient equity in it to qualify for a second mortgage, equity loan, or line of credit, you may have to get creative in order to fund a college education.

Adding It Up

A **fixed** interest rate means that the rate charged for the loan is fixed for the entire term of the loan, whereas a **variable** interest rate "varies" or changes based on some predetermined interest rate, i.e., the prime lending rate. A fixed rate allows you to know what your monthly cost of the loan will always be. Variable rates enable your monthly payment to go up or maybe go down.

You could get a second job, or have your child find a job to help pay for his or her college expenses. If your parent or parents are still living and have assets that they'll pass along to you or your child at the time of their deaths, you could consider asking them for a gift now. We'll get into that topic in much more detail in Part 6, "Preparing for the Future."

Many families have come up with creative ways to finance children's educations. If you can't afford to pay outright for college, it doesn't mean that you're not a good parent.

Be frank with your son or daughter about your financial situation, and see if he or she has any ideas. And, remember that the price of an education varies tremendously from school to school.

Extras, Spending Money, Cars, and Credit Cards

It's very common for students to earn their spending money themselves. Your son worked at summer accumulating $2,500 and this should tide him over until he comes home next summer. If you're generous and can send him a check in addition to all the other costs of college, congratulations.

But earning it and spending it wisely over the course of the school year is a wonderful learning experience. If your child earned $2,500 and is in school for 9 months, he has $275 per month to spend, including Christmas and birthday gifts. You might need to help him by sending him only what he can spend each month, or he might need to watch it carefully himself. If he overspends one month, he needs to get a job until next month.

You'll need to decide if your child can take a car to school, is a car really needed at school, or are they just used to having a car at their disposal. Are you comfortable with them being miles away in case there is an accident or breakdown and you need to go get the car?

Many colleges don't permit freshman to have cars on campus, while other schools don't have any restrictions. You should receive an auto insurance discount when your child is away at school and their car is at home, so know a car on campus will increase your car insurance costs, plus most colleges charge parking fees. Using the car increases daily gas expenses. Do you really want them to have a car?

The greatest problem with college students is credit card debt. The average amount of credit card debt accumulated by college graduates keeps mounting to new heights with each new graduating class. Current college seniors have over $7,500 in debt.

If you want your child to have a credit card, have the card company (a local bank) set a low enough limit so your child can't keep borrowing. Credit card interest is not deductible and the rates are prohibitive. The credit card companies send the cards to your child's college address. Many of the companies are borderline predatory. Discuss with your child the uses of a card and maybe have them use their debit card rather than having a need for a credit card.

The Least You Need to Know

◆ College is expensive, but some are much more affordable than others.

◆ There are traditional types of college accounts, and some newer ones that may offer specific advantages.

◆ Financial aid is available to many, and there are resources available to help you find out if you qualify.

◆ Some schools may be too expensive for you to afford, even if your son or daughter qualifies for financial aid.

◆ You may be able to use your home equity to get a loan to help pay for your child's college expenses.

Chapter 9

Wedding Bells

In This Chapter

- ◆ The high cost of a wedding
- ◆ Understanding who pays for modern weddings
- ◆ The biggest wedding costs
- ◆ Cutting expenses to reduce wedding costs
- ◆ Knowing when to stop spending

Your son or daughter is getting married, and you (hopefully) couldn't be happier. Seeing your child in love and happily looking forward to a wonderful day is a rewarding and wonderful experience. Or perhaps you're planning to tie the knot, whether for the first time, or not.

If you're going to be involved with planning and paying for a wedding, you'll no doubt experience some concerns about the cost of the event. Your concerns certainly are valid. The average cost of a wedding these days is $19,000, for an average of 200 guests, according to *Brides* magazine. Keep in mind, though, that $19,000 is the average cost. That certainly doesn't mean you have to spend that much.

In this chapter, we'll look at wedding costs, who pays for wedding costs, and some suggestions for keeping the wedding within budget.

Your Baby's Getting Married

Your little girl (or boy) is getting married, and you just can't believe it. How can your baby be old enough to be getting married? How can *you* be old enough to have a daughter who's getting married? Whether you believe it or not, it's happening.

Her brand-new ring sparkles as she shows it off to everyone she meets. Her face lights up as she talks about her dress, her flowers, who she and her fiancé plan to invite, which photographer they plan to hire, where the wedding and reception will be held, and what they'll serve at the reception.

While your daughter's head is filled with visions of beautiful dresses, flowers, guests, dinners, cocktails, appetizers, photographers, and so forth, your head is filled with images of writing checks, handing over credit cards, opening yet more accounts for bills, and counting out your cash. How in the world are you going to pay, or help to pay for this wedding? Don't despair. Times have changed, and steadily increasing wedding costs have forced families to re-evaluate how they'll pay for the events.

Who Pays for a Wedding These Days?

As you probably know, tradition had it that the bride's family paid the majority of the wedding costs. This was great for the groom's family, but could cause serious pocketbook stress for the parents of the bride.

As tradition dictated, the bride's family would cover the costs for goods and services listed as follows:

- ◆ Engagement party
- ◆ Cost of the ceremony, including location, music, rentals, and all other expenses
- ◆ Entire cost of the reception, including location, food, beverage, entertainment, rental items, decorations, and wedding cake
- ◆ Bride's wedding dress, veil, and accessories
- ◆ Wedding gift for the couple
- ◆ Bridesmaids' bouquets
- ◆ Bridesmaids' luncheon
- ◆ Photography
- ◆ Flowers

Money Morsel

While the groom was traditionally responsible for paying for the honeymoon, some families of either the bride or groom now pay for the honeymoon as a wedding present to the couple.

The groom's family, on the other hand, was traditionally responsible these expenses:

- Rehearsal dinner
- Travel and accommodations for the groom's family
- Honeymoon
- Wedding gift for bride and groom

As you can see, tradition was not financially kind to the bride's family. Fortunately, at least if you're looking at the situation from the viewpoint of that family, times have changed. Rather than burden one family with practically the entire cost of a wedding, it is common practice these days for both families—and sometimes the bride and groom—to share expenses.

Some modern options for paying for a wedding include:

- The bride and groom pay for the entire wedding
- Expenses are divided evenly between the couple, the bride's family, and the groom's family
- Each family covers the cost for the number of guests it invites
- The bride's family and groom's family split the expenses evenly

How you decide to divide the costs of your son's or daughter's wedding depends primarily on the financial situation of each family, and of the bride and groom themselves. Circumstances and common sense—not tradition—now dictate who will pay what for a wedding.

If your daughter is marrying a man who comes from a wealthy family, your future in-laws may offer to pay for the entire event. Or they might pick up one or two of the big costs, such as flowers or liquor at the reception.

Maybe you've been stashing away money ever since your daughter was born for the sole purpose of someday giving her a beautiful wedding. If so, you may want to cover most of the expenses.

If the bride and groom are older, as many couples are these days, they may each have been working for five years or more, have some money saved, and be perfectly willing to pick up some of the tab.

The best way to decide who will pay for what is for both families (or all the families that apply) and the couple to sit down together and have a frank discussion about what each party can afford to contribute. Some people are terribly uncomfortable discussing their finances in front of others, so be sensitive to that. Separate meetings are sometimes necessary, but it's best if you can get everyone together at one time to brainstorm and share information.

Only when you learn how much money each family and the bride and groom can chip in can you know what kind of wedding to begin planning.

Don't feel bad if you're a parent of the bride and can't afford to pay for the entire wedding. Very few people expect that anymore. And, don't offer to pay for something you can't afford. There's no law that says every wedding has to cost more than $15,000, or $10,000, or even $5,000.

Don't Go There

Starting out thousands of dollars in debt is great stress for a newly married couple, who may still be paying off college loans or planning for a family. If your son or daughter is considering taking out a wedding loan, do everything you can to discourage him.

Some couples, or their families, decide they simply must pull out all the stops for a wedding. They want nothing but the best, even if they can't afford to pay for it. To facilitate their dreams, they take out wedding loans.

Companies that offer wedding loans, such as the MBNA America Bank, will tell you that it's great to take out a loan, so you can have exactly the wedding you want. Information on MBNA's Web site (where you can actually apply online for a loan) tells the bride to go ahead and order beef for her guests, instead of chicken. She should get that designer gown, MBNA says, instead of buying one off the rack. As you can imagine there's a catch involved, and it's a huge one.

The small print at the bottom of the ad tells you that MBNA will set your interest rate at between 12.99 percent and 27.99 percent, depending on your credit rating. We'll tell you right now that anyone who takes out a loan for a wedding at nearly 28 percent interest is crazy. She'd do better to charge the whole thing on a credit card and pay it off over time.

If you feel you absolutely must take a loan to pay for a wedding, don't even think about a wedding loan. Look at a home equity loan instead, for which the interest rate would be much lower.

Wedding Costs

What are the main expenses involved with a wedding? The percentages probably haven't changed much since your own wedding, although weddings today tend to be a bit more elaborate and include more extras than they did 20 or 30 years ago.

While it's the big expenses—the food, liquor, music, photography, flowers, and so forth, that come to mind—remember that little costs can accumulate quickly, and every "extra" you choose will boost the cost of the wedding.

Consider a new fad, for instance—wedding bubbles. It used to be that guests showered the bride and groom with rice as they exited the place of the ceremony. Then we started substituting birdseed so our feathered friends could clean up the mess without risking their well-being.

Nowadays, guests are encouraged to surround the bride and groom with bubbles as they exit. Companies that sell wedding favors claim that bubbles are better because they're ecologically safe, they don't stain anything, and they're much more fun for everyone. These bubbles come in a variety of containers, all of which can be enhanced by tying on ribbons that match the wedding colors.

Depending on where you buy them and what kind of container you choose, these wedding bubbles can be a little pricey. A box of 24 little bell-shaped plastic bottles of bubbles is available at an online wedding store for $12.95, plus shipping costs. You'd need five boxes for 200 guests, adding on about $65 plus shipping to the cost of the wedding. If you want to get fancy, you can pay extra for personalized labels to attach to the wedding bubbles.

> **Don't Go There**
>
> Don't feel that you need to provide all kinds of favors to your guests. Most people already have more "stuff" than they know what to do with, and a little ceramic wedding couple is just something else to worry over.

Wedding costs vary tremendously, depending on the guests and what is important to the bride, groom, and their families. Typically, however, you can count on the percentages of costs listed as follows:

- Reception: 40 percent of the total wedding budget
- Honeymoon: 20 percent of the total wedding budget
- Bridal attire: 10 percent of the total wedding budget
- Flowers: 8 percent of the total wedding budget
- Photographs: 7 percent of the total wedding budget
- Miscellaneous (such as special parties, wedding bubbles, and so forth): 7 percent of the total wedding budget
- Music: 3 percent of the total wedding budget
- Stationery items: 3 percent of the total wedding budget

You can use these percentages as a guide when planning for your son's or daughter's wedding, or your own wedding, for that matter. If you know the amount of the total wedding budget, you can figure out roughly how much you're likely to end up paying for each category of expenses.

Saving on Wedding Costs

We think everyone should save money whenever possible. Money saved really is money earned, especially when it's well invested.

Go Figure

Some insurance companies now offer wedding insurance, just in case the caterer decides to file for bankruptcy and go out of business two days before the event, or somebody steals all the wedding gifts. You even can buy insurance that pays you if it rains or snows on the day of the wedding. Check out Weddinguard at www.weddinguard.com for an example of what's available.

If you're paying for or contributing to your child's wedding, remember that your donation buys you some say in how the money is spent. If she wants to hire limousines to transport herself, the groom, and the wedding party from the ceremony to the reception, and you think that some nice cars driven by special wedding guests will do just fine, be sure to make your opinion known.

If you're paying the costs outright, you can simply refuse to shell out for limos, despite the fact that your daughter is likely to be upset with you. Or you can offer to give her a lump sum that she can use however she wishes. Do point out, however, that if she hires limos and drivers, she'll need to cut back in another area.

Let's take a few minutes to think of some creative ways to reduce the cost of a wedding. We understand that you want your child's wedding to be beautiful and meaningful, and something from which she'll have wonderful memories for the rest of her life. If you can help her understand that bigger is not always better, and that less sometimes is more, you'll be ahead in the paying-for-the-wedding game.

- Limit the number of guests. Inviting 150 people instead of 200 automatically cuts your wedding costs significantly. If you figure it will cost $80 per guest for food, drinks, and so forth, you'll save $4,000 by reducing your guest list by 50 people.

- Cut back on clothing costs. Your daughter will look as beautiful in a $500 dress as she will in one that cost $3,000. Or there's a growing trend of borrowing a wedding dress from a friend or family member. We know a smart woman who wore her college roommate's wedding dress, and even recycled the bridesmaid's dresses from her roommate's wedding for her own wedding. She ended up buying one bridesmaid's dress instead of a wedding dress and three bridesmaid's dresses. Borrow or make a headpiece instead of paying a couple of hundred dollars for one. Men can opt to wear their own, nice suits instead of tuxedos, saving rental costs.

- Be nontraditional with the food. Not every wedding reception needs to feature sit-down dinner with a fruit cup and full meal. Think about a beautiful brunch, or an outdoor cocktail reception. Luncheons or teas also are options. Buffets can be less expensive than sit-down dinners because you don't have to pay servers. If you still want the sit-down, stay away from the most expensive foods—usually seafood and beef. And, buy only a small, decorated wedding cake. This is the cake the bride and groom will cut and have their photos taken along side of. And it will feed the wedding party. The rest of the guests can eat slices of cake cut from large, plain cakes. They'll never know the difference.

Money Morsel

Check out the Unique Wedding Web site, where you can shop for new wedding dresses that cost up to 70 percent less than retail prices or find a used dress. The Web site is www. uniquewedding.com.

♦ Consider the timing of the wedding. Wedding caterers—the good ones at least—are booked a year or more in advance for Saturdays in June, and often charge more for their services during these busy times. The same caterers in November, however, may be looking for business and willing to give you a break on their costs.

♦ Watch the alcohol. Wedding receptions traditionally are festive affairs, complete with cocktails, wine, and champagne toasts. Unfortunately, all this festivity comes at a high price. Be prepared to pay more for booze than you will for food at a wedding reception. If you can, supply the alcohol yourself. Many places do not permit you to do that because they make a lot of money on liquor. If you're having the reception outdoors, at your home, or in another private location, however, you probably will be able to supply your own refreshments. If not, consider limiting alcohol to a variety of beers and wines, and skip the champagne toast.

♦ Get friends and family to help out. If you've got a great amateur photographer in the family, enlist her services. If your nephew is a flower designer, get him on board. Hit up friends and family to perform services such as singing, playing musical instruments, and videotaping. Use friends as drivers instead of paying people to drive.

♦ Say no to the extras. You really don't need wedding bubbles. Or a picture frame for each guest to take home. You don't need embossed matchbooks or napkins, or elaborate flower arrangements on every table. Keep it simple and you can save significant money.

There are many ways in which you can reduce the cost of a wedding and still have a lovely, classy event that will impress your guests and create wonderful memories for your son or daughter.

Avoiding Temptation

We understand that your baby's wedding is a once-in-a-lifetime event (hopefully), and that you want it to be perfect. We can't stress, however, how important it is to be realistic about how much you can afford to spend to make those dreams come true.

Some families have no problem plunking down $20,000 or $25,000 for a wedding. Most of us, however, have to do some serious thinking and planning before we hand over that kind of money.

If you haven't been great about saving for retirement, think long and hard before spending a good chunk of whatever amount of money you have. Your daughter can live without a big, fancy wedding, but you really can't live without retirement money.

If you're going to be paying for, or contributing to the wedding costs, set a limit on what you're able to spend and stick to that amount. Do not yield to the temptation to add a first course to the wedding dinner, even if your best friend did for her daughter's wedding. Understand that your daughter will be just as lovely in a $400 dress as she will in that $2,000 model, and that a champagne toast, while nice, is not a necessary part of a reception.

With careful planning and some well-placed restraint, you can help to give your son or daughter a great wedding. Don't, however, put your future in jeopardy to do so.

The Least You Need to Know

- Weddings are festive and wonderful events, for which the average cost these days is $19,000.
- While the bride's family traditionally paid for most of the wedding costs, it is common today for both families to share the cost and for the bride and groom to contribute some of their money.
- The main costs of an average wedding are the reception, the honeymoon, bridal attire, and flowers.
- With a bit of creativity and determination, you can significantly reduce the cost of a wedding.
- We all want our kids to have wonderful weddings, but you should never spend money to do so that you'll need for your own retirement.

10

Helping Your Kids Get on Their Feet

In This Chapter

- ◆ Coping in an expensive world
- ◆ Deciding if you should help your child financially
- ◆ Loaning or giving?
- ◆ Making sure everyone understands the situation
- ◆ Dealing with a not-so-empty nest

Your son, Charlie, graduated from college last year, the same year that your daughter, Patty, was married. Charlie stayed at home with you for a while, found a job, and now is ready to move out.

Patty and her husband just told you last week that they're expecting a baby in six or seven months. All these changes are exciting, although a bit unsettling. You and your spouse are home alone now, perhaps experiencing a bit of the empty nest syndrome. You're anxious as can be to hold a little grandson or granddaughter, but maybe a bit concerned that your daughter will be over-whelmed by the challenges of being a full-time working mom.

It's natural to worry about and to want to help your kids. After all, they were your babies just a short time ago. You bandaged their knees, taught them not to run into the street without stopping first to look both ways, and sat with them until they went back to sleep after bad dreams. You held your breath as they drove off by themselves for the first time, cried when they left for college, and smiled bravely as she walked up the aisle to be married.

Your work with your children probably never will end. You'll continue to worry, to offer advice, and to lend a helping hand. But how much should you help them financially? This is a tricky question, and a very subjective one. Some parents help out their kids financially their entire lives, while others cut the purse strings the day the child leaves the house.

In this chapter we'll explore the possibilities of helping out your kids financially, and look at some of the areas in which they might need some help.

The Cost of Getting Started

It's no secret that it costs a lot of money to live comfortably in America: housing, transportation, food, entertainment, and clothing. It all adds up ... fast. And, when you're just starting out on your own, managing your finances can be particularly challenging.

Let's have a look at what it might cost for a college graduate who's starting his first job in a city not within commuting distance from your home. Let's say that Charlie grew up in Detroit, graduated from Michigan State University, and has landed a job in his field (computers, what else?) in Denver.

ACCRA, a nonprofit organization that started out in 1961 as the American Chamber of Commerce Researchers Association, compares the cost of living in various cities across America and produces a well-regarded Cost of Living Index.

According to ACCRA, it would cost Charlie just a little more to live in Denver than in Detroit. The average rent in Denver is $861 a month, compared to $802 in Detroit. If Charlie decides to stay in Denver and buy a house someday, he can expect to pay somewhere in the neighborhood of $243,424, which is a bit lower than the Detroit's average home price of $258,350. Food costs are higher in Denver than in Detroit, as are medical and some other costs. On the whole, the cost of living in Denver is 0.07 percent higher than the national average.

Money Morsel

You can find ACCRA's Cost of Living Index on the organization's Web site at www.coli.org.

Regardless of whether Charlie lives in Detroit, Denver, or someplace in between, he's going to need substantial funds to get started in a new city.

The question is, should you help him financially, or allow him to find out what the world after college is really like?

How Much Should You Help?

Only you can decide if, and how much, you'll help your kids once they go out on their own. If you've supported him all his life and paid his way—or helped to pay his way through college, you may well feel, as many parents do, that you're off the hook. You've gotten him this far, and now it's time for him to make it financially on his own.

That doesn't necessarily mean that you'll never crack open your wallet and hand him a twenty or two. And you may still buy that lamp or set of sheets that you find on sale at the department store for Charlie to use in his new apartment. You'll be happy for he and his girlfriend to share the big house you rent at the beach this summer, and you're always glad to take them out to dinner when they're in town.

Basically, however, you might feel that your days of being responsible for financially supporting Charlie have ended.

Remember, though, that we've been assuming Charlie has graduated from college and is heading for a fairly good job with a decent starting take-home pay. As you know, that's not always the case.

But what if Charlie didn't have the benefit of college and is trying to make it on his own with only a relatively low-paying job? Or what if he's finished college, but hasn't been able to land a job in his field? What if his girlfriend just told him that she's pregnant and they're going to get married? Or he's been sick and unable to work? Or he's trying to pay back college loans while getting started in his own apartment and pay for the car he needed to buy so he could drive to work?

Many young people come out of college seriously in debt. If he's been to graduate school, he may be even further in the hole.

A recent survey by Nellie Mae, provider of more student loans than any other nonprofit firm in the country, shows some frightening statistics about college grads and debt. The survey of 2,500 men and women who had just graduated from college reveals that their average debt was $18,800. That's compared with $8,200 average debt a decade ago. Students just coming out of graduate school averaged debt of $24,500. That includes education loans and other debt, such as credit cards and automobile loans.

Don't Go There

A study by the National Foundation for Credit Counseling shows that 64 percent of all students graduating from college owe at least $1,843 on their credit cards. Twenty percent have credit card debt of $10,000 or more.

If your son or daughter has worked hard to get through college, took out loans to pay her way, and is struggling to pay off her debt so she can move ahead financially, should you help her if you're able to? If so, how much?

This is basically a philosophical question, for which the answer varies dramatically from family to family. Some parents feel very strongly that their financial obligation ends when their child turns 18, while others continue supporting kids for years and years.

If you do decide to help out a son or daughter financially so he can move on or improve her current living situation, to what extent would you do so? Consider the possibilities listed as follows:

- You'll repay his college loans, with the understanding that your financial obligations end at that time.
- You'll give him the first couple month's rent and security deposit for his new apartment.
- You'll continue to have her live at home, paying no rent and not contributing to any of the household expenses.
- You'll set her up completely in an apartment and pay half of her rent until she's financially established.
- You'll buy a small, fairly inexpensive car for him to drive back and forth from work, and then tell him that your financial support has ended.
- You'll promise to provide the down payment for his first house, regardless of when it is that he buys the home.
- You'll promise to pay for her wedding, or to help pay for her wedding.
- You'll give your child no financial support, either because you can't afford to, or you choose not to.

Don't Go There

Don't assume that, if you decide to help out your adult son or daughter financially, that it gives you the right to control his or her life. If you feel that contributing money gives you a right to impose your opinions, be sure your son or daughter realizes that before accepting your gift.

Money Morsel

Some health insurance policies allow you to include your child until she turns 23 years old. You may be able to help her out by keeping her on your policy until she gets a job that includes health coverage.

All these are possibilities for ways you could help out your kids if you choose to do so. Let's face it. Nearly everyone can use a little financial help now and then. Whether your child will get it from you, or have to see another source, is between you and her.

To Loan or to Give?

If you decide that you do want to help your son or daughter to get on his or her feet financially, should you loan money or give it outright?

Again, there's no really clear answer. You may feel that giving your child money without any expectation of repayment is a loving act, or even a parental obligation. Or you may feel that the only responsible means of helping your grown child is to make him repay money, just as he would have to if he borrowed from any other lender.

You might base your decision of whether to loan or give depending on how much money is involved or whether you think your child will really appreciate a financial gift. As a society, we tend to use money for many purposes, other than simply buying what we need and want. Some people use money as a means of control or to manipulate another person or a situation. Some people give money in an attempt to patch up old wounds or reconcile a broken relationship.

Some thoughts to keep in mind if you're considering loaning or giving money to your grown child are as follows:

Money Morsel

If your grown child is buying a home and you want to help, ask your accountant or financial advisor about the possibility of finding a financial institution that allows you to pledge securities instead of selling them, allowing you to give the cash down payment to your child.

- ◆ Maybe you're in a financial position that allows you to comfortably loan or give money to a grown child. You're responsible first for your own financial future, and jeopardizing it will not help you or your child in the long run.

- ◆ Don't loan or give if it causes problems between you and your spouse or partner. Again, creating trouble for yourself will not make your child happy, and you may end up resenting her for taking the money.

- ◆ Don't attach conditions or strings if you loan or give money, other than how the loan will be repaid. Loaning your child money for a home does not mean you get to choose the house and all the furnishings.

- ◆ If you loan or give money to your grown child, don't be judgmental about the reason for which they need it. Don't, for instance, point out that you've never taken a cruise and perhaps their money could be better spent elsewhere. It's your decision whether or not to offer money. If you do, be gracious about it. You'll only breed resentment by questioning their judgment.

- ◆ Be sure that you're comfortable with loaning or giving money. If you suspect that your daughter's marriage is in serious trouble and that your soon-to-be-ex-son-in-law may take off with your $10,000 loan, hold off for six months or a year until you see how the situation resolves itself.

◆ Don't loan or give money to try to patch up a rocky relationship you have with your grown child. Your money would be better spent on family therapy. As The Beatles told us decades ago, money really can't buy you love.

Regardless of whether you decide to loan or give money outright, it's extremely important that everyone understands exactly the terms of the arrangement.

Keeping It All Up Front

As you no doubt have found out along the road of life, money can cause major disagreements amongst family members.

In a survey of married couples, more than half of them said that, sooner or later, money is the most important concern in marriage. Many of the couples also said that money is their most frequent source of disagreement.

What parent hasn't argued with her kids about money? What kid hasn't argued about the green stuff with his folks?

The point is, money can be a volatile subject, especially if the parties involved have different views or expectations concerning that money. If you give money or make a loan to your kids, everyone had better have the same understanding of the conditions. There's no way you want to hand over $10,000 with the assumption that you're going to get it back, while your son and daughter-in-law are thanking you profusely for your gift. Talk about a sticky situation!

When you get a loan from a bank, credit union, or other lender, there's no question about how it will work. You'll fill out a loan application, and a loan officer will do some sort of credit check on you. That's to be sure you don't have a history of skipping out on loans or have so much debt already that there's no way you're going to be able to repay this loan.

> **Don't Go There**
>
> If your child has proved to be consistently irresponsible, you shouldn't loan him money. If he's not repaid you for loans in the past, or is not working to get money on his own, there's no reason you should enable him to continue being unaccountable for his actions. You want to help, but you'd actually only be encouraging his irresponsibility.

Once you're approved for the loan, you agree to pay off the amount of the loan and the interest, set at a certain rate, over an agreed-upon period of time. If you don't pay it, you face serious consequences, including the loss of the home or auto for which you needed to borrow money, or legal action.

If you loan money to your grown son or daughter, the first thing to do is to make sure everyone understands that the money is a loan, not a gift. Cement this understanding with a written agreement. If an agreement concerning money isn't put into writing, it can tend to become a little fuzzy over time. You might think your son already paid you back, when he's really only returned half of the money. Or your daughter may just forget to give you your payment some month.

Decide if you're going to charge interest on the loan. If you do, it presumably will be lower than what a lending institution would charge, but the amount of interest you set is up to you. Write out the terms of the loan, and make sure both you and your child sign it.

You may want to include a *promissory note,* which is a written promise of repayment by an agreed-upon time.

You could ask your lawyer to draft a simple loan agreement, or type up your own agreement on your computer. Just make sure it includes the following:

- ◆ The names and relationships of all involved parties
- ◆ The date the agreement is acted upon
- ◆ The amount of money loaned
- ◆ Interest rate (if applicable)
- ◆ Over what time period the loan will be repaid
- ◆ At what time intervals (week, month, etc.) the loan will repaid
- ◆ The amount to be paid at each interval
- ◆ Signatures of all involved parties, including two witnesses

Adding It Up _____

A **promissory note** is a written document in which the person who receives the loan gives unconditional promise that he'll repay a specific amount of money to the lender, either upon demand, before, or on a certain date and time.

Money Morsel _____

An online source of free legal forms is Work-At-Home, located on the Internet at www.visitorinfo.com/Work-At-Home/free-legal-forms/free-online-legal-forms.htm.

Or you can get copies of basic business forms from a business supply store, or find forms online that you can download and use.

Regardless of how you decide to make a loan official, be sure that all parties understand and agree to the conditions of the loan. Being casual about lending money—perhaps especially to a family member—is not a smart move. Many families have suffered irreparable damage over money issues, and you certainly don't want yours to become one of them.

It's equally important that your son or daughter understand if you're giving the money as a gift. Just make sure everyone is on the same page, regardless of the conditions you place on the money.

Boomerang Kids

Sigh … your kids are out on their own. The house is tidy and quiet. You don't need to stop by the store every other day for milk, bread, and orange juice. You and your spouse or partner are free to come and go as you please. You've even started playing tennis together again for the first time in 15 or so years.

Just when you think you've got it made, one—or maybe more than one—of the kids is back.

There are about 65 million boomerang "kids" between the ages of 18 and 34 who still live at home with the folks. The reasons are many. Some young people try, and find out they simply can't manage on their own. Some experience emotional, health, or psychological problems that prevent them from living on their own. Others simply realize a good deal when they see it, and continue to hang out where life is easy and they've got it made.

If you're making life at home so wonderful that your child is reluctant to leave, you need to take a look at what's going on and decide how you'll handle the situation. Perhaps you don't want him to go. While that may be understandable, it's probably not the healthiest situation for your kid. Providing free room and board, along with laundry and housekeeping services, isn't giving your son a very accurate view of the real world.

While we all love our kids, most of us don't want them hanging out with us forever. It's natural and healthy for children to move on and establish lives that are independent of ours.

Experts give the following advice for dealing with those boomerang kids who just can't seem to leave the nest.

- Determine an amount of time the adult child will stay with you. Help him to set a goal of getting out on his own. Offer to have him live with you for a year, and then urge him to find his own place.

- Encourage your dear one to get out on her own by saving the rent she gives you while living at home, and giving it back to her—with whatever interest you've earned on it—at the end of a year. Do so, however, with the stipulation that she uses the money to cover her first month's rent or to pay the security deposit on an apartment.

- Determine up front what she's expected to contribute. Discuss what you expect her to pay to live at home, and what she'll do to help with household chores. Will she be responsible for doing her own laundry, for example?

- If your child's not working and can't afford to contribute financially, make sure he does his part in other ways, such as lawn work or cleaning.

- If your child is in trouble with credit card or other debt, resist the temptation to bail him out. Do, however, encourage him to meet with a credit counseling service to work out how he'll repay the debt.

- Be sure she has the insurance she needs. If she's no longer covered under your health care policy and has no health care benefits of her own, she may need to get individual coverage. Also, make sure she has auto insurance.

- If your child is a full-time student under the age of 24 or earns less than $2,900 and you're footing the bill for more than half of his support, you may qualify for a tax deduction. If you're a single parent providing more than half of the support for your adult child, you may be able to get a tax advantage by filing as head of household instead of a single taxpayer.

Whatever you do, don't make your child feel that she's failed by coming back to your home. She may be no happier about the arrangement than you are, and likely feels bad that she's had to come home.

Discuss problems and issues as they arise, be straightforward about your expectations, and be patient while your child gets himself back on his feet.

The Least You Need to Know

- Your son or daughter may need some financial and moral support when just starting out on his or her own.

- Whether or not you'll help your adult child financially is a personal decision.

- If you help your child financially, you'll need to decide whether you'll give the money as a gift or a loan.

- If you loan money, make sure the terms of the loan are written down and everyone understands the agreement.

- If your grown child moves back to the family home, you should establish some ground rules up front.

Part 3   Hearth and Home

Housing can, and often does, become an issue at this stage in our lives. If your kids have grown and moved out, you might feel a bit lost in your big, family home. Maybe you're thinking of getting something a bit smaller and more manageable, with all the amenities you'd like. Perhaps you're anticipating having an elderly parent come to live with you, and need to make some revisions to your home to accommodate her. Or maybe you're thinking that a vacation home sounds like a good idea.

Regardless of how or why your housing needs may be changing, you can bet that accommodating the changes will cost you some money.

In Chapters 11 through 14, you'll learn about different types of mortgages and which one may best fit your homeowner profile. And we'll also deal with how you might best sell your home if you decide to move.

To Stay or Not To Stay?

In This Chapter

◆ Looking at changing housing needs
◆ Considering having an aging parent move in
◆ Deciding to build a new home
◆ Choosing a builder
◆ Renovating the home you have

Whether or not you regard your home as your castle, it's no doubt a very important place to you and your family.

As discussed briefly in Chapter 3, "On the Plus Side," our homes are much, much more than just structures in which we live. They're the places where we've watched—or are watching—our children grow up. They're where we invite our friends to come for dinner parties, celebrate holidays with people we love, and take off our shoes and just relax. They're safe places—places where we can laugh, cry, or express our frustrations with the world. We spend a lot of time decorating our homes, choosing wallpaper, furniture, and accessories. Our homes reflect the personalities of our families.

Even if you've moved several times due to job relocation or other factors, you've probably managed to make a home in each location. Most people feel a need to find a place and make it their own. In short, most people are connected emotionally to their homes.

It's this emotional connection—along with financial and practical considerations—that can make decisions concerning your home difficult. As you get older, you might find that your home doesn't work for you as well as it used to. Perhaps there are too many rooms but not enough closets in any of them. Maybe you live in an old home that demands constant upkeep and repairs. Scraping peeling paint may not be as enjoyable a pastime in your 40s or 50s as it seemed in your 20s or 30s. You may be thinking that it's time to make a change concerning your home.

If that's the case, be prepared to think long and carefully about what to do. Should you leave your home for a smaller one? Should you remodel? Should you finally build the dream house you've always wanted? Should you ask your aging parent to move into your home? What will your house be like when all the kids have moved out? Should you scale down on your housing, so you're able to save more for retirement? These decisions aren't easy ones, and they rarely can be made without a certain level of discomfort.

If Your Housing Needs Are Changing

Maybe you have the perfect home—one that you've worked on for years to make exactly the way you want it. And perhaps you fully intend to stay in that house for as long as you live. You just can't imagine living anywhere else.

> **Go Figure**
>
> Builders are spending a good bit of time these days researching the wants and needs of baby boomers regarding housing. They're looking at the boomers' spending habits, lifestyle preferences, hobbies, number of grandkids, and so forth in order to be able to provide the perfect home for a potentially huge market.

Many people, however, find that their housing needs change as they get older, and what used to be the perfect house is now something with which they're a bit discontented.

Statistics show that more and more baby boomers are moving. The trend these days is not to buy a house when your children are young and live in it until you die or are forced to move. Middle-aged men and women are moving—not necessarily because they have to, but because they want to.

They no longer want to spend all day Saturday cutting grass and trimming hedges. Or they want to live in a house that's built on the edge of a golf course, making their favorite hobby more accessible. They want a smaller home, with features that may not have been practical while raising children.

Of course, some boomers will move to accommodate job changes. And some will move because their health is changing, and they want to make sure they've got a home in which they'll be able to live comfortably.

Let's take a look at some of the major reasons that middle-age people might consider changing their housing situations.

Health Issues

If you're in your mid-50s and you've developed severe arthritis in your knees, the practical thing to do is to start thinking about moving to a house where everything is on one level. The last thing you'll need when you're 65 or 70 is to be lugging heavy laundry baskets up and down your basement stairs to get to the washer and dryer.

Most people, however, are not eager to address future needs. And, as you can imagine, delaying action on housing issues can lead to serious problems.

We've probably all known people who have remained living in their homes much longer than they should have. This is a frequent dilemma of elderly people, who realize that the upkeep of a home is getting to be too much to handle, but remain unwilling to address the problem and make a move.

Often, by the time they finally admit there's a problem and start thinking of moving into an apartment or assisted living facility, the thought of relocating is so overwhelming that they simply stay put.

Anyone who's ever moved knows it's not easy. It's mighty hard physical work, for one thing. And it can be an extremely emotional task. Sorting through a lifetime of possessions, many that hold special memories or significance, is a difficult job. Add to that the actual chores of packing and moving, and the thought of relocating can seem absolutely impossible.

> **CAUTION** **Don't Go There**
>
> If you see that your aging parents are falling into the wait-too-long-to-move trap, encourage them to consider finding a more manageable place to live before it becomes absolutely necessary. Waiting until they're forced to move limits their options and causes unnecessary stress.

Many older people get stuck in bad situations because they didn't take action soon enough. It's always better to address housing issues before you have to.

So if your arthritic knees are making it more and more difficult for you to get up and down those basement stairs to do the laundry, sit down sometime soon and give some thought to your housing situation. It's better to start looking for the perfect one-story home now, than to wait for 10 years and be forced to take whatever you can find because you can no longer manage steps.

Too Much Space

A four-bedroom house with a big family room and separate playroom was great when your three kids were living at home. Now that they've moved out, though, the big house seems a little excessive—not to mention a bit lonely.

Sure, it'll be great to have some extra rooms for future grandkids, and it's nice to have a guest room always made up. Somehow, though, the house just seems too big.

Go Figure

It used to be that a person would buy a home, fully expecting to stay in it until he died. These days, we're much more likely to move in our 50s, 60s, or 70s. This is partially due to the great increase in life expectancy during the past century. While people in 1900 could expect to live 45 years, today, 4 out of 5 of us will live to see 65, with a 50 percent chance of living past 80.

If you're a couple, or maybe even single living in a family home, you're likely to feel a bit like a marble rolling around in a trash can. While many people hang on to their family homes (due in many cases to the emotional attachment), a growing trend is to move into something more size-suitable for one or two people.

Too Much Yard

Your huge backyard served as a playground for all the neighborhood kids while your children were growing up. Now, it seems to exist only to cause you headaches and cost you money.

Let's face it. Any property maintenance means work, and a large property is more work. You've either got to do it yourself, hire someone else to do it, or bribe your teenager. There's grass to cut, hedges to trim, fertilizer to spread, weeds and insects to control, gardens to maintain, and trees to trim. In the winter, there's snow to shovel, ice to chip … need we go on?

If you're like many people, these outdoor chores become tiresome as you get older. You don't relish the thought of waking up Saturday morning and fueling up the lawn mower. You'd much rather head out for a round of golf or tennis, but there you are, tied to your property.

Some people find great enjoyment and satisfaction from maintaining a large property. Many others, however, consider a large property to be an inconvenience, and perhaps even a reason to consider moving.

Just Not Quite Right

You've lived in your house for 20 years now, wishing every day that you had a two-vehicle garage instead of a single. You're sick and tired of having to brush snow off of your car and scrape ice from the windshield every time there's a storm.

Or maybe you've had it with the lack of closet space in your home. Perhaps you're sick to death of hauling groceries up from a shelf in the garage because there's not enough cabinet space in your kitchen to store them. Or possibly your house has no powder room or central air conditioning. Maybe your street has gotten very busy over the years, and your neighborhood is no longer the quiet place it once was. Or perhaps many of the old neighbors have moved out, and it seems that the entire neighborhood is looking a bit run down and feeling a little forlorn.

Some drawbacks concerning your home are easy to overlook, while others can cause a bit more angst. If you've always hated the chandelier that hangs over your dining room table, for instance, you can easily replace it with a new one. The layout of your family room, however, is a bit more difficult to alter.

We're often forced to live in homes that aren't quite right because we can't afford to alter them, or we don't have the time or ambition to do so. Sometimes, however, these little imperfections are what spur us to consider, and actually make, major housing changes.

Welcome Home, Mom

As members of the sandwich generation, it's quite likely that many of us will at some point find ourselves caring for aging parents.

The level of care-giving will vary from person to person. Some of us will only need to lend a hand with yard work, writing checks, or driving to doctors' appointments, while others will assume much greater responsibility for a parent's care. Some of us will invite aging parents to move into our homes with us.

> **Go Figure**
>
> More than seven million are caring for older people who need help with at least one daily task, such as dressing, bathing, or eating. These caregivers include spouses, adult children, other relatives, and friends.

Deciding If You Can Do It

Wanting to help out Dad by having him move in with you is a loving and giving gesture. It also could be a huge mistake for you, your parent, and your entire family.

The desire to help a parent who can no longer cope on his or her own can be powerful. After all, Dad always took care of you, right? Now it's your turn. If you and Dad haven't gotten along since you were a kid, however, chances are that it's not going to happen now. And moving into your house could just be a recipe for disaster.

If you're thinking about moving an aging parent into your home, there are some things you'll need to consider. Keep in mind that, unless you live alone, your decision will affect your entire family. It's not one to be made lightly. For example, consider the following:

- **Space limitations.** Think carefully about how much space you have in your home. Shared living tends to work best in large homes, or those with separate bedroom and bathroom facilities. Will a family member have to give up a bedroom to accommodate Dad? Will you need to install grab bars beside the toilet and in the tub of the family bathroom? If your space is very limited, but you're determined to have Dad move in, consider renovating a basement or attic to create more space, or putting on a small addition.

- **Practical matters.** Other than space, what other limitations might your home have for an aging parent? Perhaps the hallways aren't wide enough to accommodate Dad's wheelchair, or there are more steps than he's able to handle.

- **Family dynamics.** Maybe you and Dad have always been best pals and have never spoken a word to each other in anger. If your husband can't stand to be around your father, however, you're asking for serious trouble if you insist on moving dear old Dad in. Moving your parent into your home will affect not only you, but your entire family. Will your kids still feel free to invite their friends over to hang out, or will they be afraid of disturbing Granddad? And how will Granddad react to their music and late-night entries? Never move an aging parent into your home at the risk of jeopardizing your relationships with your own family members.

- **Amount of care.** If Dad can dress, bathe, feed, and generally care for himself when he moves in with you, you'll have a much easier time of it than if he's unable to cope with these tasks of daily living. Think about how much time and energy you really have to care for an elderly parent in your home. If you work, will you be able to manage care-giving in addition to your job? Could you arrange for someone to come in and help Dad while you're at work? Will Dad be alone all day and bored silly?

Money Morsel

If you're smack in the middle of your own life and helping to care for an elderly parent, check out *The Complete Idiot's Guide to Caring for Aging Parents*, by Linda Colvin Rhodes, Ed.D., it's a wonderful resource covering all sorts of important issues.

These are only a few issues you'll need to address before deciding whether or not having Dad move in is the right thing to do. Call a family meeting and let everyone have his or her say before making a decision.

Financial Implications

Having an elderly parent move into your home bears some similarities to bringing a baby home from the hospital. No matter how you look at it, it's going to mean extra work and responsibilities. And it's going to cost money.

Chances are, before Mom moves in, you'll need to make at least some minor adjustments to your house. Perhaps you'll need to install handrails on stairways that don't have any, or remove slippery carpet from the steps. You may have to install a ramp to accommodate Mom's wheelchair, or replace a small shower with a larger one in which there's room for Mom to sit down.

Money Morsel

A new trend is Elder Cottage Housing Opportunity, or ECHO housing. ECHO homes are modular units that can be moved onto your property for as long as they're needed. Mom lives in the ECHO home, in close proximity to you and your assistance. When the additional housing is no longer needed, it can be removed. Find out more about ECHO housing at Senior Resource's Web site at www.seniorresouce.com/hecho.htm.

These kinds of changes to your home probably won't put you on the road to bankruptcy, but what happens if you need to renovate an attic or basement, or put on an addition in order to make your house livable with an extra person?

If you're going to spend a lot of money to make your house suitable for Mom, and she's got the means to help, you may ask her to pitch in to help pay for the renovations. If she doesn't have the money to do so, however, you'll need to carefully assess your financial situation and determine whether or not it makes sense to spend big bucks.

Handling It Emotionally

As difficult as the financial and practical aspects of having an aging parent move into your home may be, the emotional matters are likely to be even harder.

Watching a parent who once was strong and vibrant struggle to just walk down the hallway or get up from a chair is extremely difficult.

Dealing every day with someone who might be cranky and miserable is draining and wearing. You

Don't Go There

If you know in your heart that having Mom come to live with you is sure to end up badly, don't invite her anyway, just to ease your conscience or make her happy. You'll both be better off in the long run if you make an acceptable, alternative arrangement.

should realize that care-giving is difficult, and by having your parent move into your home, you may be stepping into an always-on-duty type of situation.

If you decide to invite Mom to move in with you, be sure you have backup. Ask siblings to help out, either by taking Mom to their homes sometimes, or by staying with her at your house to give you a break. If you don't have siblings or other close family members, contact your local Area Agency on Aging (check the Blue Pages of your phone book) for referrals to individuals or agencies that provide respite care.

Considering a Brand-New Home

You may reach a point where you, or you and your spouse or partner, will think about buying a brand-new home. If so, you'll no doubt be in for some exciting days—and perhaps sleepless nights—ahead.

There are, of course, some definite advantages to buying a brand-new home, as opposed to remodeling the home you have or buying an already constructed home. You can get pretty much whatever type of house you want, and you also can choose where it will be located. You can get a log cabin in the woods a luxury home on a golf course, or a traditional Colonial in a development. When building a new home, you get to call the shots. Let's look at some of the advantages, and possible disadvantages, of moving to a brand-new home.

Getting Exactly What You Want

The home-building industry is licking its collective chops at the prospect of retiring baby boomers, whom builders are anticipating will spend big bucks to get the homes they want—and can afford.

Baby boomers are an affluent group, overall. They're also liable to retire, or semi-retire, earlier than their parents did. And, studies show that while relocating retirees traditionally opted for condos; apartments; or smaller, already constructed homes, many boomers will buck the trend and go for brand-new. And, the building industry is predicting, they'll be willing to spend a lot of money to get the features in a house that they want. Some of the features baby boomers are showing they like are listed as follows:

- Oversized master suites with matching walk-in closets, and bathrooms with his-and-her sinks, a Jacuzzi tub, and so forth.

- Large entertainment room. Once the kids have moved out, many people opt to eliminate the traditional family room and go instead for a large room in which to hold both formal and informal gatherings.

◆ Home office. As the way we work changes, many people are making home offices a priority. Many baby boomers say they'll only partially retire, and continue working on a limited basis from home.

◆ Exercise room. Many people would rather work out at home than go to a gym, making in-home gyms or exercise rooms popular options.

◆ Small guest bedroom for visiting family. It's not that boomers don't want their kids and grandkids to visit, it's just that they don't want the guest rooms to detract from the size of the more-used rooms.

◆ Good-sized homes on small lots. This is a popular trend in the building industry. The focus is on the home, not the yard.

Houses with these features frequently are built in a country club-style setting, with golf, tennis, swimming, and other activities available. That setting is becoming increasingly popular but definitely is not for everyone. Perhaps you'd rather have a house in the woods or on the shore of a lake. Buying a brand-new house gives you the option of expressing your own lifestyle preferences.

Money Morsel

If would like some help with home buying and selling, check out *The Complete Idiot's Guide to Buying and Selling a Home, Third Edition*, by Shelley O'Hara and Nancy Warner. It will get you on the right track with home finances and mortgages. If you're getting ready to move, pick up a copy of *Moving Without Madness: A Guide to Handling the Stress and Emotions of Moving*, by Arlene Alpert.

Leaving Your Home and Neighborhood

If you decide to buy a new home, you'll leave behind the home in which you've been living, and along with it, your neighborhood.

Moving from one home to another is stressful, there's no question about it. Even if you're moving because you want to, relocating from one home to another is ranked right up there on the stress meter with losing a job or having a baby.

While the need to sort out, clean out, and pack a houseful of long-accumulated possessions might be the obvious reason for stress, don't overlook the emotional and psychological aspects. It's difficult to leave a home in which you've raised kids or celebrated holidays. Maybe you're moving from the home you've lived in since you were married. And you might be leaving a neighborhood that's been a source of support and friendship to you over the years.

We tend to think sometimes that close neighborhoods are a notion that went out of style with Ozzie and Harriet. Neighborhoods, however, are alive and thriving all over the country, in cities and suburbs, alike.

Many people build very close, family-like relationships with their neighbors. If you're going for the new home, don't underestimate the effect that leaving your 'hood might produce.

Getting the Home You Want

If you've decided to have a new home built, there are some guidelines you should keep in mind in order to assure that your experience is a positive one.

♦ Get a clear understanding of your wants and needs. Write down exactly what features you want in your new home. If you love to cook, for instance, you might want special features in your kitchen. Or if that arthritic knee is getting worse, you may want to build a one-story home.

♦ Find a good, reputable builder. You can start by checking the real estate section of your Sunday paper to get an idea of who's building what types of homes in your area. Contact your local Home Builder's Association for referrals to reputable builders. Or your local Chamber of Commerce may be able to recommend a builder in your area.

> **Don't Go There**
>
> Don't assume just because a builder has a lot of business that he's the person you should choose for your new home construction. Overly busy builders may be seriously behind schedule or may hire less-than-qualified workers to try to keep up with their business.

♦ Check out the work of several reputable builders. Visit some homes under construction and examine the quality of the work. If you're not knowledgeable about construction quality, take someone with you who is. Take notice of the quality of the materials used. And, talk to the people living in the homes the builder you're considering have built. Builders should be willing to give you the names of some customers. If they're not, a warning flag should go up. Ask customers whether they're satisfied with their new homes, and find out if the work was completed on time. Ask if they would buy another home from the same builder.

♦ Talk to your builder. Once you've chosen a builder, sit down and talk with him about exactly what you want in your home. He should be willing to alter existing plans to give you what you want.

♦ Pay close attention to the builder's warranty and service-after-the-sale provisions. It may be tedious reading, but be sure to carefully read the terms of the warranty, and know exactly what kind of service the builder provides once you've move in. New construction typically requires some "adjustments," so be sure your builder is willing to come back until everything is to your satisfaction.

Remember that if you decide to buy brand-new and have a home built, you're in charge. Overseeing the construction of your new home will require your time and attention. Keeping a close eye on what's going on, however, can save you lots of grief and future problems.

If you're too busy to keep a close watch on what's going on while your home is being built, you might consider hiring a home inspector who will watch for you. Check your phone book for some names, or approach someone you know who has good knowledge of the building industry or who is familiar with new home construction.

Adapting the House You Have

While building a new home may be an attractive option, it certainly isn't the only means of getting the house you want.

Many people choose to renovate the home they have instead of building a new one. Maybe you live within walking distance of nearly everything and wouldn't consider giving up that convenience. Or, your neighbors are also your best friends, and you can't stand the thought of moving away.

Renovating the home you have can provide you with the features you want, without the hassle of moving. It also is usually less expensive to adapt a home than to build a new one.

Most home-improvement projects appreciate in value over time. With careful planning and common sense, home fix-up projects can be a wise investment.

> ### Go Figure
>
> The *Chicago Tribune* reported recently that more dollars are being spent on home improvements than on new home construction for the first time in history, and that more than 60 percent of American homes are at least 20 years old.

It's important, however, not to overimprove your house. There's a danger of owning a house that's valued at much more than any other home in the area. Buyers generally are unwilling to pay more than 10 or 15 percent more for a house that's been improved than they would for an unimproved version in the same area.

Also, additions or major remodeling need to be done well, so your house looks good when the construction is finished. We've probably all seen homes that practically scream out "new addition" as you drive by.

If you decide to renovate your current home, follow the guidelines listed in the preceding section for finding a builder, and make sure he knows exactly what it is you want to do. Don't cheap out on design, materials, and construction if you hope to get your money back on the home when it's time to sell it.

The most common renovations involve kitchens and bathrooms, according to the Remodeling Council at the National Association of Home Builders. Homeowners are also adding great rooms (combined kitchen and family rooms) master-bedroom suites, and home offices.

If you're thinking of remodeling, take a look at the big picture. Once you find out about how much your project will cost, figure out what percentage of value you're adding to your home. If your home (along with most of the others in your neighborhood) is valued at $120,000, and the addition you're planning will cost $60,000, you're increasing the value of your home by half. Is it feasible to think that you'd be able to sell your home for $180,000 when other homes in the area are selling for $120,000?

> **Go Figure**
>
> Statistics show that adding a second full bathroom to your home significantly increases its resale value. If you have two baths, adding a third one brings a lesser return upon resale.

And consider how long you plan to live in the home. It doesn't make sense to sink $40,000 into a house you'll be moving out of in two or three years.

Only you can decide whether to stay or not stay in your current home. Sometimes, such as when there are serious health concerns, the choice becomes obvious. Usually, however, it's a judgment call that you'll only be able to make after careful thought and consideration.

The Least You Need to Know

- Changing housing needs are likely to make you consider moving, or renovating the home you already have.
- Health issues, the amount of maintenance required, and the size of a home are common factors in changing housing needs.
- If you're considering having an aging parent move in with you, you'll need to carefully review all the pros and cons before making your decision.
- If you decide to build a brand-new home, take steps to choose a builder who's experienced and reputable.
- Renovating the home you're in might be a great idea, but be sure you don't add too much more to the house than you'll be able to recoup when you decide to sell it.

Chapter **12**

A Home Away from Home

In This Chapter

- ◆ Considering all the angles
- ◆ Tax advantages of owning a second home
- ◆ Relaxation and a place to entertain
- ◆ Understanding the cons of owning two homes
- ◆ Buying a timeshare unit

Nearly everyone looks forward to vacations. Some of us tend to be creatures of habit, revisiting the same places again and again. Others are far more adventurous, seeking new experiences and locations.

Either way, you may have at one time or another considered buying some sort of vacation property. Maybe you love the shore and have thought about a beach home. Or perhaps you've considered buying a timeshare property that would allow you to trade and travel far and wide.

In this chapter we'll look at the pros and cons of owning a second home, and help you decide whether it might make sense for you.

Thinking About a Vacation Home

For you and your family, there's nothing better than your annual three-week trip to Cape Cod, Massachusetts. You've rented the same cabin every summer for the past 12 years, and you know every nook and cranny of that little home away from home.

Your kids have grown up catching frogs in the pond across the lane, and some of their best friends are other kids who vacation at the same place. Sitting on the screened-in porch with a cool drink is the perfect wind-down after a long day at the beach. You treasure the time you have together there and look forward all winter to when you can pack the suitcases and head back to the cabin.

If that scenario sounds familiar, you may have considered the possibility of buying that cabin, or a similar one. That way, you could make the trip whenever you wanted to, and you'd always have the cabin to enjoy. Once your kids have families of their own, they could use the vacation home. On the other hand, how much time would you really be able to spend there? Could you get away for more than three weeks? Would you use the house on weekends, or would your kids' activities make that impossible? Is there a possibility that you'd move to your vacation home when you retire? Would the money you'd need to buy the cabin be better spent somewhere else?

Don't Go There

If you're thinking of buying a vacation home, look carefully at what's happening in the area in which the home is located. If the area is overdeveloped, overregulated, or has very low property values; the economy hits rocky times; or high inflation makes mortgage rates too high for most people to afford a mortgage, you may not be able to sell the home if you no longer want it.

Owning that cabin might be a happy dream, but you shouldn't even consider buying a second home unless you're sure you can afford to do so. Many people have rationalized the cost of a vacation home, and ended up losing big bucks on it.

Before you get too carried away with the thought of a little home away from home, consider the questions listed here:

♦ Would you use a second home primarily as an investment property, or a cozy hideaway to be available whenever you and family want to use it? If you can make enough money by renting the property to cover many of the expenses involved, it may make better financial sense to buy than if you're going to only use the house for your family vacations.

♦ Do homes sell quickly in the area you want to buy, or may you have difficulty getting rid of the house if you no longer want it?

◆ Will the location continue to be a good one for you? If your kids love the beach, but you and your spouse or partner only tolerate it, think carefully before buying that shore house. Kids get very busy as they get older, and before you know it, they have jobs, are going to college, or even getting married. Make sure it's a place that you'll continue to enjoy.

◆ Is the vacation home within reasonable travel distance, or will it be too expensive and time consuming to get there? A ski cabin in Vermont sounds great, but if you live in Georgia, how often will you realistically be able to get there to use it? The closer you buy to where you live, the more likely you'll be to use the second home.

◆ Have you considered all the costs involved with buying and owning a second home? There will be settlement costs. You'll probably have to buy some furnishings for the house. It's a lot easier to store sheets and towels in the cabin than to pack and transport them each time you visit. There are costs involved with maintaining a vacation home.

◆ Will you be able to relax there? Buying a handyman's special as your vacation home and fixing it up might be an affordable way to acquire a second home, but do you really want to spend your vacation time scraping paint and rebuilding the deck?

Don't Go There

Many people have lost their enthusiasm for a vacation home because they buy one that's difficult to get to. It doesn't take long to get really tired of working all week, driving six hours to your cabin, spending a day there and then turning around and driving six hours home.

Whether or not to buy a second property is a big decision. You've got to live someplace, so buying or leasing a first property is a no-brainer. When you've already got a perfectly fine home and are considering buying a second one, however, you're likely to spend a lot of hours weighing the pros and cons.

Perhaps the next section, which deals with the tax advantages of a second home, will help you make your decision.

Tax Advantages

You've probably heard that owning a second home provides some tax relief—and, it can. There are some special tax rules and regulations that apply to second properties, however, and they can be a little confusing. Hang in there, we'll try to make this as clear as possible.

To figure out what type of tax breaks you might get as related to your vacation home, you need to know how you'll use the property, and how the Internal Revenue Service will categorize it.

Your vacation home will be considered a residence if you use it for personal purposes at least part of the year. If you rent it all year, it's considered to be a rental or investment property.

The first rule to remember is that you can't deduct the mortgage interest on your vacation home as home mortgage interest on line 10 of Schedule A if it's not considered to be a residence. Refer to the IRS Web site at www.irs.gov/forms_pubs/forms.html to select and print a copy of Schedule A.

Money Morsel _____

Vacation homes come in many packages. Your vacation home could be a house, a condo, a cabin, or a duplex. It also could be a boat or a recreational vehicle. To qualify for a tax deduction, your vacation home needs to have a bathroom, kitchen, and a place to sleep. It's a good idea to pay a visit to your accountant before you buy a vacation home. Ask her about tax advantages for rental properties and residences, and have her run pro forma returns under different scenarios to see how your income tax return may be affected.

That doesn't mean, however, that you can't rent a vacation home and still have it be considered a residence. It's all a matter of timing.

The IRS says in order to have your vacation home qualify as a residence, you need to spend at least 14 days there, or 10 percent of the amount of time that the property is rented.

Let's say that you own a home on a lake, very close to some good ski areas. The location makes your home attractive to skiers and snowmobilers in the winter, and to families and others who enjoy the lake, hiking, and so forth in the summer. There's a big demand for these properties, and you have no trouble renting your home for 210 days out of the year.

You might think the rental income is great, but if you don't use the house for at least 21 days, the IRS will consider the home to be a rental property and you won't be able to deduct your mortgage or real estate taxes entirely on Schedule A. Part of the mortgage interest will need to be declared against the rental income on Schedule E of your tax return. Refer to the IRS Web site at www.irs.gov/forms_pubs/forms.html to select and print a copy of Schedule E.

On the other hand, if you own a vacation home and rent it for less than two weeks, you get a tax break because you don't need to report the rental income on your tax return. All that rental income is, essentially, tax free.

If your property is considered a residence, but you rent it for more than two weeks a year, you'll need to report the rental income. You'll also be able to take advantage of some allowable tax deductions, but since it's a vacation home, you can't have more expenses than income. You can come out to zero, but the IRS doesn't permit you to take a tax loss on a vacation home.

The income and deductions offset each other when you rent a vacation home for more than two weeks. Deductions include the following:

- Mortgage interest
- Upkeep
- Maintenance
- Mortgage insurance
- Utilities
- Real estate taxes
- Insurance
- Depreciation
- Supplies and miscellaneous expenses

The trick is, rental deductions, on a vacation home, can't exceed gross rental income, less interest, taxes, and costs to advertise the property. If you rent out your beach home for 12 weeks, for instance, at $1,000 a week, your rental income will be $12,000, less the interest, taxes, and advertising costs.

If all the deductions listed earlier total more than the $12,000 of rental income received, you won't be able to list the loss (the excess expenses) on your income tax return.

If you use your vacation home as a rental property, the system changes. First of all, you can't use the home for more than 14 days or 10 percent of the time that it's rented. The second difference is that passive loss rules kick in on rental property. Passive loss is when you lose money from a *passive activity*, such as renting property or participating in a limited partnership.

If you lose money on your rentals—that is, if the expenses you can deduct are greater than the income from your rental property, the loss can be offset by passive income. You can claim up to $25,000 of losses in a year from vacation home rentals if your income is less than $100,000. If your income exceeds $100,000, the allowable loss decreases until income reaches $150,000, when the allowable loss is eliminated.

Adding It Up

You might think of watching TV as a **passive activity,** but the tax code defines passive activity as an activity in which you do not materially participate, such as real estate rentals and limited partnerships..

You also may be able to deduct the value of your rental property over a period of years. This is called depreciation, and is intended to reflect the wear and tear on a property and its contents over time. Depreciation applies to a home and its contents, but not the value of the land.

In summary, try to keep these simple rules in mind when considering possible tax advantages of owning a vacation home:

◆ If you don't use the property, all your expenses are deductible against the rent.

◆ If you rent the property for less than 14 days a year, the rent you receive does not have to be reported on your tax return.

◆ If you use the property for more than 14 days a year, your expenses are prorated against your income.

Tax considerations shouldn't be the only reason you consider buying a vacation home. Hopefully, you'll find lots of other ways to enjoy it, too.

Other Advantages

We live in a busy, stressful world that seems to spin faster and faster with every passing day. Finding time to relax and do nothing, or relax as you participate in activities that you enjoy, seems to get more and more difficult as you deal with the obligations of home, kids, work, aging parents, and so forth.

There's no question that it's a lot easier to relax and enjoy when you're removed from the situations that cause your stress. To that end, a vacation home that's not too far away from your primary residence can be a real lifesaver.

Sharing your vacation home with friends and family also can be very rewarding. A couple we know invites their whole family to spend the Thanksgiving weekend at their beach house on the Jersey shore. It's become a family tradition that grows every year.

Don't Go There

Resist the temptation to do so much entertaining that your vacation home starts to resemble a bed-and-breakfast facility, with you as the chief cook and maid.

Another couple enjoys loaning their Florida vacation home to their grown children and their families during times of the year when the couple isn't using the house. Although financial issues definitely will be factors in deciding whether or not to buy a second home, remember that there advantages that can't be accounted for in dollars.

The Downside of Vacation Homes

While you'd like to restrict the imagery concerning your second home to tranquil walks on the beach in the moonlight, or quiet afternoons on the lake with a fishing pole in your hand, things don't always work out as we plan.

Some of the less-than-happy considerations you should think about before signing the sales agreement on a second home include those listed here:

◆ **Unforeseen disasters.** Hurricanes. Floods. Fires. Unfortunately, because many vacation homes are near the coasts, they're prone to storms and storm damage. You can spend a lot of anxious hours in front of The Weather Channel when there's a hurricane or tropical storm blowing up the coast toward your vacation getaway. Many lenders will require extra insurances on vacation properties due to these possibilities.

◆ **Regular maintenance and upkeep.** The grass doesn't stop growing just because you're not there. Nor does the roof keep from leaking, the squirrels from finding their way inside, or the paint from peeling off the front door. If you rent the home, you'll need to get someone in to clean it between rentals, and someone else to check on the place when you're not in the area. There are service companies in areas that have a lot of vacation properties. You'll probably be able to find someone to do the work, but you'll have to pay, of course.

◆ **Problem renters.** This is an unpleasant possibility, but one you should consider if you plan to rent your property. Friends with rental properties have found sliding doors pulled from their tracks, screen doors kicked in, carpets stained, and windows broken. Plus, there's the possibility of rowdy renters. You can have a rental agent handle the bulk of renter-related problems, but you'll still need to deal with the devastation left behind.

◆ **Bad timing.** Friends bought a place at the beach and had a great time vacationing there with their kids for two years. After that, the kids no longer wanted to leave their friends every weekend to go to the beach house. They were involved with too many school activities, and the parents ended up feeling frustrated because they weren't getting the use they'd hoped for out of the house. They managed to sell the place after a while, but they took a loss on it.

Money Morsel

Be sure to collect a refundable security deposit if you rent your vacation home to someone you don't know. Consider renting only to people who have been referred by friends or acquaintances.

◆ **Deed restrictions.** Consider the possibility that a planned community, property association, or condominium may impose restrictions on how often, and to whom, you're allowed to rent, or even loan your property. Make sure you understand all restrictions on a property before you buy.

Not wanting to be gloomy pessimists, we'll stop considering the less-than-desirable aspects of owning vacation property right here. The point is, buying a second home is not a step you should take without lots of careful consideration.

What About a Timeshare?

If you get a call or information in the mail offering you a free or greatly discounted vacation at a popular tourist destination, chances are that you've been targeted as a potential purchaser of a timeshare.

Timesharing, basically, is when individuals purchase the right to spend a specified amount of time each year at a specific place. Most timeshare agreements allow you to trade with owners in different locations.

Timeshares were hot commodities 15 or 20 years ago, and then became less popular for a while. Sales are on the rise again, however, increasing by 14 percent during the past 6 years. More than 1.7 million Americans currently own timeshares, according to the American Resort Development Association.

If a timeshare company identifies you as a potential buyer, it may offer you, your spouse or partner, and maybe some other family members a couple of free nights in a hotel or motel. It probably will throw in some other incentives such as free or discounted meals, shopping, and admission to area attractions.

In exchange for the free stuff, you've got to agree to spend a couple of hours with a salesperson who's trying his darnedest to get you to plunk down $10,000 or so to buy a timeshare offered by his company. He'll tell you why his timeshare company is the best, and show you catalogs of all the great places you'll be able to visit when you trade timeshare locations with other owners. He'll probably show you a couple of timeshare models that are nearby, and then ask you to commit on the spot to buying one.

> **Go Figure**
>
> The average timeshare owner is 49 years old, earns $70,000 in annual income, is married, well educated, and has children.

If you've done your homework and decided that a timeshare is for you, you may enjoy one of these presentations and the opportunity to buy. Just remember, however, that many of these salespeople use high-pressure tactics and don't give you the opportunity to sleep on your decision.

The average price of a timeshare is $10,500, which normally guarantees you the use of your timeshare for one week per year for the rest of your life. Prices vary based on the time of year you'll use the unit, and its location and size. Buyers traditionally put down 10 percent, then pay the balance over the next 7 years.

For the privilege of owning a timeshare, you get to chip in for property taxes, general upkeep, furnishings, and maintenance. Those costs average about $400 a year. An upside, however, is that you can get a mortgage to buy a condo and deduct the interest you pay on it.

Timeshares are interesting concepts, and many people think they're great. Most timeshare deals allow you to trade for different locations, allowing you to test out new spots without the cost of having to rent a house or hotel room while you're there. Some timeshare deals allow you to buy a week a year and use one or two days at a time, making them attractive to businesspeople.

Don't Go There

Most timeshare companies are happy to give you a loan, but they usually come at a much higher rate than a mortgage you could get on your own. Don't be talked into taking a company loan.

According to the Better Business Bureau, you should keep the following tips in mind if you're considering buying a timeshare unit.

- A timeshare is not a real estate investment. It is a pre-paid vacation accommodation. All expenses associated with a timeshare should be looked at as vacation expenses.

- Make sure the timeshare property is in a location you don't mind visiting again and again. And check to see if you're bound to the same date each year, or if the dates that you can use the facility are flexible.

- Make sure you understand all the implications of what you agree to at signing.

- Determine if the unit is a deeded interest or a right-to-use unit. Deeded units may be more expensive, but they can provide some tax benefits (deductions) and can allow a buyer to have a voice in the management of the resort.

- Buying a timeshare is a long-term commitment. Make certain the developer or owner of the timeshare resort has long-term plans for managing the property.

- Many timeshare resorts are affiliated with exchange programs that allow owners to exchange their weeks for weeks at different locations. Keep in mind, however, that there is no assurance that the exchange program will be able to provide the time-share owner with another accommodation that is desirable or available at the time the owner wants to swap. Also be aware that there is no guarantee a timeshare development will continue to affiliate with an exchange program.

- Maintenance fees can rise as the property ages and upkeep becomes more expensive.

Money Morsel

For more information about timeshares, including secondary sales, check out the Timeshare Users Group online at www.tug2.net.

♦ Money paid toward the purchase of a timeshare should be kept in an escrow account until the title to the unit is free and clear.

♦ Consider all costs associated with buying a timeshare, including travel costs.

A drawback of buying a timeshare is that you might have trouble getting what you want for it if you decide to sell. New timeshares are being built constantly. The company that sold you your timeshare generally won't buy it back, leaving you on your own to sell it.

There is a secondary timeshare market, which is something to consider if you're thinking about buying a unit. You can get some terrific deals on timeshares that have outlived their usefulness and now are burdensome to the owners.

Timeshares have their own set of advantages and disadvantages, all of which should be carefully considered before you buy. Try to avoid the high-pressure sales that come along with those free vacations, or be well prepared with questions and background information before you get into that situation.

The Least You Need to Know

♦ There are many, many factors to consider before deciding if buying a vacation home is the right move for you.

♦ There are definite tax advantages to owning a second home, but you need to understand the laws and regulations.

♦ Your own vacation home is a great place to relax and entertain family and friends.

♦ Vacation homes present their own problems and challenges, and you should be aware of the possible problems before you decide to buy.

♦ Timeshare units are vacation opportunities that have been increasing in popularity.

Paying for a New Home or Second Home

In This Chapter

- ◆ Figuring out what you can afford to buy
- ◆ Keeping extra costs in mind
- ◆ Examining payment options
- ◆ Understanding mortgages and loans
- ◆ Taking a good, hard look at what's involved

If, after long bouts of debating, deciding, and redeciding, you've finally concluded that you're going to take the plunge and buy a new home, this is a must-read chapter for you.

You've found the perfect home, in the perfect neighborhood. It's convenient, it's accessible to your friends, to the shops you frequent, and if applicable, to your kids' schools. It's got the extra bathroom you've always wanted, and the closets are absolutely huge. The kitchen is fabulous, with plenty of cabinet space and a work island in the middle. It's got an entryway that you just love, and even the guest bedroom is spacious. So you're not crazy about the color of the carpeting, but you can live with it—at least for a little while.

Getting ready to move is an exciting time, there's no question about it. It's also a busy time, and a very expensive time. If you don't watch it, those expenses can add up shockingly fast.

New curtains to match the bedspread you already have. New shower curtains, too. Oh, heck. You might as well buy that sofa that you saw on sale. It will fit much better against that large wall than the smaller one you already have. And, of course, you'll want the love seat, too. You see what we mean? In just one paragraph, we've managed to spend thousands of dollars.

Maybe your excitement is due to the fact that you're buying a second home, as discussed in Chapter 12, "A Home Away from Home." You lie awake at night, looking forward to the time you'll be able to hear the ocean from your bedroom window.

Regardless of whether you're buying a primary residence or a second home, there are many, many financial issues to consider. In this chapter, we'll have a look at how you can judge what you can afford to pay for a house, and what payment method will work best for you. We'll tell you how to determine the value of your home, and find out how much equity you've got in it. It's information you've got to have before signing on the dotted line.

Knowing What You Can Afford

Let's make something very clear, right away. Having a mortgage counselor deliver the good news that you and your spouse can afford to buy a $200,000 home, by no means compels you and said spouse to head out in a frantic search for such a place.

Being able to afford a particular mortgage payment on paper is a lot different than being really able to afford it. Just because a formula says you can handily pay $1,500 or $2,000 a month on your house doesn't mean you've got to find a place that costs that much.

If you're going to borrow money for a home, you should borrow an amount that also allows saving for your other financial goals. Are your college savings well funded and up to date? How about your retirement accounts? And don't forget about the cash you'll still need for entertainment, recreation, and vacations—not to mention groceries.

Money Morsel

If your credit card debt has been creeping upward, do everything you can to reduce it before applying for a mortgage. Doing so will reduce your total debt and put you in a better financial position for getting a mortgage.

When you apply for a mortgage, a lender will review your net worth statement and your credit history, look at your current income, and see what sort of debt you already have.

He'll take into consideration expenses such as day care costs, monthly parking fees, and the cost of your daily commute. Once he's got a handle on your financial situation, he'll assess the impact that a new mortgage will have on all that, then decide if you can afford the property.

Remember, though, just because he or she says you can afford it, doesn't mean you want it.

Most lenders use a debt-to-gross-income ratio of between 28 and 36 percent. That means that your total debt, including mortgage, taxes, car payments, credit card debt, and so forth, should fall somewhere within 28 and 36 percent of your total income.

A couple earning $80,000 per year (that's $6,666 per month), for instance, can have a monthly debt repayment schedule of between $1,800 and $2,400 per month. See the following table to get an idea of what you might be able to afford a month in debt repayment. Remember that your mortgage is only a part of your total debt repayment. These figures are based on a 28 percent total debt-to-income ratio.

Annual Income	Annual Mortgage Payment	Monthly Mortgage Payment
20,000	5,600	466.67
25,000	7,000	583.33
30,000	8,400	700.00
35,000	9,800	816.67
40,000	11,200	933.33
45,000	12,600	1,050.00
50,000	14,000	1,166.67
55,000	15,400	1,283.33
60,000	16,800	1,400.00
65,000	18,200	1,516.67
70,000	19,600	1,633.33
75,000	21,000	1,750.00
80,000	22,400	1,866.67
85,000	23,800	1,983.33
90,000	25,200	2,100.00
95,000	26,600	2,216.67
100,000	28,000	2,333.33

It's basic, but very important to keep in mind that a bigger mortgage means less money elsewhere. Unless you're manufacturing money in your basement, you've got a limited amount. You may have gotten pretty comfortable with your old mortgage, or maybe even had your old home paid for. Maybe you've been paying all your bills, eating out whenever you wanted, and still had extra funds to put aside in savings.

Just remember that a larger mortgage payment, or a second mortgage payment, can cause your discretionary income to vanish. Think back to when you bought your first home. Remember how you scrimped and saved? Are you willing to do that again? Just be sure that you don't overextend your finances on a new mortgage.

CAUTION

Don't Go There

Don't forget about all those extra, nasty little fees like points and settlement fees that crop up when you get a mortgage for a new home. Not planning for those costs can turn settlement from a happy occasion into an embarrassing one.

Once you figure out how much you're able to afford (theoretically, at least), you can look at your overall financial picture and see where you might be able to cut down in order to give you a little breathing room between your increased mortgage and other expenses. Nobody likes to have to watch every nickel they spend, but you don't want to end up house rich and cash poor (or broke).

And remember that the costs of buying and moving into a new home don't end with the mortgage.

Considering Extra Costs

The cost of moving includes far more than mortgage payments and settlement expenses. When you're thinking about moving, try to anticipate some of the extra costs that you'll encounter. If you can, talk with somebody who's moved recently to see what costs they ran into. Extras can add up fast, for example:

♦ **Furniture.** Unless you're really lucky, you're going to need some new furniture for a new home. The pieces you have are too worn, or they don't fit, or they don't match the carpets. Where there's a new house, there will be a need for furniture.

♦ **Moving expenses.** Unless you've got great friends who are willing to give up a Saturday to help you load your stuff into a U-Haul, you can expect to pay out some pretty substantial money for a professional mover. Movers charge by the hour, so save time by packing everything yourself, and move some of the smaller pieces to where the truck will be parked. If you're relocating due to work and your company is picking up the tab, keep in mind that it might not agree to pay extra costs, such as moving your grand piano.

♦ **Window treatments.** Count on about $500 per window for custom-made window treatments. That can add up pretty fast, as you can imagine. Don't worry. You probably can learn to live with no curtains, or get used to the yellow-and-orange floral drapes that are already there.

♦ **Decorating.** You can paint yourself and keep the costs down, but chances are you'd rather hire somebody and save yourself the time and hassles. Check in your local shopper's paper for painters looking for work, but make sure they carry insurance and can give you some references. Same goes for paper hangers and other contractors.

◆ **Landscaping.** Most homeowners haven't updated their landscaping for years. If you're buying a previously owned home, chances are that you'd like to make some changes. The trouble is, landscaping can be really expensive. Don't forget to consider these costs.

◆ **Appliances.** Major appliances are expensive, especially if you have to buy a houseful of them. Hopefully, at least some appliances will be included with the house you buy. If not, add them onto your rapidly growing list of expenses.

Money Morsel

Remember to consider all the extra costs you'll run into when deciding how much money to pay down on the house. It's great to have a big down payment because it reduces the size of your mortgage. It's not great, however, to be unable to afford to buy what you need for your new home.

◆ **Utility connection fees.** The transfer on your telephone, Internet connection, cable TV, and other utilities can really add onto the cost of moving.

◆ **Travel expenses.** If you're relocating for your job, you may have to move before your family does. If so, you'll encounter expenses traveling back to see them, or having them come to see you.

◆ **Double payments.** If you find yourself in the unfortunate position of owning two homes (more about this in Chapter 14, "Selling the House You Already Have"), you'll have to count on paying double house payments, utility bills, property taxes, and so forth, until the old house has been sold.

◆ **Settlement costs.** Need we say more? Settlement costs average about 3 percent of your home's purchase price.

◆ **Repairs and maintenance.** Your current home will need to pass an inspection in order to satisfy the buyer's mortgage company. You may not have minded the older fence around the pool, or the garage roof that looked like it might need replacing in a few years. If you're interested in keeping the deal together with the buyers, however, you may have to do a little upgrading in order to pass the inspection.

Deciding How You'll Pay for It

If you've decided to go ahead and buy a new home, chances are that you'll need to borrow some money, at least temporarily. If you've got a lot of equity built up in your current home, and are buying something that's less expense or about the same price as where you're living now, you may only need to borrow money for a short time. You borrow to pay for your new home, then repay the loan when your current home sells.

If you've always lived in an apartment, however, or are buying a second home, chances are that you won't have the cash available to buy your home outright. Very few people pay 100 percent of the price of a home before they move in. Most folks, and chances are that you're one of them, will need to get a mortgage and make monthly payments on their home.

Getting a mortgage sounds simple, but the problem is that there are many kinds of them out there. The trick is deciding which kind of mortgage is right for you. Get ready for a quick, crash course on mortgages, and then we'll show you a profile of what types of mortgages seem to work best for certain types of people. You can figure out where you best fit in, and what type of mortgage you might consider.

Mortgages

The two most common types of mortgages are *fixed rate* and *adjustable rate*. Fixed-rate mortgages are those on which you agree to pay a certain amount of interest every month for as long as you have the mortgage. If your mortgage rate is 7 percent, you'll pay 7 percent every month from the time you get the loan, until it's completely paid back.

An adjustable-rate mortgage is a loan on which the interest rate varies. For that reason, your monthly payments don't stay the same.

The interest rate on an adjustable-rate mortgage rises and falls in line with changes in overall interest rates. The typical rate changes once a year—and usually can't rise more than two points annually or six points over the life of the loan.

Adjustable-rate mortgages generally offer lower beginning interest rates than fixed-rate loans, and you generally don't have to pay points if you get this type of mortgage. Remember though, that points are really prepaid interest, so if you don't pay them up front, you'll end up paying over the life of your mortgage.

Some other types of mortgages include the following:

Adding It Up

A **fixed-rate** mortgage is one where the interest rate remains constant over the life of the loan. An **adjustable-rate** mortgage normally has the same interest rate for a specified time, after which the rate may fluctuate.

◆ **Hybrid mortgage.** This kind of mortgage mixes fixed and adjustable-rate loans. There are different types of hybrids, among them are balloon mortgages and two-step mortgages. Hybrids allow you to pay a certain amount of interest for a while, and then change to a different rate, either higher or lower. A balloon mortgage allows you to pay a lower-than-normal interest rate for a while, and then requires you to pay the off the balance of your principal in a lump sum payment. Even though you could refinance a balloon mortgage to get a more traditional one, that particular type of mortgage isn't for everyone.

- **Graduated-payment mortgage.** This type of loan allows you to start out paying less than the full monthly payment that you'd have with a traditional mortgage for the same amount. Your payments gradually increase as you get further into the life of your loan. The interest rate is usually fixed, so you don't face the risk of unexpected increases you would have with an adjustable mortgage. This type of mortgage can be advantageous for someone buying a second home, because it allows lower total payments in the early years, giving the borrower time to pay off his first home or other debts.

- **Assumable mortgage.** This is when the buyer assumes the mortgage of the seller. There are advantages if the seller got the mortgage when interest rates were low, and they've risen dramatically.

- **Seller financing.** This is when the person selling the house provides financing to the buyer, and the buyer repays the seller instead of to a mortgage lender.

- **Jumbo mortgage.** These are, as the name implies, large mortgages, and they generally carry higher interest rates than regular ones. A loan of more than $275,000 currently is considered a jumbo mortgage, but the amount increases at regular intervals.

- **Biweekly mortgage.** You pay twice a month instead of once on this kind of mortgage, and it has the attractive benefit of shortening the length of your loan.

In addition to different types of mortgages, you can pay them back over different periods of time. The most popular payment periods are 15 and 30 years.

If you choose a 30-year mortgage, you get to pay less each month because your loan is spread out over a longer period of time. A 15-year loan means higher payments, but you can usually get a slightly lower interest rate. And paying the mortgage off in half the time results in big savings overall.

There are, however, some advantages to a 30-year mortgage. Mortgage interest is 100 percent tax deductible, and having a longer-term loan allows you to claim the deduction for many years. Also, if you're paying less per month on your mortgage, you may have more money to invest.

> **Go Figure**
>
> The total interest paid on a 15-year mortgage with a 7 percent interest rate is $46,350. Total interest on a 30-year loan at the same interest rate is $104,632. Big difference!

Checking Out Your Profile

The Pennsylvania Institute of Certified Public Accountants has come up with a set of mortgage guidelines, based on a borrower's profile. Read it over and see where you think you fit in, and what type of mortgage may be best for you.

- **The Lifer.** For borrowers who will stay in their home for many years, a fixed-rate mortgage may be the best. You pay slightly more in the first year than you would with an adjustable-rate mortgage, but you lock in the low fixed rate for the long term. It may be worth paying points up front to get a lower interest rate that will save you money over the years of the loan.

- **The Mover.** If there's a possibility that you may move again during the next few years, an adjustable mortgage might be best for you. You get a lower rate in the early years than with a fixed mortgage. And, because you'll be moving, you needn't worry much about the adjustable rate creeping up on you.

- **The Income Climber.** If you expect to receive pay raises, pay off debts, or experience increases in income due to an inheritance or some other reason, consider a graduated payment mortgage. Monthly payments will gradually rise on a fixed schedule.

Money Morsel

Today's adjustable mortgages don't offer the really big initial savings that they did in the past. Even the Mover might be better off locking in a low long-term rate through a fixed mortgage.

Adding It Up

Fannie Mae is a security issued by the Federal National Mortgage Association, which is backed by insured and conventional mortgages. Monthly returns to holders of Fannie Maes consist of interest and principals payments by homeowners on their mortgages.

- **The Well-Heeled Buyer.** If making a big mortgage payment isn't a problem, consider a mortgage for 15 or 20 years, instead of 30. You'll pay off the loan faster, and save a bundle on interest.

- **The First-Time Buyer.** If you can afford the monthly payments but don't have the savings for a 10 or 20 percent down payment, look around for a mortgage that requires little or no money down. One such loan is the Flexible 97 mortgage backed by *Fannie Mae*. It allows a down payment with an unsecured loan from a family member, something that isn't permitted with most traditional mortgages.

These profiles can give you an idea of what type of mortgage may work the best for you. It's a good idea, though, to talk to a mortgage counselor or your accountant before making a final decision.

If you're thinking about buying a vacation home and you have built up a fair amount of equity in your primary home, you might think about getting a home equity loan.

Home Equity Loans and Lines of Credit

Loans based on the equity in your home generally can be obtained at lower interest rates than nonsecured loans, and the interest is normally tax-deductible.

If you need cash out of your home, you probably don't have to refinance into a new first mortgage. Consider adding a second mortgage or getting a home equity loan. Second mortgages are loans you get on top of your primary mortgage, and they're not part of the national market. Held by local lenders, the interest rates on them can vary tremendously, so be sure to shop around.

Home equity loans are generally paid back over a much shorter time period than mortgages. Review your entire loan situation with your lender, looking at whether it's best to refinance everything into one loan or to add a home equity loan to your first mortgage. The lender will be able to provide you with comparison costs and total interest paid.

Using your home as collateral for a loan puts your home at risk if you should default. You should carefully assess your borrowing needs and your ability to repay before you decide to borrow against your house.

There are two types of equity loans. The first, a fixed, lump sum amount, is known as a home equity loan. Usually taken out for a car or home improvement project, there is a fixed term to the loan. That is, the interest rate and your monthly payment will remain fixed over the life of the loan.

An equity line of credit enables you to draw against a credit line as the need arises. You can pay for the kids' braces, car repairs, or whatever. Instead of borrowing a fixed amount of money, a line of credit qualifies you for a certain amount of credit. You can borrow up to your credit limit, if needed, but you don't need to. The monthly repayment amount depends on what you've borrowed and the interest rate charged is variable. Lines of credit generally carry higher interest rates than home equity loans.

Money Morsel

If you're interested in an equity loan, be sure to do some comparison shopping. Lending institutions are competing fiercely with one another to sell home equity loans. Find a lender that charges a good rate, with minimal fees.

Swing Loan

A swing loan is a mortgage loan necessary to tide you over when you need to buy a property while you already own another one. Some cases in which a swing loan comes in handy might be when one spouse gets a new job and goes off to the new location while the rest of the family stays behind. The spouse who's already moved finds a great house, flies the rest of the family out, and they agree to buy it, despite the fact that their original home isn't even up for sale, yet.

Or perhaps you have no intention of moving, but quite by accident, you find the house you've always wanted. You're afraid of losing your dream home, so you make a bid and start looking for a swing loan.

Swing loans are interest-only loans, using the first property as collateral for the second property. They're usually executed as equity loans on first property.

Swing loans require you to sign a mortgage note that collateralizes the first house. You'll pay interest only until the first property is sold. When you sell the property, you repay the loan and satisfy the mortgage.

Construction Loan

Construction loans are available to finance new construction. You can be a first-time homeowner and need a construction loan, or you can already be a homeowner who requires one while you build a second home.

The bank agrees to give you a specified construction mortgage, usually with four equal draws or payments to the contractor. When the contractor requests a draw, an inspector is sent to the property site to verify that the builder has completed everything that's been agreed upon to date.

To request a construction home loan, you'll need to take your building plans and a purchase contract to your lending institution. Although all lending firms are different, most require an initial settlement, which is held in escrow until spent.

A construction mortgage is interest only while the property is being built. Once the construction is completed, the bank has a formal settlement, any overages are accounted for, and a standard mortgage (with principal repayment and interest) begins.

The Least You Need to Know

◆ It's very important to know exactly how much you can afford to pay in debt each month, while keeping your debt-to-income ratio between 28 and 36 percent.

◆ There are many extra costs associated with moving from one home to another, and you need to be sure to factor them in with your total expenses.

◆ There are different methods of paying for a home, and you should find out about everything available before deciding which method you'll choose.

◆ Mortgages come in many flavors, some of which are more appealing than others to particular types of buyers.

Chapter 14

Selling the House You Already Have

In This Chapter

- ◆ Selling your home on your own
- ◆ Finding and working with a realtor
- ◆ Timing your settlement date
- ◆ Selling a house is expensive business
- ◆ Making the most of packing and moving
- ◆ Coping with the actual move

There are many issues involved with moving, not the least of which is how to sell your current home.

If you're thinking of buying or have already put a deposit on a new home, you're no doubt very excited and probably a little nervous. Will you really be able to afford the new house? Will you like the neighborhood? Will the neighbors like you? Where will everybody sleep? What colors should you use in the living room?

It's easy to get so involved with the new house that you overlook the very important fact that you've got to sell your old house.

In this chapter we'll look at some aspects of selling the house you already have. This is important information because selling your home can be tricky if you don't know what you're doing. Even if you've sold a house or two or three in the past, it's a good idea to review the finer points of working with a realtor, settlement costs, and so forth.

Hire a Realtor or Sell It Yourself?

Many people are tempted to try to sell their own home, bypassing the services—and fees—of a realtor. Realtors usually charge between 6 and 7 percent commission on the sale of your home, which can add up to a lot of money, depending on the value of your property.

The National Association of Realtors reports that about 13 percent of homes are sold by owners, without benefit of a professional realtor. A theory behind owner selling is that, because you're saving the realtor's fees, you can sell the house for a few thousand dollars less, and that will cause it to sell more quickly.

Some people have had great success selling their own home and swear they'd never do it any other way. And maybe you will, too. Before you decide to go the FSBO route (realtor lingo meaning "for sale by owner"), carefully read the information that follows, and think long and hard about what you may be getting yourself into.

If you're going to sell your own home, you'll need to invest significant time to do so. You'll have to be around to show the house when it's convenient for potential buyers. You'll probably need to do some work on the home to make it as attractive and sellable as possible. You'll need to arrange for advertising, open houses, and research your selling price.

Money Morsel

If houses in your neighborhood are so much in demand that potential buyers line up outside every time a for sale sign goes up, you may have little trouble selling your home yourself. Just be sure you adhere to all the legal and financial guidelines.

The first question to ask yourself is if the time and energy required to sell your own home is worth the money you'll save.

If you have many obligations at work or otherwise, you might simply not have the time required to market and sell your own home. Or you may not have the personality to do it. Remember that you have a lot of yourself invested in your home. How will you feel when a potential buyer criticizes your decorating scheme or sniffs at the size of the kitchen? You've got to be able to remain calm and impassive, as though you're a third party instead of the owner of the house.

The biggest mistake that FSBOs make, according to professional realtors, occurs with pricing the home. Almost everybody thinks their home is worth more than it is, and why wouldn't you? You're emotionally connected with your home, which greatly increases its value in your mind.

Somebody walking through your home for the first time, however, probably isn't going to feel the emotional connection that you do.

Determining a Price for Your Home

You've got to know the value of your home if you're going to put it on the market. The following are some ideas for determining what your house is worth:

◆ Check out the real estate transactions. Look in the real estate section of your local paper and see what houses in your neighborhood are selling for or have sold for. Remember not to price your house too much higher than those around you, even if you've made improvements the others don't have. You want to get your money back from the work you've done, but you don't want to price your home out of competition.

◆ Talk to your neighbors. In every neighborhood, there are some folks who know exactly what's going on. And they're usually willing to share the news. Find out what the Smiths got for their house last fall, or what the Joneses are asking for theirs. Just be sure that your information is reliable.

◆ Hire a professional appraiser. This is the best way to determine the value of your home, because he's trained to know exactly what it's worth. Many people assume the value reported on their tax assessments is correct, but you shouldn't rely on it, even if it's been done recently.

Once you know what your house is worth, consider special circumstances that might affect what you ask for it. If the market is particularly strong, you might add 5 or 10 percent of your home's value to its appraised price. Don't get too greedy, though. Overpriced homes don't sell. Likewise, if the housing market is at a crawl in your area, you may have to shave a percentage of its appraised value off your asking price.

 Don't Go There

Trying to get an extra couple of thousands of dollars out of your home by setting your asking price higher than the appraised value can backfire on you, especially if you're selling the home yourself. Savvy buyers know you're avoiding a realtor's fee by selling yourself and may resent that you're still asking a higher price than other sellers.

Advertising Considerations

If you're putting your home on the market, you've got to let prospective buyers know that it's there. There are some effective methods for doing this, but you've got to be ready to spend a little money.

The first thing you should do is figure out a marketing budget. This will include the cost of everything you're going to do to attract potential buyers, get them into your home, and follow up with them once they've been there.

Think about which newspapers will best advertise your property. Don't limit yourself to just your local paper if you think your home may be attractive to folks outside of your immediate area. For instance, if you live close to a major highway that makes your area an easy commute to a city 40 miles away, you might consider placing some ads in their nearby city papers.

Homes located further away than the immediate suburbs of a major city normally are less expensive than those that are closer. People looking to live within commuting distance without paying the high prices of homes in the immediate suburbs may well be attracted to your area.

Money Morsel

Don't skimp on the ad for your home to try to save money. Remember that realty companies use photos in many of the advertisements for homes they're selling, so consider using a photo of your home, as well. Your ad is likely to be the first contact with your home for prospective buyers, so make it as impressive as possible.

Regardless of where you advertise, make sure your ad is professional-looking and attractive. The advertising departments of most newspapers have staff to help you get an ad ready. Or you could hire an ad agency or graphic design firm to make an ad for you.

If you prepare your own ad, use others that have appeared in the paper as guidelines. Be sure that you list the best features of your home, but don't exaggerate by using words like "prestigious" or "spectacular" if they don't apply.

If you're well versed with the Internet, you might consider setting up a Web site on which to advertise your home. More and more people are house hunting online, and the Internet is full of realty company sites that contain their listings.

Be sure to buy at least one attractive, weatherproof "for sale by owner" sign for your yard and several "open house" signs that you can place at appropriate locations to alert potential buyers.

And, don't forget to prepare a fact sheet to give prospective buyers when they come to see the house. Many realtors now place these sheets, which list pertinent information such as price, square footage, and features of the house, in a waterproof box next to the sale sign on the lawn. Pick up a sheet prepared by a realtor to see what yours should include.

Legal Considerations

If you don't have a realtor, be sure to work with a lawyer (preferably a real estate lawyer) who can review contracts and advise you on other legal matters. Some forms you'll need to have include the following:

◆ Deposit receipt

◆ Offer to purchase

◆ Seller's disclosure form

> **CAUTION**
>
> **Don't Go There**
>
> If you've already assumed the responsibilities of a realtor, don't—under any circumstances—try to be your own lawyer, as well. In our litigious society, it's imperative that you get competent legal advice.

Some people selling their own homes have gotten into big trouble by not disclosing certain information about their homes or through other mistakes.

If you live in an old home that may contain lead paint or asbestos, for instance, don't even think of selling it without first disclosing that information. Have the home tested for radon and termites, and any other possible problems.

Be especially careful to avoid even the appearance of discrimination when you're selling your house. If a physically disabled person wants to see the house, for instance, you can't legally say something like, "I won't show you the house because you wouldn't be able to get around in it. It's got a lot of steps."

It is unfair under the law to discriminate in a real estate transaction on the basis of race, color, religion, national origin, gender, handicap, and presence of children in a family.

And if you're involved with financing, be sure to consult with your lawyer about terms and agreements. Work carefully with your attorney to assure you come through selling your house legally unscathed.

Practical Considerations

If you're going to try to sell your home, you'll want prospective buyers to see it at its very best. Perhaps a fresh coat of paint wouldn't hurt. How about cleaning all the windows and washing the curtains?

A few other tips for getting your home in tip-top condition are as follows:

- Check the roof and gutters to see if they need to be cleaned or repaired.
- Make sure the shrubbery is trimmed and the lawn neatly cut. If it's autumn, keep the leaves raked.
- Check to be sure all the plumbing is in good working condition.
- See that all the appliances are working properly.
- Make sure the caulking around tubs, windows, showers, and sinks is in good condition.
- See that the house is clean; consider having the carpets cleaned if they're dirty.

Once your house is in shape and you've determined a fair price, got your advertising in place, and considered all the legal aspects, you're ready to launch it onto the market. Good luck!

If you decide, on the other hand, that you don't have the time, energy, or personality to sell your own house, don't feel bad. There are plenty of realtors out there who will be glad to do it for you. The trick is, how do you find a good realtor with whom you'll want to work?

Finding the Right Realtor

Having an experienced, competent realtor can be a huge comfort to those unfamiliar with the ins and outs of selling a home.

Money Morsel

Ask your agent to go through the listing agreement with you, asking any questions you have on points you don't understand. Understand what happens if a sale falls through, if the buyers can't obtain a mortgage, and so forth. Keep a list of questions and concerns you think of in between visits with your realtor.

Your realtor will pre-qualify prospective buyers, saving you the hassle of having to clean up and clear out for somebody who can't begin to afford your home. She'll take care of all the paperwork involved with selling your house, present to you all offers received on your property, and advise you whether or not to accept those offers.

There are lots of realtors around—just check out the yellow pages of your local phone book. If you're relocating and looking for a realtor, you could call the chamber of commerce or the local board of real estate agents in the city to which you're moving and ask for a recommendation. Or you could trust an established firm in that city to hook you up with a good realtor.

Other tips to keep in mind when you're looking for a realtor include the following:

◆ Ask around. If you know somebody who just sold her home, ask about her experience with her realtor. Personal recommendations are a great source of information. Remember, though, that just because your friend liked—or didn't like—her realtor, doesn't mean that you'll feel the same way.

◆ Conduct an interview. If you get a lead on an agent, give him a call and ask to meet. Get a feeling for his personality and work background. Ask a lot of questions about the market, your property, and how his agency operates. And ask him for recommendations of folks with whom he's worked recently.

◆ Ask other professions for recommendations. Call your attorney and ask for a reference. Area bankers, mortgage agents, your financial planner can provide information about real estate agents that can be helpful.

◆ Make sure that he's a member of a multi-list service that provides a listing of all residential property in your area. This makes your property accessible to many more people. Also, be sure your realtor will list your home on the Internet.

◆ Look at the realtor's experience level. Has she been in the business for a period of time? Is she a full-time agent or is this a part-time job? Someone who works full-time in the business is generally up to date with the latest regulations and market trends.

◆ Be sure that he's familiar with the various mortgage companies, home inspectors, and other services within your community that you might need.

◆ Consider your comfort level. Chances are that you're going to be spending a significant amount of time with the realtor you hire. Be sure that it's somebody with whom you're comfortable and will want to work with.

Other traits to look for in a realtor include diplomacy and communication skills, honesty, understanding, and familiarity with your area.

Whether you hire a realtor or sell your home yourself, you need to pay close attention to details. There are a lot of legal and financial implications involved, and you can't afford to neglect or overlook anything.

Money Morsel

For more information on buying a new home and selling your current home, refer to *The Complete Idiot's Guide to Buying and Selling a Home, Third Edition*. It is full of helpful hints and educates you on the entire process.

Timing Is Everything

If all is right with the world, you'll sell your house (quickly, of course) to a perfect family who promises to love and take care of the property just like you did. Meanwhile, a house that you've had your eye on for three years will just happen to go up for sale on the very day the great family makes an offer on yours.

Your offer on the new home will be immediately accepted, you'll set up an appointment with the movers, and start packing your belongings. Everything will go as planned, and one day soon you'll have settlement on your old home at 9 A.M., your new home at 10 A.M., and be moved into your new house by dinner time.

That's a great scenario, but real life rarely works out that perfectly. Timing is extremely important in buying and selling homes. Improper timing can make the process a lot more difficult. Let's look at some timing possibilities, and see how you might be able to time events to your best advantage.

The Ideal Situation

Most financial advisors and mortgage counselors recommend that you sell your old home before buying a new one. And selling the old house first has some real advantages.

If you know that your house sold for $175,000, you can better gauge your house search. You know how much proceeds you realized from the sale of your home, and how much down payment you'll be able to make on your new home.

And if you sell your old home before you buy your new one, you're likely to reap the benefit of pre-qualifying for your new property. Pre-qualifying is when you provide the bank with your financial information before applying for a mortgage, and the mortgage counselor tells you just how much mortgage you qualify for.

This allows you to narrow your search of homes, and shortens the amount of time it takes to get a mortgage once you find a place to buy. It also displays to the seller that you're a serious buyer with means to pay for the house.

Adding It Up

Settlement is the final closing of the sale of your home. It is the settling of property and title on an individual or individuals, at which time your lender hands over money to the seller and you assume the mortgage.

Selling your house before you have another one, however, also carries some risk. If, for some reason, the buyer wants to move in immediately, you could be left without a place to live for a while.

The ideal situation is to be able to sell your property (for the price you wanted, of course) and set a *settlement* date that gives you time to find another house before you need to be out of yours. Once you find your new home, you schedule the settlement date for a day or two before, or the same day, as settlement on your old house. This gives you time to move your belongings from one home to the next while still having a roof over your head.

As you know, however, ideal situations often elude us.

Congratulations, You Own Two Homes

Just imagine that you're out driving around one Sunday afternoon and suddenly, you see it. It's the house you always wanted, but have never seen before. And it's got a sale sign in the front yard. The minute you saw it, before you even noticed the sign, you knew you were destined to live there.

You go right home and grab your spouse, babbling all the while about this perfect house. Your excitement is contagious, and by six o'clock that evening you've made an offer. You lie awake all night, planning where you'll put the piano and what color curtains you'll get for the guest room.

The next day, you learn that the seller has accepted your offer, and you set a settlement date for 30 days out. You're absolutely thrilled, until you suddenly realize that unless you sell your current home within a month's time, you'll own two homes.

How in the world could you afford two homes, even if it's just for a little while? Well, know that while this situation sounds frightening, it occurs all the time. Most buyers who already own a home will agree to make an offer on a new home with the contingency that they must sell their current property before buying the new one. This delays settlement for the sellers until they've sold their house. If a cash buyer comes along, however, the seller does not have to hold the house for the contingent buyer.

If you missed the section on swing loans in Chapter 13, "Paying for a New Home or Second Home," flip the pages right on back there and read up on this nifty innovation that allows you to buy a home before you sell the one you're in.

Swing loans are mortgage loans that use your first property as collateral for the second home. You'll be required to sign a mortgage note, but you'll only pay interest until your first property is sold. When you sell the property, you repay the loan and satisfy the mortgage.

> **CAUTION**
>
> **Don't Go There**
>
> Don't be overly optimistic about selling your home quickly if real estate sales in your neighborhood have been at a standstill for the past six months. If sales are down, it's not a good idea to buy a new home before you sell your old one unless you've got enough money to hold two mortgages for a period of time.

Owning two homes is sometimes necessary. If you're going to be in that position, just be sure that you think through how you'll manage financially until your current house is sold.

Where Is the Nearest Hotel, Please?

On the other end of the owning-two-homes spectrum is the dilemma of being temporarily without a home. Sometimes, a house sells much faster than anticipated, or its sale is contingent on the buyers being able to move in very quickly, forcing the sellers to make settlement on their home before they've bought or settled on a new one.

Being between houses isn't completely bad, although most people avoid it if they can.

Go Figure
Most contractors try to stay pretty well on schedule with new construction, but sometimes delays occur. If the buyers of the new construction timed their settlement in anticipation of the pre-delay construction schedule, they could be in for a period of homelessness.

On the plus side, you will have sold your house, clearing the way for you to go ahead and look for a new one. On the minus side, you'll need to find a place to store your furniture—not to mention yourselves—until you find a new home, wait for your settlement date, or wait on new construction.

Many people bunk in with family rather than stay in a motel, but you probably know how living with relatives can get a bit, shall we say, stressful? Hopefully, your timing will work out right, and you can avoid this situation. If your timing problem is due to a construction delay, ask the builder to reimburse you for hotel costs.

Deciding on a Settlement Date

Normally, the buyer stipulates the date of settlement. If that date or time isn't convenient for the seller, the realtors should try to find a time that is mutually acceptable.

Something to think about is this. The longer the time period between when you sign the sales agreement and the date of settlement, the greater chance there is that something may go wrong to prevent settlement. One of the parties could lose his or her job, illness could occur, or the buyers might find another house that they like better.

So if you're anxious to sell your house, don't drag your feet when setting a date for settlement.

Costs Associated with Selling

You expect that buying a house will be an expensive undertaking. Somehow, though, you just don't anticipate how expensive it will be to sell a home.

Let's take a quick look at some of the expenses involved with selling your house. If you're working with a realtor, he or she should be able to give you an idea of what all these costs will total. Or a mortgage counselor can help you. Some costs to keep in mind include …

- Mortgage points. Each point is 1 percent of the amount of your mortgage.
- The mortgage appraisal and mortgage application fees.
- The credit report the mortgage counselor will request before approving your loan.
- A pesky 1 percent transfer tax.
- Notarization fees.
- Tax certification.
- Flood plain certification.
- A deed (also called documentation) preparation fee.
- The real estate commission.
- Any expenses paid by the seller on behalf of buyer. Sometimes a buyer doesn't have the cash required for settlement, so he pays a higher price for the property and the seller assumes some of his settlement costs, such as points.

Try to get a pretty good idea of what all those costs will add up to before you commit to selling your home.

Preparing for a Move

Moving is a tiring and stressful time. Any advance planning you can do may make the event a little easier. As soon as you find out when you'll be moving, make a list of everything you need to do.

Prioritize the jobs on your list, and try to estimate about how much time you'll need for each task. Then start enlisting help.

Older kids can pack up their own stuff. Be sure to encourage them to use the occasion as a chance to get rid of all the items they no longer use. Ask other family members to help you. This isn't a time to be shy, or to think you can do everything yourself.

Packing and moving is a great chance to get rid of all the unnecessary stuff you've accumulated. If you haven't looked at your college textbooks in 22 years, for instance, chances are that you don't need them.

Take the items you won't use to Goodwill, the Salvation Army, a women's shelter, or your church or synagogue's bazaar. Thoughtfully decide where the items can best be put to good use. Any items you give to charity can be listed as charitable contributions and deducted from your income tax. Just be sure to get a receipt from the charity and itemize what you've donated.

The following table is a listing of suggested price ranges for gifts of donated property to charity, in good condition. The IRS requires proof of the donation and documentation supporting its appraised value.

Donated Goods and the IRS—a Taxpayer's Guide

Furniture		Ladies Clothing	
Studio couch	$50 to 200	Dresses	$4 to 25
Kitchen set (table/two chairs)	$65 to 120	Suits	$10 to 85
End tables	$16 to 65	Shoes	$2 to 12
Coffee table	$25 to 90	Coats	$10 to 80
Washing machine (working)	$50	Skirts	$3 to 15
Vacuum cleaner (working)	$20 to 60	Blouses	$2 to 8
Dryer	$60	Handbags	$1 to 4
Refrigerator	$60 to 150	Hats	$2 to 8
Gas stove	$60 to 150	Sweaters	$3 to 8
TV (b&w)	$50 to 70	Slacks	$4 to 20
TV (color)	$15 to 200	Bathrobes	$4 to 12
Dresser w/mirror	$45 to 150	**Men's Clothing**	
Chest	$35 to 100	Suits	$20 to 85
Wardrobe	$30 to 80	Jackets	$10 to 45
Bed (double, box spring/mattress)	$50 to 200	Shoes	$2 to 12
Bed (single, box spring/mattress)	$35 to 80	Slacks	$4 to 20
Mattress (double)	$25	Shirts	$2 to 5
Mattress (single)	$15	Overcoats	$20 to 60
Folding bed	$20 to 60	Sweaters	$4 to 8
Sofa	$50 to 350	Belts	$3
China cabinet	$60 to 200	**Children's Clothing**	
Trunk (wood)	$15 to 30	Coats	$5 to 15
Floor lamp	$12 to 30	Snowshoes	$5 to 10
Table lamp	$8 to 20	Shoes	$1 to 6
Upholstered chair	$25 to 80	Dresses	$3 to 6
Convertible sofa w/mattress	$90 to 300	Pants	$2 to 5

Furniture (continued)		Children's Clothing (continued)	
Desk	$45 to 150	Shirts	$1 to 2
Bicycle	$20 to 60	Boots	$2 to 4
Radio	$10 to 35	Sweaters	$3 to 5
Crib w/mattress	$10 to 85	**Sporting Goods**	
Playpen	$10 to 30	Fishing rod	$3 to 15
Dry Goods		Ice skates	$3 to 15
Bedspreads	$5 to 20	Roller skates	$3 to 15
Pillows	$4	Tennis racket	$3 to 15
Sheets	$2 to 5		
Drapes	$10 to 20		
Throw rugs	$3 to 5		
Blankets (synthetic, double)	$5 to 12		
Curtains (single window)	$2 to 6		

Consider having a big yard sale or garage sale. Or you could take clothing and household items to a consignment shop. Preparing for a move also is a good time to update your records.

Be sure to call a moving company as soon as you know the date on which you'll be ready to go. A company representative should either come to your home or give you an estimate over the phone of how much it will cost to move your belongings. Look for a reputable firm that's had some experience. Do as much packing yourself as you can to cut the movers' time and save money. Don't forget to mark the boxes as to where they go in the new house.

After your mortgage has been approved, make a list of everyone you'll need to notify. These will include the following:

- Cable company
- Telephone company
- Newspaper carrier
- Trash hauler
- Utility companies
- Postal service

Advise all of them of when you'll be moving and make arrangements to have services transferred to your new home, if applicable. Keep a list of what you've done and who you've spoken with.

Go Figure

June, July, and August are the busiest months for most moving companies, due to families wanting to move while the kids are on summer vacation. If your move falls in one of those months, be sure to call early.

When the Big Day Arrives

Hopefully, all your advance preparations will pay off, and you'll be calm, cool, and collected on your moving day.

Try not to think of all the work you'll have after your belongings are moved but to focus on what's happening at your current house.

The movers will have questions concerning what goes to the new house and what stays, so at least one person needs to be available. Another person can go on ahead to the new house to direct the movers there.

Moving is stressful, there's no question about it. Try to stay as calm as possible, and know that your life will soon begin to get back to normal.

The Least You Need to Know

- There are advantages to selling a home on your own, but you've got to know what you're doing.
- A good realtor can help keep you out of legal and financial trouble, as well as provide reassurance and guidance.
- Ideally, you'll move out of one home and into the next without overlaps or gaps in the timing.
- There are a lot of hidden costs to selling a house, and you'll need to figure out in advance how much they add up to.
- Packing and moving can be stressful, but provide great opportunity for cleaning out and starting over.
- Moving day will be easier and proceed more smoothly if you've coordinated everything ahead of time.

Part 4   Life Changes

We don't always know what the changes will be, but every one of us will experience many of them as we get older. There are all kinds of changes in our lives. Some are good, and others we wish we could avoid.

Some of us will change jobs because we want to, and others will need to find a new job after losing theirs. Perhaps you're thinking of getting remarried. Or maybe you're struggling with ending an unhappy marriage through divorce. You might have lost a parent recently, or even a spouse.

Chapters 15 through 19 will help you to prepare as much as possible ahead of time for life changes, so you can better deal with them when they occur. And since all major changes affect your finances, you can be sure you have the necessary resources for coping with change.

Chapter 15

Knowing That Nothing Stays the Same

In This Chapter

◆ Knowing that change will happen
◆ Dealing with change can be difficult
◆ Identifying different kinds of changes
◆ Figuring out how to cope with change
◆ Knowing when to look for help

One thing of which we can be certain, is that nothing stays the same. Our days pass by, one spilling into the next so seamlessly that we often don't notice all the changes occurring around us.

One day, though, you glance in the mirror and for a moment you barely recognize the person looking back at you. Or you look at your 18-year-old son and wonder when he stopped looking like a boy and started looking like a man.

The seasons change again and again. The paint peels off the window sashes, and you call the painter to come and take care of it … again. Carpets, furniture, and cars wear out and need to be replaced. You change jobs. You move. One of your best friends dies. Kids graduate from high school, then from college. They move away. They move back. They get married, divorced, and then married again. They have babies. You retire and move yet again.

Life is full of changes. Some are subtle—like the onset of gray hair. Others, like the death of a spouse or close friend, can knock us down and make us think we'll never get up again. Not all change, of course, is bad. Maybe you've recently received a great promotion at work or found out that you'll be spending a year in England as part of your company's expansion plans. Major changes, however, whether good or bad, rarely occur without challenge.

Change may be difficult, but it's inevitable and necessary to our lives. Learning to deal with change effectively is the key to successfully navigating the twists and turns in life. As Benjamin Franklin so succinctly stated, "when you're finished changing, you're finished."

Folk singer and songwriter Woody Guthrie spoke of change a bit more colorfully than Franklin, but his message is basically the same. Guthrie said, "Life has got a habit of not standing hitched. You got to ride it like you find it. You got to change with it. If a day goes by that don't change some of your old notions for new ones, that is just about like trying to milk a dead cow."

Woody's dead cow analogy is an interesting one, to be sure, but he's right. We can't avoid changes in our lives, so we've got to be ready to make the best of them.

Coping With Change Isn't Easy

Change is rarely easy, but life would be pretty stagnant and boring without it.

Many people resist change, finding it far more comfortable to drift along day after day in the same old routines. They eat the same kind of cereal for breakfast—every day. They shop at the same grocery store every week, buy their gas and coffee at the same convenience store, drive the same route to work every day, contribute every year to the same charities, and sit in the same pew every week in their church or synagogue.

Go Figure

A bumper sticker expressing our general reluctance toward change was spotted recently. It said, "Change is good. You start."

While routine is not a bad thing, it can become really stifling if carried to the extreme.

Not everyone balks at the thought of life changes. Some people, in fact, embrace change. They view change—most change, anyway—as being positive, and call it opportunity. Others see change as threatening and something to be feared.

Those who embrace change must be in the minority, however, because experts say that resisting change is a natural human reaction.

Being uncertain about the future, as we often are when change is occurring, can be a very uncomfortable feeling. Sure, it was just fine when you were in college to have not a clue as to where you'd be living when classes started up again in the fall. You figured that if you couldn't find a spot in the dorm, there would be a friend of a friend somewhere who'd be looking for somebody with whom to share an apartment.

Somehow, however, that kind of uncertainty becomes much less acceptable, and far more stressful, as we move out of youth and into middle age.

Business leaders fully recognize the need for change, and go to great lengths to encourage employees to effectively cope with the changes that occur in the workplace. Motivational speakers who teach coping techniques are in demand at seminars and conferences.

Your attitude toward change plays a big part in how you'll deal with it. If you view all change as bad, it sure won't happen easily for you. If you look at change as opportunity, you'll be more open to it and willing to make it work.

Work and job-related changes are so significant to people in their 40s and 50s that we're going to spend several chapters discussing them. For now, however, let's look at what other kinds of changes could be waiting for you.

Types of Changes You May Encounter

Change comes in many forms, often when you least expect it.

A car accident could cause paralysis and leave you in a wheelchair for the rest of your life. Or you could win 50 million dollars playing the lottery and decide to move to a secluded Greek island.

Your boss may come into your office and announce that you've been transferred to the company's Indiana facility, and you'll be leaving New York City at the end of the month. Or your youngest child could show up at the door one day, wondering if her old room is still available for her use.

Let's take a quick look at some of the changes people in their 40s and 50s are likely to encounter.

- ◆ **Work changes.** We spend a significant amount of time discussing job-related changes in Chapters 16, "Job Changes," 17, "Dealing With Losing Your Job," and 18, "Going Out on Your Own." Be aware, however, that changes in the workplace are common at any age, including middle age.

◆ **Financial changes.** Financial changes could result directly from work changes or from other events such as inheriting money, selling a home, or cashing in some investments.

◆ **Physical changes.** While most of us will not encounter serious health problems in our 40s and 50s, nearly everyone notices some changes in their physical condition. Blood pressure may begin creeping upward, or you notice a nagging pain in your back every time you play a couple of sets of tennis. You've had to trade in your glasses for bifocals or are considering LASIK surgery. Most women experience menopause during their 40s or 50s. You have a good measure of control over your physical condition by how well you choose to take care of yourself, but we'll all experience physical changes as a normal part of aging.

> **Go Figure**
>
> The divorce rate in the United States was at around 50 percent in 1999, according to the U.S. Census Bureau. That's up from 43 percent in 1988. And the bureau estimates that if the divorce trend continues, the rate will climb to 60 percent before 2010.

◆ **Domestic and relationship changes.** Your spouse of 23 years comes home one day and tells you that she wants a divorce. Or, having been divorced for several years, you finally meet Mr. Right and decide to remarry. Your last child moves out and you begin suffering from a big-time case of empty-nest syndrome. Your first child moves back home—with her six-month-old baby—and you begin longing for the empty nest. These sorts of changes can continue through middle age. Your attitude toward change will help determine how you deal with it.

◆ **Spiritual changes.** It's not uncommon for external changes—such as a divorce, illness, job loss, or death—to spur spiritual change. You may accommodate spiritual change through meditation or join a discussion or prayer group. Perhaps you'll begin attending religious services or attend more regularly than in the past. You may discover spirituality in music, art, sunrises and sunsets, gardening, fly-fishing, mountain climbing, or traveling to new places.

◆ **Living changes.** You sell your home on the three-acre lot and move to a brand-new condo, where your outside work is limited to sweeping off your deck and watering the pots of geraniums. With all that extra weekend time on your hands, you and your spouse decide to take up mountain biking. The next thing you know, you've joined a biking club, installed a bike rack on the back of the car, and are traveling to spots you've never heard of to bike on steep and rocky trails. You make a lot of new friends, and you're both in better shape than you have been for years. Using change to your advantage can result in positive changes in your life, regardless of age. You can either respond positively or sit around your condo on weekends, wishing you hadn't moved from your home. Change is all about choices.

◆ **Personal change.** Stuff happens. Your husband goes off to work one day as usual, and three hours later you get a call that he's been taken to an area hospital. By the time you get there, he's died from a massive heart attack. Or your best friend from the time you were in third grade moves to a city halfway across the country, leaving you with a huge void in your life. Your wife, a lawyer, is accused, and then convicted, of stealing money from clients. The story, along with photos, plays out for weeks in your local newspaper. Your daughter is going through a very difficult and ugly divorce, and you feel powerless to help her.

These are no doubt the most difficult kinds of changes we face, and the events that really test strength of character.

Don't Go There

When bad stuff happens, some people have a tendency to withdraw from family and friends, preferring to "deal" with the changes on their own. If that's your tendency, try to avoid it. Experts say this is not a healthy reaction to change, and that it's much better to talk about and deal with your feelings than to isolate yourself.

It's difficult to predict how you'll handle these sorts of life changes. You might think that you'll always be strong when tragedy occurs, only to find when it does that you're completely devastated and feel totally helpless. Or you may absolutely dread any sort of change, only to end up thriving from it when it occurs.

Let's look at some means of coping with life changes.

Strategies for Handling Life Changes

Experts say that when change occurs, it's important to recognize and acknowledge it, rather than trying to ignore or avoid it. Once you acknowledge change, you can effectively work toward accepting it. Some tips for dealing with change are listed here. Although some of them may seem obvious, they're all important.

◆ **Try to not be afraid of change.** Accepting that change may occur at any time can help you to adapt when it does. Routine might be comfortable and reassuring, but acknowledging that it could change at any moment will help you to better cope when it does.

◆ **Get a support system in place.** It's better to have a support system in place before change occurs than to try to establish one when it does. Hopefully, you've got good friends with whom you can share problems and concerns. Perhaps you could talk with a clergy member or have a relationship with a counselor. Rely on family members for help—they're the people who love you most and want to help. People who have strong support systems normally come through stressful situations far better than those who don't. They also stay healthier, live longer, and are generally more successful.

◆ **Take care of yourself.** When change occurs, it's important to pay attention to your physical and emotional health. Change produces stress, which can have very real and serious health consequences. Get enough rest, eat well, and take time every day to get some exercise, even if it's just a 15- or 20-minute walk. Reach out for friends or family members, and talk about how you're feeling. Continue with activities that you enjoy, such as playing the piano or hiking in the woods. You might consider joining a yoga class or getting a massage.

◆ **Take charge of change.** If your job situation is changing rapidly, and the changes aren't for the better, take the bull by the horns and do something about it. Ask your boss if you could be reassigned to a different area. Or think about looking for a new job. If your changes are occurring because your spouse has withdrawn from you and your relationship has badly deteriorated, ask if he or she is willing to see a marriage counselor. If the situation is impossible, and the relationship past saving, you may want to consider ending it. Doing something is almost always better than doing nothing because it gives you a sense of having some control over the situation.

Money Morsel

A friend in a high-paying health care administration job saw the writing on the wall when her job responsibilities were cut in half. Figuring that she was on her way out, she contacted a headhunter, negotiated a terrific severance package with her company, and resigned from her job. Four months later, she started a new job with a comparable salary, while still benefiting from her severance pay. This is a great example of someone who anticipated, acknowledged, and acted offensively in the face of change.

◆ **Don't blame yourself for changes you can't control.** Many of us have a tendency to blame ourselves when a life-changing event occurs. "If only I wouldn't have let him use the car, the accident wouldn't have happened." "If I'd set a better example when she was young, my daughter wouldn't be getting a divorce." "If I was 20 pounds lighter, my husband wouldn't be having an affair with his secretary." You get the picture. Change will keep happening, regardless of how we feel about it. Blaming yourself when it does is not productive, and will not help you to effectively deal with changes.

We'll all face major changes in our lifetimes. And while learning how to deal with change is extremely important, it sometimes is more than we're able to do on our own. If that's the case, you may need to find some help.

Knowing When You Might Need Some Help

If your wife comes home from work one night and tells you she's met somebody else, she no longer loves you, she wants a divorce as soon as possible, and there's a moving truck waiting outside to take half of your furniture to her new apartment, you're bound to be more than a little shaken by the experience.

You'll no doubt experience a dizzying range of emotions. You may well spend some time in a state of shock, unable to comprehend what's happening. You'll be angrier than you've ever been in your life. You'll feel incredibly hurt and betrayed. You may wonder what you did to trigger the situation and go through a period when you blame yourself for her leaving. You may one day beg her to come back, and tell her you never want to see her again the next. You'll mourn the end of your marriage, and wonder about your future.

If you're *mentally* and emotionally *healthy*, you'll eventually begin to heal. You'll accept what has happened and get on with your life. In time, you'll become open to new relationships, perhaps even seeking them out. You'll learn to deal with your ex-wife in a civil manner, and eventually you'll remember the good times you and she had together.

If you find you're unable or unwilling to accept what's happened and move on with your life, you probably should look for help. Some people resist seeking help because they perceive it as a sign of weakness. Experts, however, say most people encounter within their lifetimes a period when they could benefit from the help of a counselor or therapist.

Help is available in many forms. Some people think that contacting a counselor or therapist will result in a prolonged period of intensive therapy. They have visions of lying on a couch recounting their life stories while the therapist scribbles notes and mumbles to himself.

Adding It Up

Physicians describe **mental health** as being able to maintain mental balance during times of emotional stress. If you lose that balance, you may need to get some help to restore it.

Don't Go There

If you suspect you're suffering from depression, call your doctor and make an appointment. Millions of people are being treated for depression, most with good success. Don't ignore symptoms of depression, which include persistent fear, feelings of worthlessness, sadness and crying, trouble sleeping, constant tiredness, trouble concentrating, eating disorders, and loss of interest in sex.

In reality, counseling or psychotherapy is not like that, at all. A counselor or psychologist may feel it's necessary to see you only one or two times. You don't have to lie on a couch, and a counselor of psychologist does not judge your character.

If you're still uncomfortable with counseling or therapy, consider attending a support group. Many churches and synagogues offer these groups for people dealing with changes such as the loss of a spouse, parent, or child; separation or divorce; and illness. Support groups in your area should be listed in the blue pages of your telephone book.

And check the Blue Pages of your phone book for mental health services available in your area. Many communities offer counseling services and other mental health resources. Some of these services may be available at little or no cost, depending on your ability to pay.

Keep the following considerations in mind if you're wrestling with the idea of looking for some help:

- Nearly everyone experiences a period in life where they could benefit from professional help.
- There is no shame in seeking help for an emotional problem.
- Finding help can allow you to move past your problems and get on with your life.
- Taking the initiative to find help is a sign of strength, not weakness. It is a step in taking control of your life.
- Living with depression, or in a prolonged depressed state, isn't necessary. Most doctors and therapists recommend a combination of medication and counseling to treat depression, and it's usually done successfully.

Change happens, and when it does, it's up to each of us to deal with it the best we can. Preparing for change is as simple as acknowledging that it will occur and having a support system in place for when it does.

Remember that not all change is bad, but even good changes can cause stress. And if you find you're having problems coping with change, keep in mind that there is help available.

The Least You Need to Know

- Something in life we can count on is that nothing ever stays the same.
- Being open to change can help make it easier to deal with when it occurs.
- Change comes in many flavors, including physical, personal, relationship, work, financial, life, and spiritual.
- There are strategies we can use to make dealing with changes easier and more successful.
- If you find you're unable to cope with changes as they occur in your life, it's a good idea to get some professional help.

Chapter **16**

Job Changes

In This Chapter

- Keeping up with changes in the workplace
- Understanding when a voluntary job change makes sense
- Coping with an involuntary job change
- Considering the classroom
- Keeping a positive attitude during job changes

A job, or perhaps a career, used to be something that was fairly constant in the life of an average person. Men and women prepared for jobs in school or through on-the-job training. They'd find work with a good company and settle in—barring any unforeseen circumstances—until retirement time rolled around.

That scenario is practically unheard of in 2001. These days, we train for jobs differently than we used to. We not only switch jobs, but entire careers—three or four times. We job share. We work from home. We work from home while keeping an eye on our kids or grandkids. We have more options than we used to, and we know it.

In this chapter, we'll look at the ways in which the workplace is changing, and how we may fit into this constantly shifting picture. It's important to examine, because, after all, few factors affect our finances more than our jobs.

The Changing Workplace

The workplace in America is changing, and will continue to change as we move further into the twenty-first century. Many of these changes are due to technological advances, and others result from shifts in the numbers of workers, and their ages, ethnicities, educations, and so forth.

The U.S. Department of Labor released a report called "futureworks," which examines the changing face of the American workplace and workforce. Some of the highlights of the report are listed as follows. Please note that all percentages have been rounded to the nearest whole numbers.

- The population of the United States is expected to grow by nearly 50 percent in the next 50 years. By the year 2050, the population will increase from about 275 million now to about 394 million people, due largely to immigration. This indicates a much larger pool of workers than we have presently.

- Because immigration will account for two thirds of the population increase, the face of the American workforce will change dramatically. The white population is predicted to drop between 2000 and 2050 from 73 to 53 percent, while the Hispanic population will increase from 10 to 25 percent. The black population will remain fairly steady, rising only from 12 to 14 percent, and the number of Asians and Pacific Islanders will jump from 3 to 8 percent.

- Baby boomers, who collectively have dominated the American workforce for the past 20 years, will reach retirement age (65) between 2011 and 2029. The average age of the workforce will rise as the boomers get older, and their retirements will precipitate many changes. Increasing numbers of younger workers will be affected by the demands of working while caring for elderly parents (those elderly parents will be us).

Money Morsel

You can request a copy of "futureworks" by calling 202-219-6001, extension 123.

- More Americans are graduating from high school than ever before, and more are going to college. Almost 83 percent of all people who are 25 or older have completed high school, and 24 percent have graduated from college. That's way up from 30 years ago, when only 54 percent of people in this age group had completed high school, and fewer than 10 percent had graduated from college. While education overall is on the rise, however, the numbers vary dramatically among ethnic groups.

Asian Americans had the highest high school completion rate in 1997 at more than 90 percent, while graduation rates for blacks and whites were just about the same at 86 and 88 percent respectively. Hispanics, however, saw a high-school graduation rate of only 62 percent. It's clear that the level of education a person has greatly affects his potential for earning. The disparity in education rates between ethnic and racial groups indicates future disparity in earning levels.

◆ Women continue to work more, while men are working less. While in 1950 only one third of all women held jobs, 60 percent were working in 2000. On the contrary, the percentage of men working fell from 86 to 75 percent during the same time period. In addition, women are more likely to work full-time in the future than they have in the past, and all year long, rather than just during the months when their children are in school. And increasing numbers of women are starting their own businesses, of which about 60 percent are run from home.

◆ The number of manufacturing jobs in the United States will drop dramatically in the next several years, while the number of service-related jobs will increase. The number of agricultural jobs will decrease significantly. Industries and businesses that are looking at big growth include child care, health care, and residential care facilities.

> **Go Figure**
>
> According to the U.S. Department of Labor, the average worker holds 9 jobs by the time he's 32 years old.

◆ While the highest-paid jobs will continue to require the best educated workers, the majority of new jobs will require an Associate's degree or less. This will give un-skilled workers more job opportunities, but their wages won't be high.

◆ E-commerce will continue to impact the American workplace, and will give more people with disabilities a chance to find jobs that employ computer technologies. It's estimated that total e-commerce will top out at $1 trillion by 2005.

◆ Computer technology will continue to cause swift and extensive workplace changes. The U.S. Department of Commerce estimates that by 2006, nearly half of all workers in America will be employed in industries that either produce, or extensively employ information technology, products, and services. Computer technology also allows workers to operate from places other than the traditional office. Many workers already do at least some of their job from home, while others use computers to file reports and keep in touch from remote locations.

As you can see, there will be many changes in the American workplace during the upcoming years. We'll need to be aware and keep up with the changing workplace in order to remain competitive workers until we retire.

Voluntary Job Changes

If you're intrigued by all these changes occurring in the work place, you may have considered changing jobs yourself. Gone are the days when you expected, and were expected, to work for the same company—often doing the same job—for years and years. And it's increasingly easy to prepare or train for a new job while you're working.

Money Morsel

If you've decided to change jobs and may be without one for a period of time while you look for a new one, try to increase your savings by 20 percent for at least several months before you leave your current job. This will give you a financial buffer in the event that you're unemployed.

Colleges, business schools, and technical schools cater to working adults by creating programs that offer classes at times other than normal working hours, or through Internet communication. And workplaces experiencing shortages of skilled workers are more receptive to hiring workers who are middle-aged or even older, than they may have been previously. We can change careers several times, moving around to find jobs that are more challenging, better paying, or just more fun.

So maybe you're thinking of changing jobs. Perhaps you've even been offered a different job at a higher salary. Congratulations. Before you jump at it, though, take a few minutes to think about the suggestions and points listed as follows:

◆ Look closely at the benefits and decide what options are most important to you and your family. Do you require an excellent health care plan? Are you looking for a 401(k) plan where the employer matches generously, short and long-term disability benefits, or supplemental life insurance that you can purchase through payroll deductions?

◆ Is a new employer perhaps so anxious to get you on board that he'll offer some additional perks such as extra vacation days, a signing bonus, or stock options? It can't hurt to ask.

◆ Keep an eye toward retirement. At this point in your life, you've got to think long term. Make sure the company you're looking to join has a good pension or 401(k) plan, and check out other retirement benefits that might be in place.

◆ Does the company offer benefits such as profit sharing, dental and vision coverage, or free memberships to a gym or health club? Will it pay some percentage of your kids' college costs? Can you buy additional vacation time? What's the sick leave, personal days, and bereavement policy like?

Voluntary job changes can be exciting and rewarding. Make sure, however, that a job change makes financial sense, both in the short and long runs.

Involuntary Job Changes

While voluntary job changes can be stimulating and ego-boosting, involuntary job changes usually are pretty much of a drag—at least initially. American workers learned this en masse following the September 11, 2001, terrorist attacks on our country.

While Americans enjoyed a pretty good stretch of low unemployment in the late 1990s, the twenty-first century has not started out as fortuitously. The U.S. economy already was faltering before the attacks, which resulted—in addition to mass death and destruction— in widespread layoffs and unemployment.

It's unclear how quickly our economy will recover, but it's a sure bet that many, many people will face the challenges of unemployment for months to come.

And, although the American employment situation has become unexpectedly grim, there have been periods previous to this that have made U.S. workers wary about their job situations. Extensive downsizing occurred in the early and mid-1990s, many of the cuts affecting middle management types, who were then forced to take lower-paying, less skilled jobs.

Even then–U.S. Labor Secretary Robert Reich advised Americans during that period to rethink the issue of job security and accept that layoffs would occur.

"Job security is a thing of the past," Reich said. "People are going to have to get used to the idea of involuntary separations—sometimes four, five, or six times during a career."

Fortunately, the involuntary separation rate has dropped since those mean, lean years of downsizing in the 1990s, but, make no mistake about it, workers are still being unwillingly moved out of jobs, especially in the aftermath of the terrorist attacks.

It's not easy to leave a job in which you're comfortable. You know the routine, you know your co-workers, and you know where everything is. If you lose that job and are forced to move on, you're likely to suddenly feel that you've gone back to square one. You have to learn a new job in a new company, not to mention ask somebody to show you how to use the copier and point you in the direction of the coffee room.

Being forced to find a new job is nowhere near as comfortable or desirable as polishing up the old resume because you've willingly decided to launch a hunt for the perfect post. Still, losing a job doesn't mean that you're not a good worker, or a good provider, or a good person. Stuff happens, and involuntary unemployment is one rather unpleasant part of that stuff.

> **Go Figure**
>
> Department of Labor statistics indicate that of all displaced workers, those who are in their fifties or older have the most difficult time finding new employment.

If you find yourself looking for a new job because you have to, rather than because you want to, don't despair. The following are some tips to remember if you suddenly find yourself without a job.

◆ Work with an outplacement counselor to see what other jobs are available. Many companies provide a counselor to help laid-off employees find another job. If your company doesn't provide this, ask if it will pay for you to hire a counselor privately.

◆ Take advantage of any sort of retraining program your former employer may offer. Many companies will pay for training for employees who are laid off. Some even provide offices for employees to use as a base for job hunting.

◆ Negotiate the best severance package you can get. If your employer needs to down-size, and you're in a fairly high-paying position, he may be willing to give you a nice severance package when you leave.

◆ Network, network, network. Come on, you've been around for a while now, and surely have met lots of folks along the way. Don't hesitate to use your contacts to get an idea for what jobs may be available, to meet other people who may be able to help you, or even to get introductions to people in authority within their companies. Statistics show that more people find jobs through other people than through job ads. Remember that people generally really like to help others when they can.

Money Morsel

The Department of Labor funnels money to states to help pay for retraining for people who have been displaced for their jobs. To find out if you might qualify, check out the Web site of the department's Employment and Training Administration. You'll find it on the Internet at www.wdsc.org.

◆ Don't get discouraged if you don't find another job right away. And don't take the first job that comes along if you know it's not right for you.

◆ Be creative. Remember that traditional jobs, those in which you show up at the office every morning at 8:00, take a quick lunch break, and head for home at 5 or 6 P.M., are not the only kind of employment opportunities out there. Perhaps you have skills that would allow you to work from home, or another location. Maybe you'll decide it's time to start your own business (much more about that in Chapter 18, "Going Out on Your Own"). Don't trap yourself by limiting your job search to the kinds of job you've always had.

While involuntary job changes can be difficult, most people who undertake them do so successfully. Keep a positive attitude and try to focus on the things in life that mean the most—your family, friends, and place within the community.

Heading Back to the Classroom

If you find yourself unexpectedly without a job, you may feel that you need to find another one as quickly as possible. Or depending on circumstances, you might be inclined to look into a completely new area of work.

If you choose the latter, chances are you'll need some sort of retraining. You might decide to head back to the classroom. If you don't have a college degree, you may decide that now's the time to get one. If you have a Bachelor's degree, you might want to tack on enough extra credits for a Master's or Ph.D.

Money Morsel

If you do enroll at a college, find out if there's a re-entry program or support services for adults. Many schools offer these types of services, which are designed to provide counseling and help meet the particular needs of older students.

Thinking about heading back to the classroom after 20, 25, or 30 years in the workplace can be daunting, but if you decide to head back, you'll certainly be in good company. So many older people have gone back to college that they're no longer called "nontraditional students." The U.S. Department of Education reports that nearly 40 percent of all college students are over the age of 25.

If you've been laid off and are considering going back to college, try to negotiate education expenses as part of your severance package. Or check with the school you're considering to find out what grants, scholarships, low-interest loans, or tuition payment plans might be available. You also may be able to get some tax advantages if you're enrolled in college.

Hopefully, you'll be able to attend courses close to home, so that commuting expenses are the only added expenses to the tuition costs. If you're going back to get a teaching certification or accounting degree—or even a complete change of career—compare the costs of area colleges. Be sure to find out how much each one charges per credit hour, and how many credits you'll need to get the degree you want.

In Chapter 8, "Paying for College," we talked about the HOPE Scholarship Credit (the tax credit for the first two years of post-secondary education) and the Lifetime Learning Credit (this credit is available for a unlimited number of taxable years). If you find yourself back in the classroom, be sure you take advantage of these tax advantages. Lowering your taxes can help to pay tuition costs. Other types of grants, aid, and loans were also discussed in Chapter 8.

Check with personnel at the college you're interested in attending to see if you might take a standardized test, such as the CLEP or DANTES, to give you a head start. These tests measure knowledge you've already attained, and many institutions grant credit to students who successfully complete these standardized exams. And, be sure to ask if the school in which you're interested offers credit for life or work experience. Some colleges allow students to demonstrate that they've mastered the principles of particular courses through their prior experiences.

As you know, technology has had a tremendous impact on education during the past several decades. One result of these technological advancements is the opportunity for distance learning.

> ### Go Figure
>
> Adult college students typically have higher overall grade-point averages than students who attend right after high school.

Distance learning is any learning that takes place while the instructor and student are geographically removed from one another. Distance learning can be accomplished by mail, video, interactive or cable TV, or satellite broadcast. The most popular method, however, is via the Internet. There are real advantages to distance learning, such as being able to manage your time and schedule, and, in some cases, being able to work ahead.

Another area worth looking into is an external degree program. This applies to people who have accumulated college credits over the years from one or more institutions, but haven't obtained a degree. An external degree program may allow you to transfer a portion of your course work, reducing the time it would take you to get a degree.

Whether or not to go back to school is a big decision that will affect your time, your family, and your finances. It may, however, be a smart move if you're looking to move into a different job area.

The Least You Need to Know

◆ The American workplace is changing quickly, and will continue to change as we move further into the twenty-first century.

◆ Changing jobs voluntarily can provide a great opportunity to refresh your outlook by trying something new.

◆ Involuntary job changes are difficult, but can result in positive changes in the long run.

◆ Returning to college offers many opportunities and challenges for older students.

Chapter 17

Dealing With Losing Your Job

In This Chapter

- ◆ Reacting to losing a job
- ◆ How your job and your personal identity are related
- ◆ Working to preserve relationships
- ◆ Financial implications of job loss
- ◆ Smart strategies while you're unemployed
- ◆ Knowing you're not alone

Nobody likes to think about losing his or her job. It's stressful. It can be depressing. It can shake the very foundations of who we see ourselves to be. Studies have shown that someone who loses a job often experiences a range of emotion similar to those of a person who has learned that he or she has a terminal illness, or who is grieving the loss of a loved one.

The emotions and reactions aren't as intense, of course, but one who loses a job may experience feelings of denial, anger, depression, and finally, acceptance.

Not everyone experiences this range of emotions, but losing a job can trigger an intense reaction, to be sure. In this chapter, we'll take a look at why our jobs are so important to us, and what you can do if you find yourself in the jobless zone. Whether or not you had any idea that your job would end, you're bound to be at loose ends for a period of time when you're first unemployed.

Downsizing and Other Dirty Words

We don't, fortunately, hear as much today about downsizing as we did in the past couple of decades, but, rest assured, it still happens.

About 10 million jobs were lost to downsizing between 1980 and 2000, and downsizing didn't stop at the turn of the century. Downsizing typically occurs in companies that hope to cut costs and improve performance—often to please their shareholders. They often leave behind them a trail of damaged and demoralized former employees.

Downsizing is a current term, but it's not much different than layoffs, job elimination, managed reductions, or good, old-fashioned firing. And if it happens to you, chances are that you'll have a difficult time dealing with it. So why is it that our jobs are so important to us? Sure, we get paid for doing our jobs, but there are a lot of ways to make money.

The psychology of how we identify with our jobs is fascinating and may shed some light as to why many people are so traumatized when their jobs end.

You Job and Your Identity

Think about meeting somebody for the first time at a cocktail party, your church, a school function, or a friend's house.

You strike up a conversation, introducing yourself and perhaps your spouse or partner. You might talk about the party or other event, move on to the weather, and ask about each other's kids or other family members.

Before long, however, it's almost a sure bet that one or the other will ask, "So what kind of work are you in?" or "What do you do?" Our jobs give us a sense of identity. To go from having a job to not having one can leave a person not knowing where he stands.

Imagine that you teach history at a small college in New England. Your entire life may well be tied to the life of that college. The other faculty members and their families are your friends—sometimes they seem more like family. Your social life revolves around concerts, plays, parties, and other events associated with the school. Your kids go, or plan to go to school there, and your spouse volunteers at the child-care center. You even attend services at the church on campus.

One day, you learn that enrollment has dropped enough so that a position in the history department must be eliminated. And, guess what? Being the newest professor, you're out of there. You not only experience the loss of a job, but many other losses, as well.

Your relationships with friends still employed at the college may change. You may not feel like attending plays and concerts there for a while, which will affect your social life. If your kids were going there tuition-free because you were a faculty member, you may have to rethink college plans. Suddenly, you're likely to feel as though you've been cut adrift. No wonder you feel angry and depressed.

A job loss can, in a minute or two, make a person stop feeling like a breadwinner and start feeling like a burden. Job loss tends to be especially difficult for a person who is the primary, or sole, earner for a family. When not dealt with positively, job loss can cause feelings of isolation, fear, anger, loss of status, worthlessness, and depression. You may feel ashamed to tell your family and friends that you've lost your job. You might feel as though you're no longer a respected member of the community.

Try to be frank and honest about your circumstances, and don't make excuses for what happened. Remember that many other people—probably some of your own friends and family members—also have lost jobs due to downsizing or other circumstances. Look to the people who care about you for support and guidance. Who knows? Maybe one of them will have a hot tip on a job opening.

Bridges Aren't Built to Be Burned

If you lose your job, at all costs resist the temptation to "get even" on your way out by telling off your boss, or your coworkers, or your secretary. Don't kick the trash can, steal a stapler, or do anything to mess up the computers. Don't whine or pout, or tell lies about somebody else to make yourself look better.

Getting downsized, laid off, fired, or whatever you want to call it, can be extremely upsetting and really hard on the ego. And it can be very tempting to retaliate against the person or people you feel are responsible. A sizeable percentage of violent acts in the workplace are by former employees who are angry at being fired.

Life, however, seldom turns out as we anticipate. Many people have found their way back to companies at which they were previously employed, and many more would have liked to but couldn't because they'd destroyed their bridges.

Don't Go There

If you feel severely depressed after losing your job or extremely angry for longer than seems normal, don't hesitate to get help. We can't always handle problems on our own, and there's no shame in admitting that you're having trouble coping. Not seeking help can result in serious health and emotional problems.

If you're fired, you're by all means entitled to ask the appropriate person why it happened. You should know for your own peace of mind the reason for your termination. When you talk about your change in job status, be as polite and respectful as possible, even if you're seething inside. Feel free to express your opinions and speak up on your own behalf, but don't say anything for which you'll be sorry later.

If possible, sit down for 15 minutes or so and jot down your questions or the points you want to make when you speak to your boss. Remaining as calm as possible, and having an idea of what you'll say will give you a real advantage.

Practical Concerns When You're Not Working

Along with the emotional issues you'll deal with if you lose your job, there will be some real practical concerns, as well. Will you be able to meet all your expenses? What will happen when your unemployment pay runs out? How will you find another job?

A joint poll in February 2001 by *USA Today*, CNN, and Gallup showed that more than 30 percent of workers could last only one month without hitting severe financial trouble. An additional 15 percent said they could last only one week.

There's no question that unemployment raises a whole raft of concerns—many of them related to finances.

In this section, we'll examine those concerns and others and give you some tips on managing your finances while you're out of work.

How Not to Deplete Your Savings Account

When you lose your job, life becomes a bit uncertain. Even if you got a nice severance package and will be collecting unemployment compensation pay, you'll need to rethink your financial situation.

Don't Go There

Don't succumb to the temptation to use credit cards in order to maintain the lifestyle you had while you were working and getting a regular paycheck. You can pull off the credit thing for a while, but it will catch up with you big time—guaranteed.

If you have considerably less money coming in during unemployment than you did while you were working, you'll need to tighten the proverbial belt and keep a close watch on your spending.

One of the first things you'll need to do is file for unemployment benefits. Be sure to do this as soon as possible after losing your job. You won't receive any benefits for one week after being laid off, but if you don't go within the first week, you'll lose more benefits.

You can file for unemployment benefits for up to 26 weeks within a one-year period. Most unemployment benefits will equal about 50 percent of the salary you had been earning.

If you have an emergency fund, and hopefully you do, you can use that money to tide you over until you get reorganized. That's the purpose of such a fund, and you can congratulate yourself for having had the financial forethought to establish one. Don't consider the fund to be income, but know that it's there to fall back on when you run short. Review Chapter 2, "Figuring Out Where You Are in Life," for more information about emergency funds.

Even with an emergency fund, however, you'll want to limit spending until you're more certain about what's going on. As discussed in Chapter 6, "The Big, Expensive Parent Trap," most people find variable expenses easier to cut than nonvariable ones. Variable, discretionary expenses are especially prime candidates for cuts.

Just as a reminder, your nonvariable expenses, sometimes called fixed expenses, are those such as mortgage, car, and insurance payments. Those expenses also are nondiscretionary expenses, which means they're not optional. Your health club fee is a nonvariable expense because you pay the same amount every month. It's not necessary, however, so it's called a discretionary expense.

Variable expenses include the electric bill, your food costs, and the amount of money you spend on clothing. They're called variable, obviously, because the amount you'll spend varies. The electric bill and food costs are nondiscretionary expenses, because you've got to pay for electricity and you've got to buy food. Clothing costs, however, are discretionary expenses.

Take a minute to identify areas in which you can cut expenses. If you're like most people and eat out often, you can save a bundle by cutting out restaurants—including fast food. It's a lot less expensive to cook and eat at home. Clothing is another obvious area in which you can cut back. Conserve electricity and water, avoid using your car when you don't have to, and make coffee at home instead of driving into Starbucks when you pass by. Drop the health club and run on the track at your local high school instead. Or dig out that stationary bike from the basement and climb on.

Money Morsel

A great idea, if you can work it out, is to trade services. If you teach piano lessons, for instance, and a friend is a hairdresser, offer to give her son every third piano lesson for free in exchange for haircuts.

Money Morsel

If you get a severance settlement when you lose your job, it's a good idea to put as much of it away as you can. You can't know how long you'll be out of work, and chances are you'll be very glad to have that money as a backup a little further down the road.

There are many ways in which all of us could save money. We know a family that actually saved money when the husband got laid off at work. They lived on his unemployment payments while they systematically cleaned out every cupboard and closet in the house. They cleared out everything they didn't want or use, and sold it, either at yard sales or to consignment shops. Antiques went to a local auction center. Their cellar and attic were cleaned out, and they made some extra cash to help tide them over until the husband found another job.

Is Everybody Covered?

When we're employed, we tend to take insurance that our employers provide for granted. Only when we no longer have the coverage do we fully appreciate it.

If you lose your job, your employer should give you information about how to continue your health coverage through a program called *COBRA*. COBRA allows you to extend your health care coverage under your former employer's plan after you leave your job. Unfortunately, you'll have to pay for the insurance, but at least you'll be covered.

Adding It Up

COBRA stands for the Consolidated Omnibus Budget Reconciliation Act of 1985. It requires most employers with group health plans to allow terminated employees the opportunity to extend their coverage. To learn more about this program, check out www.cobrainsurance.com on the Internet.

Be sure to check with the human resources department of your company about continuing coverage for you and your dependents.

Many people get life and disability insurances through their employers, in addition to health coverage. If that's the case for you, you may be able to deal directly with your employer's insurance carrier to extend that coverage. If not, you should talk with an insurance agent about getting life and disability coverage through another carrier.

Financial Strategy Planning

It's nice to think you'll find another job within a week or so of losing one, and perhaps you will. Chances are, however, it will take longer than that—maybe much longer—to find a job you want.

For that reason, it's important to take some time to strategize your finances. The first thing you should do is to realistically assess your situation.

Figure out exactly what income your family has. This shouldn't include an emergency fund or severance pay that you've put away but may include the following:

- Unemployment compensation
- Income of spouse/children
- Interest from saving accounts
- Union assistance
- Dividends from investments
- Income tax refunds

Next, make a list of all the bills you're responsible for paying, and compare that balance against your income. We've already discussed the areas in which it may be easiest for you to cut expenses and save money, so be sure to consider those. If you think you're going to have trouble making your required payments, however, consider these strategies.

- If you have a mortgage, you may be able to renegotiate payments so that you'll pay less each month until your regular income resumes. Of course, this will extend the overall life of your mortgage but perhaps can help you to avoid a current problem.

- If you're paying rent and think you're going to have a problem making the payments, talk to the landlord before you run out of money. People are more likely to be sympathetic if you explain your situation, rather than simply not paying what you owe.

- Discontinue direct payment of bills from your checking account. While this is normally a convenient service, discontinuing it at this time will allow you more flexibility in deciding which bills to pay at specific times.

- Discontinue automatic payments into investment accounts, college savings, or whatever. You'll need to meet your bills first.

Money Morsel

People over 40 are protected from employment discrimination based on age by the Age Discrimination in Employment Act. If you feel that you were fired, or are not being hired, because of your age, you can contact a lawyer or find out more about the act from the U.S. Equal Employment Opportunity Commission. It's on the Internet at www.eeoc.gov/laws/adea.html.

- Check the yellow or blue pages of your phone book to see if there's a consumer counseling agency in your area. These agencies often offer their services for free or at a nominal cost.

- Check with the utility agencies with which you deal about a budget plan that may lower your monthly payments.

- If you have a cash value life insurance policy, you may be able to borrow money from it, if necessary. Ask your insurance agent for more information.

Go Figure

Being laid off may seem like a tragedy when it first happens, but many people find it turns out to be a positive occurrence in the long run. To get a different perspective on being laid off, read *Congratulations! You've Been Fired*, by Emily Koltnow.

- Consider taking a temporary job in order to generate more income. Remember that even if you're getting unemployment pay, you can still earn up to 40 percent of your unemployment benefits without penalty. If you're earning $300 a week in unemployment, you can earn up to $120 in salary.

If you plan carefully, chances are you'll pull through a period of unemployment relatively unscathed. Don't think, however, that you can continue to live in the same lifestyle that you did while you were working.

Resources to Help You

If you're having trouble during a period of unemployment, there are numerous resources to which you can turn for assistance.

Check to see if your community has a career services center that may offer free counseling and facilities. Career centers, both private and publicly funded, will help you to write or update a resume, identify potential jobs, and contact potential employers. You also might consider a career coach, who will personally work with you to find another job.

And, don't overlook online career resources. They are numerous, with many concentrating on specific job areas such as science, medical, sports, or nonprofit organizations. For some reassurance about finding a new job, read "Job jitters? Stay calm. Hiring still outstrips firing" on the *U.S. News and World Report* Web site at www.usnews.com/usnews/nycu/work/articles/010226/nycu/career.htm.

Remember that losing your job isn't the end of the world, and it shouldn't be a source of shame or extreme anxiety. Many people have said in hindsight that losing a particular job was the best thing that ever happened because it gave them a chance to rethink where they were in life and what they wanted.

The Least You Need to Know

- A typical person may experience feelings of denial, anger, depression, and eventually, acceptance upon losing a job.
- Many people link their job to their identity, which can make losing the job very traumatic and difficult on an emotional level.
- Don't burn bridges with your former employer, no matter how much you might be tempted to do so.

◆ If you lose your job, you'll need to assess your financial situation and plan for how you'll cope with a reduced income.

◆ You should employ all necessary strategies to insure your finances remain on track during the period in which you're unemployed.

◆ There are many resources to assist people who are unemployed and looking for another job.

Chapter 18

Going Out on Your Own

In This Chapter

◆ Considering the possibilities of starting your own business

◆ Minimizing risk through planning and preparation

◆ Dreaming of the rewards of being an entrepreneur

◆ Remembering to keep retirement in mind when going on your own

◆ Comparing the benefits of working at home to renting or buying an office

Most people, at one point or another, consider what it would be like to have their own business. Think about it. If you had your own business, you'd have no boss. You could work whatever hours you wanted. You'd make lots and lots of money because you're smart, hard working, and dedicated. Once you got the place running smoothly, you could take the winters off, pack up your golf clubs, and head for someplace warm. Sounds great, doesn't it? Well, starting and running your own business can be great, but it's not for everyone—for sure.

Entrepreneurs, those hardy souls that embrace the work, risks, and possible rewards of starting and running their own businesses, are a special breed. According to the dictionary, an entrepreneur is a person who organizes and directs a business undertaking, assuming the risk for the sake of profit. Entrepreneurs, however, will tell you that it's a person who believes in himself or herself enough to follow through on a dream and make it profitable.

They tend to thrive on solving problems and putting out fires. They need to be able to think on their feet, make quick decisions, and accept that risk is a fact of life. They're willing to work long hours and miss family events. They're generally innovative, flexible, and able to overcome obstacles. They have energy levels that make other people look like they're moving in slow motion. They're responsible, determined, confident, and persistent. They don't give up, even when things look bleak and they haven't seen a paycheck in three weeks.

Money Morsel

If you're thinking of starting your own business, your first stop should be the Small Business Administration's Web site at www.sba.gov. It contains a wealth of resources and information about nearly every aspect of starting and running a business.

If you've been thinking about starting up your own business, you'll need to ask yourself how much risk you're willing to assume, and how hard you're willing to work. And you'll need to know that starting your own business impacts many more people than you. Your family will be greatly affected, especially if you have children still living at home. Your social life probably will suffer for a while, and you'll find little time for leisure.

If, after careful consideration, you think that starting your own business will be your most rewarding undertaking ever, you can start to consider what kind of business might make sense for you.

Entrepreneurial Opportunities

There are thousands of business ventures out there. So how do you identify one that's right for you? The first step is to take a good hard look at your personal situation. What are your financial needs? Your personal likes and dislikes? What type of business would best accommodate your family's needs?

Once you've identified those sorts of factors, you can start looking at businesses that would best fit into whatever your situation happens to be.

Considering Your Personal Criteria

Having an idea of the type of business to which you're best suited will help you to narrow your search. Some factors to consider are listed as follows:

◆ **Financial needs.** If you're the sole, or primary breadwinner for your family, you probably want to start a business with a lot of potential for earning. If your spouse is already pulling in a great salary, or you're pretty well financially established, you may have a little more latitude about what type of business to start. If you're going to need to pay for college for three kids and stash a lot more money away for your retirement, you'd better be darned sure to choose a business with great moneymaking potential.

◆ **Your personality.** What's your personality type? Are you a high-powered ambitious sort who should be looking for a business with great growth potential? Or is your personality more laid back and better suited to a slower-paced enterprise? If you can't stand kids, you sure as heck shouldn't think about opening up a day-care center or toddler gym. If you never wear anything but jeans and sweat shirts, a trendy boutique probably doesn't make sense for you. You get the idea, right?

◆ **Family concerns.** If you're a woman with three young children and a strong commitment to the PTA, you probably want a business that allows you to have some flexibility. If you're single with few personal responsibilities, a business that requires you to work for three days without stopping might work out just fine. Also consider where you may have to live to make your business work. If you've always dreamed of owning a bait and tackle shop that specializes in fancy, deep-sea fishing equipment, for instance, it will make a lot more sense for you to start the business in Florida than in Kansas.

◆ **Your health.** Many people in their 40s and 50s find that they don't have as high of an energy level as they did in their 20s and 30s. Consider whether you'll be able to handle the physical demands of starting your own business. Also, consider any physical limitations that might affect what type of business you should consider. Health considerations often can be accommodated, but some businesses might be better suited to you than others.

◆ **Your personal likes and dislikes.** If you love to get up early, enjoy being around people, and love the smell of coffee, a Starbucks franchise might be just the ticket for you. If it's impossible for you to crawl out of bed before 10 A.M., however, a bagel shop that opens at 6 A.M. is a really bad idea. If you retreat to indoors the second the temperature dips below 45 degrees, you sure don't want to think about opening a ski resort in Colorado. If you break out in a rash every time you get close to an animal, you shouldn't consider starting a pet grooming business.

Giving some thoughts to these types of issues will help you to choose a venture that matches your interests and works for your personal situation. Once you've got an idea of what you want, you can see what's available.

What's Hot and What's Not

Once you've figured out what type of business makes sense for your personality and circumstances, you'll need to see what makes sense from a business perspective. It makes no sense to sink your resources, both financial and otherwise, into a venture that has little chance of succeeding.

With the digital camera market growing by leaps and bounds, for instance, it's not a good time to open a traditional photo developing facility. You should gear your search toward growth industries—those that are expected to expand significantly in the coming years.

There are several ways to identify growth areas. One is to simply take a look around and see what's been popping up. If three new coffee shops have opened in your town during the past year, and every one has a line of people out the door every morning, you may assume, correctly, that coffee is a growth area.

Money Morsel

Don't rule out the possibility of a franchise as your business venture. A franchise agreement means that you get to sell a trademarked product or service, such as Pizza Hut pizza or CleanNet USA maintenance services. In exchange, you give the franchiser a percentage of every sale.

But don't take our word for it. Walk into your local department store and check out the housewares department. We've come a long way since our Mr. Coffee machines of the 1980s. You'll see cappuccino makers, espresso machines, seven kinds of fancy European coffeemakers, bean-grinding machines, and on and on.

A stop in the gourmet food section will reveal all sorts of coffees and coffee-related items, such as chocolate-coated stirring sticks, flavored syrups, and biscuits specially designed for dipping.

If you leave the department store and look around your community, you'll notice the fancy coffee vending areas in convenience stores, and the expanded coffee menus in restaurants and sandwich shops. It should be pretty clear that coffee is a growth industry.

If you're not comfortable with identifying growth industries on your own, you can get an idea of what's out there from government statistics. The Bureau of Labor Statistics has identified the following jobs as the 10 fastest growing occupations during the period between 1998 and 2008:

- ◆ Computer engineers
- ◆ Computer support specialists
- ◆ Systems analysts
- ◆ Database administrators
- ◆ Desktop publishing specialists
- ◆ Paralegals and legal assistants

- Personal care and home health aides
- Medical assistants
- Social and human service assistants
- Physician assistants

There you have it. Computers, law, and health care are the professions of the future. If you're thinking of starting your own business, and you happen to be a computer whiz, you shouldn't have much trouble deciding a job area in which you have a good chance of being successful.

What happens, though, if you don't have the slightest interest in computers, you don't want anything to do with lawyers, and you can't stand the thought of being around someone who's sick?

You simply don't gear your business toward any of those fields, that's all. Just because a job or industry has been targeted for growth doesn't mean you have to—or even should—jump on the bandwagon.

It's far more important to find an industry in which you're interested and comfortable, than to try to mold your entrepreneurial efforts toward an area targeted for growth. Consider your interests, your family and personal situation, and what your instincts tell you about the sort of business you should start.

Then be prepared to trust in yourself and make your dream come true.

Money Morsel

Remember that service jobs, such as housecleaning, catering, and dog grooming, are on the increase, and are expected to be even more in demand in the future. We're a busy bunch of folks in America, looking for people to do the chores we don't find the time for.

Risks of Starting Your Own Business

More than half of all entrepreneurial ventures fail. Having gotten that fact out in the open, we're now telling you to ignore it if you're considering starting your own business.

There are reasons that business ventures fail, and, when you know what they are, you can avoid them. Sure, there are risks involved with starting your own business. You could lose a lot of money. You could become estranged from your family if you put all your time and energy into work. You could lose your business to fire, an earthquake, or flood.

But there are risks involved with working for somebody else, too. You might lose your job. You might hate the job and be miserable every day of your life. You might have to take a salary cut, or become estranged from your family because you're traveling for weeks at a time.

All of life involves risk. If you go into a business, or a marriage, or anything else thinking that you'll fail, then chances are that you will fail.

Don't Go There

Many entrepreneurs try to start a business without a business plan because they're intimidated by the idea of writing one, and they end up failing because they don't have a guide. If you don't know how to write a business plan, consult the Small Business Administration's Web site at www.sba.gov. There's a model plan there that you can adapt as your own.

Most businesses fail because the person who started them didn't set goals, or failed to thoroughly think through what he would do, and how he would do it. Some entrepreneurs try to start a business without ever writing a business plan, which is a huge mistake.

A business plan is the entrepreneur's bible, and an absolute necessity. It not only serves as a road map for where your business will go and how you'll get it there, it will be an important sales document when you're trying to attract funding for your business.

If you do your homework, and adequately prepare before starting a business, chances are good that you can make it work. And remember that not attempting something you really want because you're afraid of the risk involved might be the biggest failure of all.

Rewards of Going It Alone

Why then, if the hours are long, the pay unpredictable at first, and the future uncertain, do so many people succumb to the urge to start their own businesses?

They do it because they believe the potential rewards far outweigh the risks involved, and they have enough confidence in themselves to believe they'll be successful.

Let's cut to the chase. Most people start their own businesses because they hope to make money—lots of money. And, they're drawn to the prospect of being their own boss. Other factors count, such as the opportunity to meet other people in business, or to be recognized within the business community. Basically, however, it boils down to money and freedom.

Making a lot of money is good because it gives you great freedom. Think about how nice it would be to not have to worry about how you'd pay for the kids' college educations or fund your own retirement? Think about being able to pack up on the spur of the moment and head out for an island getaway. Or taking the whole family on a ski trip to Aspen over Christmas.

Money is definitely an incentive, and one of the greatest rewards of being an entrepreneur. The freedom of being your own boss is another reward of owning and running your own business. It's nice to be able to take off for a couple of hours to watch your daughter's soccer game or to take your elderly parent to his doctor's appointment.

Of course, being your own boss also entails a lot of responsibility, but it provides a very attractive sense of freedom. One additional reward—and it's a big one—of starting your own business, is the great feeling of accomplishment that comes with having built an enterprise from your hopes and dreams.

Money Morsel

Having money is nice, but remember that it doesn't solve all your problems. Someone once said something like, "When you have money, people think you have no problems. All money means is that you don't have money problems. You still have all the others."

Thinking Toward Retirement

If you're in your 40s or 50s and thinking about starting your own business, don't be intimidated about doing so at your age. There's a lot to be said for maturity, life experience, and business perspective that only comes from spending time in the work force.

Starting your own business now may well allow you to ease out of work gradually as you get older, without having to fully retire. Many people find working part-time, with a flexible schedule, an attractive option to full retirement.

If you are considering starting your own business, however, it's extremely important to consider your financial situation as it pertains to your retirement. There's a lot of information in Chapter 21, "Investing Outside of Work," about various types of IRAs and other retirement plans, so be sure to read it carefully to help you plan for what you need.

Briefly, small business owners have several retirement options that are unique to them. One of those is a SEP-IRA, which is short for Simplified Employee Pension-Individual Retirement Account. A self-employed person can contribute a percentage of his or her income into a SEP-IRA—even if the percentage is greater than the permitted $2,000 contribution to a regular IRA.

Self-employed persons can contribute 13.0435 percent of their earnings to a SEP-IRA. That means that the more you earn, the more you can contribute. You can, in fact, contribute 13.0435 percent of income up to $200,000.

If you're self-employed and have employees, you may want to consider setting up a SIMPLE retirement plan. You'll read more about this in Chapter 21. SIMPLE plans allow employers to contribute up to 3 percent of each employee's salary into the plan. The employees can contribute matching funds into the plan.

Working at Home vs. Renting an Office

Some businesses can be run very nicely out of your home, while others work better in an out-of-home setting. A small public relations firm, for instance, could work well in a home setting, provided the work area is private and quiet enough so as to be conducive to business. A construction firm, however, which requires space to store equipment and vehicles, probably would not work well at home.

There are advantages and disadvantages (trust us on this one) to working at home. Sure, it's great to be around when your kids come home from school. It's nice to wander out to the kitchen for a cup of coffee, and to work in shorts and a T-shirt. Working at home, however, also entails a fair share of distractions. The dog needs to go outside. A neighbor, who has only a vague idea of what you do at home all day, asks you to take her to the doctor. The guy from the gas company bangs on the garage door because he needs to read the meter. You get the picture.

Money Morsel

If you decide to work from home, and many people do so very successfully, make sure that family members and everyone else understands that you're working, and that they respect your time and space.

If you're thinking of working from home, or wondering if you should rent an office, consider the financial implications listed as follows:

♦ When you rent office space, the cost is completely deductible as an expense. If you pay your landlord $400 a month, the $4,800 you'll shell out in a year is considered a real and actual expense on Schedule C of your income tax return. You also can deduct costs associated with renting, such as utilities and phone. Refer to the IRS Web site at www.irs.gov/forms_pubs/forms.html to select and print a copy of Schedule C.

♦ To be considered a home office for which you can get a tax deduction, your workspace must be exclusively and regularly used for business. You can't put a desk and computer in the corner of your kitchen, for instance, and declare it a home office because it's from there that you do desktop publishing.

♦ If 10 percent of the total space of your home is used exclusively for business purposes, you can deduct 10 percent of the costs of maintaining your home on your federal income tax. You would deduct 10 percent of the cost of your electricity, heat, property taxes, mortgage interest, water, and trash and sewage.

♦ If you have a separate phone line in your home for work, you can deduct only your business phone costs, not your personal phone. If you have only one phone line, you can deduct the percentage of time that's it's used for business purposes.

- If you own your home, you normally deduct the cost of your mortgage interest and real estate taxes on Schedule A. If your office is 10 percent of the total home space, however, you can deduct 10 percent of your mortgage interest and real estate taxes are deductible on Schedule C, and the remaining cost on Schedule A. It seems like it wouldn't matter where you take the deduction, but there are some advantages in taking the Schedule C deduction, so be sure to mention it to your accountant.

- If your office is in your home, you also could deduct 10 percent of the value of your property (excluding the value of land) as depreciation. Property can be depreciated over a period of years, with the depreciation considered an office expense. So if your home is valued at $275,000, and you use 10 percent as office space, the annual depreciable portion of your home is $27,500. If your property is depreciated over 27.5 years (the IRS tells your accountant how long you must take to depreciate the property), you have a $1,000 per year deduction for the office space.

- You can deduct the cost of office expenses, such as paper, printer cartridges, and so forth, regardless of whether you work at home or in an office. You also can depreciate the cost of more expensive items such as furniture, computers, and printers.

Money Morsel

The Internal Revenue Service has a worksheet to help you determine your home office deductions. You can find in on the IRS Web site at www.irs.gov/prod/forms_pubs/graphics/15154t02.gif.

Go Figure

If you declare 10 percent of your home as office space, 10 percent of the gain you realize when you sell the home may be taxable. This liability may be eliminated by discontinuing your home office for a few years before you sell your home.

After considering the financial aspects of working at home vs. renting an office, you'll need to look at the practical ones, as well. Will it be too stressful for you or members of your family to have you work at home? Would you have the privacy you need? After looking at all the angles, you can decide which alternative would better fill your needs.

The Least You Need to Know

- To determine what kind of business you should start, you need to consider your personality and personal circumstances, as well as the business and financial implications of various job areas.

- Risks involved with starting your own business can be greatly minimized through careful planning and preparation.

◆ Making money, having the freedom of being your own boss, and the satisfaction of growing a business from nothing are the greatest rewards of being an entrepreneur.

◆ It's important to gear your business around your financial needs, especially as those needs pertain to retirement.

◆ When deciding whether to run your business from home or from an office, you need to consider factors such as tax advantages, practicality, and the strain it may cause for other family members.

Chapter 19

Other Changes to Think About

In This Chapter

- ◆ Recognizing the difficulty of death and changing relationships
- ◆ Dealing with the financial impact of death
- ◆ Knowing how divorce affects finances
- ◆ Sorting out financial matters in remarriage
- ◆ Coping with an empty nest
- ◆ Illness and finances

While all major life changes can be challenging and difficult, death and changing relationships are among the most painful.

Relationships shift and alter with time. They don't stay the same. Children grow up and develop completely different relationships with parents than those they had when they were very young.

As parents age and grow dependent on their children, the parent-child role may reverse. Marriages that last for many years undergo transition upon transition. Marriages that don't last usually cause pain and stress to both people. Friends may drift in and out of our lives, depending on circumstances.

While changing relationships can be difficult, death is even harder to cope with. We all know that every living thing must someday die, but somehow we're always unprepared when a death occurs within the circle of people we know and love.

In this chapter, we'll explore some of the most difficult changes we encounter in our lives, and how they can affect us emotionally, physically, and financially.

Nobody Lives Forever

We can anticipate death. We can expect it. We can even be relieved when it finally comes to a person who's been very ill for a long time. We can't, however, minimize the pain that comes with losing somebody we love.

We all will face death within our lifetimes. Some of us avoid it for many years, not even losing a grandparent or family friend to death until we're in our 20s or 30s. Others encounter death early on. A parent dies in an accident, or a brother or sister succumbs to a deadly childhood disease. Either way, we all will have to cope with loss in our journeys through life.

Losing a Parent

In the natural circle of life, our grandparents should die before our parents, our parents before us, and we before our children. And generally, that's the case.

Even though we understand this cycle, it's extremely difficult to lose a parent. This is partially because losing our mother or father forces us into a new role. We are no longer the "next generation." We move from the second generation to the first. And, we lose the mother-child or father-child bond that we shared with a parent. Losing your second parent can stir up feelings of abandonment—that you're all alone in the world.

Money Morsel

You may experience additional grief when a parent dies through the grief of your children, who are mourning the loss of a grandparent. Be aware of your children's grief, but don't try to put your own feelings aside in order to comfort them. Experience the sadness together.

Whether your relationship with your mom and/or dad is great, indifferent, or difficult, chances are that his or her death will affect you on many levels. If you didn't live close to your parent, you may feel sad or guilty that you didn't have more time with him. Guilt also may occur if you didn't have a close or loving relationship with your parent. You might wish that you had tried harder to get closer or to improve the situation.

You may feel relief at death if your parent has suffered for a long time, and those feelings might spawn additional guilt. Know, however, that feeling relief upon the death of someone who has been suffering is a natural reaction, and actually an expression of your love for your parent.

And, you might feel anger or resentment toward a parent who has died. Unresolved issues can sometimes surface, and you may feel angry that Mom died before you had the chance to work them out. Or you might have the feeling that you need Dad to take care of you, and experience anger at him for leaving you on your own.

Because our relationships with our parents change so much from the time we're kids until we reach adulthood, they're usually complex and operate on many levels. When a parent dies, we experience complex emotions, as a result.

And, if your parent was elderly, chances are that other people may not fully recognize or acknowledge your loss. They'll tell you that you should be happy for the years you had with your dad, or that your mom was lucky to have a good, long life. While those sentiments are true, they don't encompass the grief you're feeling at the loss of your parent.

On a practical side, the death of a parent may mean a tremendous amount of work for you—or for you and your siblings, if you have them. You may have to oversee the sale of a home, dispose of all possessions, sort out personal property, or execute your parent's will. These topics will be covered more thoroughly in Chapter 25, "Helping Aging Parents Plan."

Don't Go There

Don't feel that there's something wrong with you if you're devastated by the loss of a parent. We each have a unique relationship with our parents, and we'll each experience their deaths differently. Don't apologize for your grief, and don't allow others to rush you through the grieving process.

If you're an heir to your parent's estate, you'll have to make some decisions about what to do with the money or property you may receive. We'll discuss that topic in some detail in Chapter 22, "Investing Lump Sums."

Many of us have already lost one or both parents. If not, chances are that you will before too long. While you can't ever fully prepare for the death of someone you love, know that you can expect to feel many different emotions on many different levels. If you find it's necessary to do so, get help from a religious leader, trusted friend, support group, or counselor.

If a Spouse Dies

Losing a spouse in middle age—whether unexpectedly or after a long illness—is a devastating experience. Of course, it's never easy to lose your wife or husband, but experiencing this loss in middle age instead of old age can be particularly distressing.

Suddenly, you're no longer a part of a couple. You've lost the person to whom you could turn for advice or consultation. Along a practical line, you've lost the other half of the team that shared financial and household responsibilities. Your children have lost a

Go Figure

About 13.7 million Americans living today have experienced the loss of a husband or wife.

Money Morsel

Funerals can range in cost from $5,000 to $10,000 or more, depending on your location and the services you choose. And if your spouse was sick before death, you may have medical expenses to pay, as well. A financial advisor can help you to prioritize bill payments when necessary.

mother or father, and especially if they're young, you may feel that you need to help them through that.

If your husband or wife dies in middle age, you'll need to pay close attention to financial matters. This is an extremely difficult task to accomplish as you're mourning the death of a spouse, but it's necessary to your future financial health. Hopefully, you and your spouse have addressed the possibility of premature death, and have planned for the eventually. At the very least, you should have a comprehensive will (more about that in Chapter 24, "You're Never Too Young to Plan").

Probably the first matter you'll need to deal with following the death of a spouse are funeral expenses. If you haven't preplanned and prepaid, this can be trying, especially if you don't have much extra money.

Many surviving spouses use benefits from their husband or wife's life insurance policy to pay for funeral expenses. And, many funeral homes are willing to wait for payment until the insurance policy has been processed and benefits paid. You can discuss this matter with personnel at the funeral home you plan to use. Or better still, designate someone else to handle these types of matters.

Assuming you and your spouse had a will, you'll need to settle your husband or wife's estate, according to the terms of the document. You should work with your family lawyer or a trusted financial advisor on this matter. It's probably not the best idea to hire someone you don't know well to settle an estate, particularly if you don't plan to be overly involved in the process. It's best to be able to hand the matter over to someone you trust in order for you to be able to work through your grief and concentrate on other matters.

Another matter you'll need to pay attention to is resolving any debt that you and your spouse, or your spouse alone, had. In some states, creditors must work through the probate process in order to collect debts that were the deceased's alone. If you and he had joint debt, however, you'll still be responsible for paying it.

Some credit card companies and retail stores will waive the late fees for debt incurred by someone who dies. They probably, however, will continue to charge interest on the money owed. You can check, or have someone else check, with creditors to see how payments after a death are handled.

Another financial matter you'll need to look into is your spouse's health care and retirement benefits. If your spouse dies while you and your children are covered by his employer's health-care plan, you may be eligible to buy temporary extended health care coverage for up to three years. You'll have to pay for it, but the cost probably would be lower than that of coverage you'd get on your own.

If your spouse had a 401(k) plan, you'll need to find out the terms of the plan so that you can plan accordingly. If he had a pension plan at work and is vested in the plan, you should be eligible to receive a percentage of the monthly benefit he earned up to the time of his death. Check with the human resources department at his place of work, or ask your lawyer or financial advisor to give a call.

You also should know that if your spouse dies, leaving you with dependent children, you might be eligible for monthly survivor's benefits from Social Security. Contact your local Social Security office for more information, or ask your lawyer or financial advisor to look into it.

After the immediate financial issues that occur after the death of a spouse have been resolved, you'll need to think carefully about what, if any lifestyle changes you'll need to make. You should develop a new budget that reflects your changed circumstances, listing sources of income, savings, and expenses.

Again, it's usually best to work with a trusted professional on these issues. Dealing with the death of a spouse consumes your time, energy, and emotional capacity. It's a good idea to get help with financial matters to assure that they get resolved if you're not entirely able to do so yourself.

Losing a Child

Losing a child is no doubt nearly every parent's greatest fear, and the most awful experience a parent can ever face. And yet, nearly 20 percent of all parents do at one point or another experience the death of a child. Government statistics estimate that 228,000 children and young adults die every year in the United States. That number doesn't include miscarriages, stillbirths, or the deaths of children who are 40 years or older.

Losing a child defies the natural cycle of life. It destroys the dreams we have for our children, and steals the legacy we'd planned on leaving behind at our deaths. It's emotionally devastating and can destroy parents who don't have the benefits of strong support systems.

A parent who loses a child may become withdrawn, perhaps because she's unable to be around other children without feeling the terrible loss of her own child. She may become bitter and resentful toward relatives and friends who still have children. If she's married, she may on some level blame her husband for the death. Or she may blame herself.

Parents believe they should take care of their children. When a child dies, it's natural to feel a tremendous sense of failure, betrayal, and loss.

Although losing a child does not normally have the direct financial implications that losing a spouse would, there can be indirect effects.

Money Morsel

Parents with a child who dies can find information, support, and encouragement from Compassionate Friends, a nonprofit organization formed to help bereaved parents and other relatives. You can find Compassionate Friends at www.compassionatefriends. org.

Parents who experience the death of a child may find themselves unable to go back to work when their bereavement leave ends. Or they may go back to work and find that they're totally ineffective at doing their jobs.

Employers generally are sympathetic toward employees who lose a child, but the degree to which they're willing to bend for an employee will vary. A bereaved employee who is finding it difficult to satisfactorily complete his work should seek counseling. Ask the human resources department what benefits may be available to cover counseling or other bereavement services.

When Friends Die

Losing friends to death is a clear and unrelenting sign of our own mortality. We expect that we'll lose grandparents, parents, and older relatives, but having a friend of about the same age die is a real slap in the face.

As difficult as it is to lose a friend, remember that you'll need to be as supportive as possible to the members of his family, who probably are feeling the loss even more strongly than you are. If there are children still living at home, you could offer to keep an eye on the kids while the surviving spouse takes care of business or if she needs a break.

Try to keep surviving family members involved with the activities they enjoyed before the death, but don't push them to participate before they're ready to. And don't get so busy caring for your friend's family that you push away your own feelings of grief for your loss.

Death is an extremely difficult part of life, but a part of life, nonetheless. Facing the fact that we certainly will one day be affected by death can help us be a bit more prepared to deal with it when it occurs.

Marital Status

A change in marital status can result in big changes to your financial situation. While middle age used to be a relatively calm period of life, many people today experience all kinds of life changes while in their 40s and 50s.

They divorce. They remarry. They become parents again after already having raised children. They become stepparents. They worry about whether their kids and stepchildren will get along. Life can be pretty exciting during middle age, and pretty hard on your finances, as well. If you're experiencing—or expect that you will experience—a change in marital status, you'll need to take steps to protect your personal financial situation.

Dealing With the Big D

While death can change marital status in an instant, it is more often divorce or separation that does so during middle age. With about half of all marriages in America ending in divorce, the big D is forcing millions of people to reevaluate their lives, and their financial situations.

Getting divorced is rarely a simple matter, emotionally. Many people see divorce as a symbol of betrayal of trust, broken promises, or failure. It causes hurt and anxiety. If children are involved, you'll need to deal with their feelings concerning the divorce, as well as your own.

If you're facing an unwelcome divorce, keep in mind that there are many support groups and other help available.

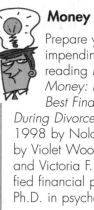

Money Morsel

Prepare yourself for an impending divorce by reading *Divorce and Money: How to Make the Best Financial Decisions During Divorce*, published in 1998 by Nolo Press. It's written by Violet Woodhouse, a lawyer, and Victoria F. Collins, a certified financial planner with a Ph.D. in psychology.

Divorce and Your Finances

While divorce can wreak emotional havoc, it also can be extremely hard on your financial situation. If you're looking at a divorce, it's extremely important to pay close attention to financial issues and make sure that you get what you're entitled to. Many people have been forced to dramatically alter their lifestyles after divorce due to financial considerations.

Basically, the legal steps of divorce, and actions you should take at each step, are as follows:

◆ **Decision to divorce.** When the decision is made to divorce, you should consult a lawyer, or begin some legal research on your own. You'll need to learn about your state's laws in regard to issues such as child custody and support, alimony payment, debts incurred after separation, valuation of marital property, and so forth. Any joint bank accounts should be frozen or closed at this time, and you should organize all financial papers and documents.

- **The couple physically separates.** Although this doesn't always happen, normally either the husband or wife leaves the household and takes up residence elsewhere. Obviously, this can cause financial problems. If you're still paying a mortgage and keeping up with the expenses of a home, finding cash to rent an apartment or other type of dwelling can be difficult.

  Each person should document all debts incurred, including moving expenses. Money spent on improvements or repairs to the marital home should be noted. Keep track of any joint bills you pay, and make sure that you have adequate insurance policies for the current living arrangement. Start thinking about tax issues at this point, deciding whether you'll file jointly or separately.

- **Filing for divorce.** One spouse files the complaint or petition for divorce, officially beginning the divorce process. The other spouse will need to file an official response to the complaint or petition.

- **Requesting temporary court orders.** One spouse files a request for temporary court instructions regarding issues such as alimony, child custody and support, and visitation. The request may also ask for one spouse to pay the other's legal fees. All child support and alimony payments should be documented in order to assure that court orders are being followed and for tax purposes.

- **Legal discovery.** Legal discovery is a series of procedures used to obtain information about your divorce case. It involves financial fact-finding, and identification and consideration of the value of all marital property. Child support and alimony payments to be made once the divorce is final will be set during this period. You should make a list of all assets such as stocks, bank accounts, real estate, automobiles, and so forth. You may need to hire a financial planner or tax advisor who specializes in divorce issues during this stage.

- **The settlement.** Following the discovery process, legal and financial settlement negotiations will begin. If both parties are in reasonable agreement concerning division of property and other matters, these negotiations can be fairly simple. Lawyers representing each party can conduct these negotiations, as can a mediator that both parties agree to use or an arbitrator with the power to make binding decisions that will be transferred back to the court. An arbitrator normally is used when a couple is not cooperative as to the division of property and other matters. The legal settlement can be long and drawn out, or fairly simple, depending on circumstances and the people involved. Make sure that all legal and financial issues—such as *alimony* and *child support*, child custody, and tax implications—are addressed at this time.

Money Morsel

Keep in mind that professionals are expensive to hire. The more amicable you and your spouse can be during the divorce process, the fewer professionals you'll need. This will have a positive effect on your financial situation.

◆ **The settlement agreement.** This is a formal document that sets forth the terms of the settlement.

◆ **The judgment of divorce.** This is the document that finalizes the divorce and ends proceedings. Once the divorce is final, you'll need to make sure that all legal documents, such as deeds and wills, reflect your change in marital status and any changes in ownership. Check all bank records, stock certificates, insurance policies, and so forth.

If you and your spouse are willing, you can work together during the divorce process to make sure it has as little negative impact on your finances as possible. Remember that a long, bitter divorce almost always costs more than an amicable one.

Adding It Up

Child support, usually paid to the custodial parent by the noncustodial parent, is money designated for the care and support of the dependent children. **Alimony** is money paid to one spouse by another, as directed by the court.

An important fact to keep in mind is that alimony (sometimes called separation maintenance) is tax deductible for the person paying and considered taxable income for the person getting it. Child support payments, on the other hand, are neither tax deductible nor considered as taxable income.

One spouse may be directed by the court to help with expenses, other than child support, which are incurred by the other spouse. These could include paying premiums on insurance policies, paying some or all the mortgage, and so forth.

As you can see, divorce is not a simple matter, financially. If it happens to you, be sure to get the professional advice that you need. Keep in mind that you may need a post-divorce budget to help you adjust to financial changes. Plan carefully to avoid unnecessary problems.

Marrying Again

Should you decide to remarry after a divorce or the death of your spouse, think carefully about how the marriage will affect your finances.

There are many issues to consider. Will you combine finances, or keep them separate? Will you be responsible for contributing toward college expenses for stepchildren? How will you handle estate planning and passing along money to your children? Can you afford to establish a new household while still helping with the expenses of your previous home?

Some financially established couples who marry in middle age decide to keep their finances separate. Others combine all their assets and liabilities. Others compromise by setting up separate, personal savings and checking accounts as well as joint accounts for household use.

Many financial experts recommend that couples who are marrying for the second time around use a prenuptial agreement, particularly if one person has significantly greater assets than the other. A prenuptial agreement (also called a "prenup," for short), as you probably know, outlines how assets will be divided in the event of death or divorce.

Go Figure
The Stepfamily Association of America reports that nearly 45 percent of all weddings are second marriages for at least one partner.

Even if you don't go for a prenup, you and your spouse-to-be should sit down for a serious financial discussion. Take a look at each other's credit reports to be sure there are no surprises. If there are kids involved, discuss matters such as allowance, spending money, and cars. Be sure that each has updated the beneficiary on bank accounts, savings bonds, and IRAs.

Discussions on matters such as these might fly in the face of romance, but there's nothing romantic about learning two months into a marriage that your spouse has tens of thousands of dollars in debt that you knew nothing about.

Another matter you'll need to discuss is your wedding. While you may be thinking only about making the event beautiful and meaningful, you'll need to consider its financial impact, as well.

If you and your spouse-to-be are very well off financially, go ahead and plan away. If it comes down to a choice between a big wedding and his next month's child support payment, however, you'd better start scaling back your plans.

The Empty Nest Syndrome

Sooner or later, most kids leave home to start lives of their own. Granted, they do this at varying rates and with varying degrees of success. Some leave, come back, and leave again. Others leave for far-off places and come back only for major holidays or events. A few never leave, but that's not what we're discussing here.

The empty nest syndrome, which is a period of anxiety or depression that some parents experience when their grown children leave home, has gotten a lot of attention over the past few years. Mind you, it doesn't happen to everyone, and usually passes after a period of time.

Considering your empty nest in financial terms may shed a whole new light on the issue. If your child has left home to go to college, you're no doubt coping with all the matters we discussed in Chapter 8, "Paying for College." If he's left home because he's financially independent now, and starting a life of his own, you may find yourself with some extra cash. If this is the case, it's a great opportunity for you to boost your retirement savings.

I Need to See the Doctor, Please

Illness can cause major, unplanned, and unwelcome changes in our lives. It also can wreak havoc with our finances. If you've learned recently that you, or someone in your family, has a chronic or serious illness, you'll need to take steps to plan for the financial implications.

Consider such questions as whether or not the illness will result in loss of income, and how your savings will be affected. If your husband is the primary wage earner, for instance, and has just been diagnosed with lung cancer, how much longer may he be able to work? And, might you be forced to leave your job in order to care for him?

Check first to see what benefits may be available through the ill person's place of employment. Someone who is already sick won't be able to get disability insurance, but if you or your family member has a policy, look over the terms and discuss how you'll use the benefits from it. Look at the terms of health insurance policies and try to anticipate any costs you may have to cover on your own.

Hopefully, you have an emergency fund containing about six months worth of wages put aside to help you to meet expenses and cover lost wages, if applicable. If the ill person is married and the primary earner for the family, the spouse may have to get a job to help meet expenses. You may choose to consult a financial advisor to help you work out how you'll deal with your changing situation.

Medicare, the federal health insurance program for people over 65, also covers certain disabled people who are younger than 65. To find out if you or a family member may qualify, go to Medicare's web site at www.medicare.gov. You'll be able to get a phone number for an office near you and can make an appointment for a consultation.

If you or your family member is able to be at home during the illness, look into community services in your area that may provide in-home help or funding for in-home help for the ill and their caregivers. These services range from unskilled help with chores such as dressing, cooking, or bathing, to fully skilled nursing care. The cost of such services, of course, varies depending on where you live and what type of help you need. Unskilled care normally can be obtained for anywhere from $8 an hour or higher, while skilled nursing care can cost upward of $40 an hour.

If you and your spouse or partner were forward thinking and had purchased long-term care insurance, be sure to check on what services are covered. Many people think long-term care insurance is for nursing home care, but most policies cover services such as home health care, assisted living care, and the cost of community-based services.

Serious or chronic illness is a great source of stress, both to the person suffering from it and for family members. Don't hesitate to talk to your doctor, a trusted friend, or your minister or rabbi about how you're feeling.

Life changes, while challenging, also can be rewarding. They allow us opportunity for growth and offer a chance for us to assess where we are in life and where we've come from. Life changes also can be financially challenging. Being prepared to deal with these changes on all levels can go a long way in bringing us through them successfully.

The Least You Need to Know

- ◆ Of all life's changes, death and changing relationships may be the most difficult to cope with.
- ◆ Losing a parent can be far more difficult than you might expect.
- ◆ The death of your spouse can have tremendous financial implications as well as being emotionally devastating.
- ◆ Divorce can wreak havoc on a couple's finances, so you need to know what to do to minimize the damage.
- ◆ If you're marrying again, you'll need to carefully address how you'll handle financial matters.
- ◆ Serious or chronic illness, either your own or a family member's, can impact negatively on your finances.

Part 5

Smart Investing in This Stage of Life

You probably know that investing your money is a good idea, but how do you know the best investments to make? Navigating the stock and bond markets can be a daunting task, not to mention trying to figure out the advantages and disadvantages of other investment vehicles.

How can you tell when it's time to sell stock that you already have, or to shift your assets away from the stock market into the bond market? What should you do if you get a lump sum of money?

In Chapters 20 through 23, you'll learn about investment opportunities at work and outside of work. You'll be challenged to examine your investment habits to be sure you're getting the most possible out of your money, and setting yourself up for a comfortable financial future. And just in case you need some help, you'll learn how to find the type of financial advisor that you need.

Chapter 20

Investing at Work

In This Chapter

- ◆ Understanding how we save for retirement
- ◆ Looking at some common types of pension plans
- ◆ And then there are 401(k)s
- ◆ Understanding the plan you have
- ◆ Planning for what you'll need

Most people look forward to retiring. They look forward to having time to do all the things they never got around to while they were working. The problem is, all those trips and activities are going to cost money. And you'll still have the upkeep on your home to think about. You'll still need to buy food. You'll still want to be able to buy presents for people, and go to the movies, and eat at your favorite restaurants.

The obvious question is, where will that money come from?

When we start thinking about retirement—as, no doubt, many of us are—we're forced to take careful stock of our finances. Will we have enough money to retire? How much longer will we have to work? Have we made the proper investments to assure that we'll be okay financially when we retire? How much will we get from Social Security?

Studies show that most people need between 60 and 80 percent as much money to maintain their standard of living during retirement as they required while working. This varies, of course, depending on factors such as health, location, and so forth. Social Security benefits for the average retiree are about 40 percent of their pre-retirement earnings. As you can see, there's a large gap between what Social Security provides and what it costs to live in retirement. If a retired person doesn't have enough money saved to make up the difference, there's a big problem.

> **Go Figure**
>
> Social Security is the primary source of income for about 66 percent of elderly Americans. And, experts say the rate of dependency is unlikely to drop in the future because of mediocre savings rates.

In this chapter, we'll have a look at some work-related investment opportunities, and see how they might relate to your retirement savings plan. Hopefully, you've invested through your company's pension plans, 401(k)s, money purchase plans, profit sharing plans or other work-related opportunities.

Basic Methods of Saving for Retirement

Very basically, there are two ways to save for retirement, regardless of whether you're saving in a job-related investment opportunity or outside of work:

- Using pre-tax dollars
- Using post-tax dollars

In this chapter, we'll be dealing with work-related investments, nearly all of which use pre-tax dollars. Nonwork-related plans are the topic of Chapter 21, "Investing Outside of Work."

All of the investment methods discussed in this chapter, then, use pre-tax dollars. That means that the money you invest in these work-related accounts isn't taxed until you take it back out of the account. This is also known as tax-deferred saving.

Retirement plans, using pre-tax dollars, fall into two types of plans:

- Qualified investing: 401(k)s, pension, and profit sharing plans
- Nonqualified investing: deferred compensation and stock options

Qualified investing is the major method, and the one with which we'll primarily be dealing. Just so you know, what they are, however, here's a bit of information about nonqualified plans.

Nonqualified plans aren't subject to the same rules and regulations as qualified plans. Deferred compensation and stock options are two nonqualified plans that are familiar to most people.

All qualified investment plans fall under the rules of the Employee Retirement Income Security Act of 1974, or ERISA. Nonqualified plans are not covered by ERISA guidelines.

Nonqualified plans usually are provided to key employees (the big guys), and used to supplement qualified plans and defer income taxes. Few of us have opportunity to be covered under nonqualified plans. So while it's good to know that they're around, they probably will have no bearing on our retirement benefits.

ERISA rules mandate that qualified plans must provide equity throughout an employer's pension fund. If an employer is going to provide a retirement benefit for his employees, the coverage must extend to all employees, within certain guidelines.

Qualified plans come in different flavors, but they all have the goal of helping you to save money for when you retire. The type of plan you have at work probably is determined by your employer, who, incidentally, is able to deduct the money he contributes to employees' retirement plans from his federal income tax. Let's look at some widely used, important qualified investing plans.

Pension Plans

The phrase "pension plan" often is used generically to refer to any sort of retirement plan offered by an employer. It could refer to a 401(k) plan, a money purchase plan, or any of the other plans we'll discuss in this chapter. If you're self-employed, and don't have the benefit of an employer-sponsored plan, you can establish your own retirement savings plan through a SEP-IRA. You can learn more about SEP-IRAs in Chapters 18 and 21.

Traditionally, however, a pension plan is an employer-sponsored retirement plan, in which the employer contributes money to a retirement fund set up on behalf of the worker. When the worker retires, he receives fixed, periodic payments, on which he must pay taxes.

Of the traditional type of pension plan, there are two kinds:

- Defined benefit plan
- Defined contribution plan

Money Morsel

Traditional pension plans used to be more common than they are now, but they're still around, especially at larger companies. Seventy-seven percent of large companies in America still offer pension plans, although most mid-size or smaller companies have 401(k) savings plans.

Both plans provide funding for your retirement. The difference is, with the defined benefit plan, the investment responsibility is on the employer, while the defined contribution plan puts the responsibility on the employee.

The defined benefit plan promises the employee a specified retirement benefit, based on a formula. The investment return risk is on the employer, who is responsible for funding and benefits.

If your company offers a defined benefit pension plan, it, in effect, promises you that if you work there for 30 years, retiring when you're 65, you'll get a monthly check for a certain amount of money (determined by the formula), for the rest of your life. The monthly pension payments are based on the number of years the retiree worked for the company and his salary during the years he worked. Different companies have different formulas for figuring out pension payments, but nearly all are based on years of service and salary.

Money Morsel

Defined contribution plans generally are considered more advantageous to younger employees who have many years to invest. Defined benefit plans tend to be better for older workers who don't have a lot of years to let their investments work for them.

Your employer is responsible for investing the money, and for being able to pay you the amount you've been promised when you retire.

A defined contribution plan, on the other hand, promises an employee the value of the employee's account at retirement—whatever that value may be.

Although the employer is responsible for providing a satisfactory investment vehicle, the investment risk is on the employee.

Let's say that your employer contributes 10 percent of your salary each year to a defined contribution account in your name. If you make $45,000 this year, he'll throw $4,500 into your retirement account. Once he's contributed the money, however, it's your responsibility. You need to decide where you'll invest it, and you bear the investment risks. Whatever is in the account at retirement time is what you have.

Under a defined contribution plan, your employer has an individual account in your name. The employer's contributions are put into the account each year, with all income and capital gains taxes deferred until the money is withdrawn at retirement.

When you become eligible to receive benefits—usually at retirement—the benefit is based on the total amount in your account. The account balance includes the employer's contributions, whatever contributions you may have added to the account, and the earnings on the account for the years of deferral.

There are three principal types of defined contribution plans. Let's have a look at what each one entails.

Money Purchase Plan

A money purchase plan is a qualified employer retirement plan in which each employee has an individual account. The employer must make annual contributions to each employee's account. The amount of contribution is determined by a pre-set formula, based on a fixed percentage, or a flat monetary amount.

The formula requires an employer to contribute a specified percentage (up to 25 percent) of each employee's compensation. Money purchase plans are expensive for the employer, and are not as common as other plans. If the employer can't make his required annual contributions, he is penalized.

Money Morsel

An employer's annual contribution to a money purchase plan is required. He can't take a year off because business is slow and profits are down.

Some money purchase plans may allow employees to add to the employer's contribution, but the employee would have to pay taxes up front on the money he contributed.

Profit Sharing Plans

A profit sharing plan is a qualified, defined contribution plan in which an employer contributes money to employees' accounts, based on the amount of profit the company has realized that year.

The employer gets to decide how much to contribute, and is not obligated to contribute anything if the company has not been profitable. Although an employer can contribute up to 15 percent of each employee's salary into his or her account, the average contribution usually is between 2 and 5 percent.

A profit sharing plan can be done in conjunction with another retirement savings plan, but sometimes it is the only type of plan available within a company. Employees may add to their employer's contribution, either with pre-tax or post-tax money.

Target Benefit Plan

A target benefit plan is an age-weighted plan that's normally used by a company that wishes to have a specified sum available for an older employee (usually an owner) at the time of retirement.

These plans are expensive, and usually employed by companies in which the owners have been unable to contribute to retirement funds while they were building up the company.

Once the company starts to be profitable and retirement money is available, the owners try to compensate for their previous lack of retirement saving.

401(k) Plans and the 403(b)

A section 401(k) plan, commonly known simply as a 401(k), is a qualified profit sharing plan that gives an employee the option of putting money in the plan (up to $10,500 per year) or receiving taxable cash compensation.

You either can take the money home as additional pay, or have the funds deposited into a 401(k) plan for you. An employer usually adds a percentage of the employee's contribution to the employee's plan.

Both your money and your employer's contribution are made with pre-tax money. That means that the income you contribute to your 401(k) isn't considered taxable income at this time. It will, however, be taxable when it's withdrawn.

> **Go Figure**
>
> Most employees like 401(k) plans because they're flexible. You're normally permitted to change the amount of money you contribute at least once a year.

The 401(k) accounts were introduced in 1982, and became extremely popular in the ensuing years. In fact, employees sometimes get frustrated when their employer doesn't provide a 401(k).

If you have a different type of plan, however, don't assume that you're being cheated by not having a 401(k). Another type of plan is likely to do as well, or perhaps even better. They're certainly preferable to no employment plan, and, 401(k)s do have many advantages. They're not, however, the only game in town.

While many employers match (or partially match) 401(k) contributions by employees, it's not required. Some employers contribute nothing. Maybe the employer can't afford to contribute to the plan, and simply offer the 401(k) as a means for their employees to contribute to a retirement fund, or your employer offers the 401(k) plan as a supplement to an already existing retirement plan.

When an employer doesn't contribute, all the contributions to the 401(k) come from an employee. The employer would pay only to install and administer the plan.

If your employer does contribute, however, it's important for you to put enough money in your 401(k) plan to take advantage of the company match. If your company matches dollar for dollar up to 3 percent of your salary, for instance, then you should by all means contribute at least 3 percent. If the company puts in dollar for dollar all of your contribution up to 6 percent, make sure you're putting away 6 percent in your 401(k).

It's important that you have a good understanding of your 401(k) plan. You should be aware of when you're able to change the amount of your contribution and move your money from one investment to another.

Employees get to decide where to invest their 401(k) funds from a list of choices provided by the employer. A greater number of choices increases the cost of the plan, so most employers provide about six choices.

Money Morsel

A good way to increase your 401(k) contribution is to automatically add any salary increases to the amount you save. You'll be glad in the long run.

If you have a 401(k), you should try not to touch it until retirement. If you need to, however, if there is a "hardship," there is a special provision that allows you to get your 401(k) money early.

Under the hardship provision, you can withdraw from the plan while you're still working for the firm that provides the plan. You don't need to quit to get your money out of the retirement plan. You just ask your employer for the money. Your employer must make sure that the reason you need the money falls within the IRS guidelines. If your need qualifies as a hardship, you'll get your money.

You don't need to repay the withdrawn funds, but you'll need to pay tax on them at the end of the year. Tax is withheld when you withdraw the funds.

Some "hardships," as specified by the IRS, include the following:

◆ First-time homebuyer

◆ Medical bills

◆ Education costs

Some plans permit employees to borrow money from their 401(k)s. It's extra paperwork for the employer, so some do not provide this option. And, some employers feel strongly that 401(k) money is retirement money and shouldn't be borrowed against, so they decline to provide a loan provision.

If permitted under your plan, you can borrow up to 50 percent of the total value of the account, up to $50,000. The loan must be repaid within a five-year period, or it becomes a withdrawal.

Many employees love the loan provision because it allows them to pay themselves the interest on the loan instead of a bank or credit union. When you repay the loan (with interest) the interest is added to your account.

There are, however, some problems with borrowing from your 401(k). If you borrow money and then leave the company, the loan must be repaid within a very short period of time.

If you decide to borrow from your 401(k) to buy a car, for instance, and then you leave the company for a better job, you must either borrow from someplace else to repay the loan, or the loan becomes a distribution, which is a taxable event.

Money Morsel

Never take a loan from a 401(k) in which the interest would be deductible if borrowed elsewhere, such as with mortgage interest. Interest paid to your 401(k) plan is not deductible.

These retirement plans are designed for retirement, and there are penalties if you take the money out ahead of time. Money you withdraw from a 401(k) is taxed at your current income tax bracket. And if you are younger than 59 and a half when you withdraw funds, a 10 percent penalty is due on top of the income tax liability.

So if you borrow $8,000 for a car, leave the company, and can't pay your loan back within the required period, you'll pay income tax ($1,200 if you're in the 15 percent bracket), plus $800 penalty. Ouch!

A good reason to borrow from your 401(k) is to repay credit card debt. If you've racked up debt and you're paying 18 percent interest on your balances, you should consider borrowing from your 401(k) to pay off the cards. You'll pay a lot less interest every month on the money from your 401(k). Just make sure that you don't turn around and create new balances on the cards.

Another problem with borrowing from your 401(k) is that the loan is invested at a fixed rate as you repay it. It's similar to having your money invested in money market funds, and you'll realize a lower rate of return.

401(k) is an IRS code section that permits this type of retirement plan (a type of profit sharing plan). If you work for a nonprofit organization, such as a hospital, charitable organization, or university, you'll fall under the IRS code section known as 403(b). Look familiar? 403(b)s mirror 401(k)s, except for until recently, the investment vehicles could only be offered through an insurance company. Now, 403(b)s can be set up through mutual fund companies and you can roll a 403(b) into a 401(k) if you go from a nonprofit to a for profit company.

Money Morsel

There are different methods by which an employer can contribute to a simple plan. If your company has this type of plan, be sure to ask your employer or human resource person for details.

Simple Plans

Simple retirement plans are relatively new. They're aimed at small employers (fewer than 100 employees), and are easy and inexpensive to administer. An employer must contribute annually to a simple plan.

An employer can set up this type of plan for very little cost. Each employee can contribute to the plan along with the employer, up to a maximum of $6,500 a year.

If your company has a simple plan, it may not have an additional type of qualified retirement plan.

Understanding Vesting

An employee must meet certain requirements in order to be eligible to be covered under a qualified retirement plan. These requirements vary from company to company.

Normal requirements are that an employee must be at least 21 years old, and must have worked for the company for at least one year. Some employers begin coverage sooner, but a year is the norm.

An employee always gets back what he's contributed to a retirement plan. Regardless of how long he stays with a company, he always takes his contributions along with him when he leaves. There are, however, regulations that determine when and how an employee is eligible to get the money his employer contributed.

A tool called a *vesting* schedule determines when you'll start to receive your employer's money if you leave the company before you reach retirement age.

You must be an employee for a minimum amount of time before you become eligible to receive your employer's contributions if you leave the company. This time period is called vesting. There are two types of vesting, cliff and graduated.

Cliff vesting means that you've got to work for your employer for five years before you're entitled to his contributions to your retirement fund. If you change jobs before you've been with the company for five years, you walk away with your own contributions, but none of your employer's.

If you do stay for five years, and then leave, you take all of your employer's contributions. It's an all or nothing deal, and something to think about if you're considering leaving a company after just a few years.

The other type of vesting is called graduated vesting. You need to stay with a company for seven years in order to get all of your employer's contributions. If you leave within a shorter time, however, you get some of his money, as long as you've been there at least three years. It's not an all-or-nothing proposition. The graduated vesting schedule is as follows:

Adding It Up

Vesting is the amount of time required for an employee to work for a company before he or she is entitled to the employer's contributions to his retirement plan.

Don't Go There

Don't walk away from what could be substantial money for the sake of a few months. If you've found another job, but are close to being vested, see if you could delay starting the other position until you're eligible for the retirement funds.

Years of Service	Vested Percentage
3	20
4	40
5	60
6	80
7 or more	100

Many employees don't understand vesting, and are unpleasantly surprised when they leave and find out they're not entitled to the money their employers contributed on their behalf.

Knowing What You Have and What You'll Need

Many people do a good job deciding how much they'll contribute and how they'll invest the money in their retirement funds, only to fall short when it comes to keeping track of the funds.

The first thing you should be paying attention to is your Social Security benefits. Call Social Security at 1-800-772-1213, and request a personal earnings and benefits estimate statement. This will tell you what you've earned, and your expected retirement benefit.

You should receive a statement from Social Security every year around your birthday, providing your income history since you began working. Upon retirement, Social Security uses a calculation based on your annual income for most of your working career, with an adjustment for inflation. You should carefully review this annual statement to see that the historical salary levels are accurate. If not, your benefit may be lower than it should be when you retire.

Don't Go There

It's tempting to throw information concerning your retirement account into a drawer without even glancing at it, but that's a dangerous habit. Mistakes happen, and if they do and go unnoticed, it could affect the amount of money you have when you stop working.

Your employer should issue a statement, at least annually, providing information about the company's retirement plan. If you have a defined benefits plan, the statement should outline the amount of benefits you'll get when you retire if you continue to work at your current job.

If you have a defined contribution plan, there's no way to know what your retirement benefit will be because the benefit is based on the value of your account when you retire.

However, an investment advisor should be able to calculate an approximate value of your account at retirement by using your current account value, the number of years until you retire, and an assumed rate of return on the investments. You, then, can use that figure as a base to calculate a monthly retirement benefit for your life expectancy.

Pension laws require your employer to provide you with the following information each year:

◆ **Summary plan description.** This explains the basic rules and features of your retirement plan, and you should get it within 90 days of becoming a participant. Review the information so you understand the plan and can maximize its benefits.

◆ **Summary annual report.** This describes the plan's aggregate financial status.

◆ **Survivor benefits explanation.** This describes the survivor benefits available to spouses under your retirement plan.

◆ **Individual benefit statement.** This isn't legally required, but most employers provide it. The statement shows your current account balances or accrued benefits. Always retain a copy for your records.

In addition, if your plan is participant directed, that is, you decide how your money is invested, request a description of each investment option, including its risk and reward characteristics, fees, and expenses.

To figure out how much money you'll need when you retire, go to one of the retirement calculators on the Internet. Some good sites are:

◆ www.vanguard.com

◆ www.troweprice.com

◆ www.fidelity.com

◆ www.kiplinger.com

A more involved calculation is available at www.analyzenow.com.

Money Morsel

If you learn from a retirement calculator that you'll need much, much more than you think you can possibly save by that time, don't panic. Consult a financial advisor to see if the calculator is accurate, and then plan if necessary.

Calculators at these sites take into account your current income, your age, and the amount of money you contribute to your retirement account. They can provide a rough estimate of what you'll require when you retire, but remember that no one can pinpoint that amount with accuracy.

These investment or retirement calculators assume an annual rate of return, an inflation factor, and they assume you'll continue to contribute at the current rate throughout your working career. All of those assumptions leave a lot of room for error, so don't depend too heavily on the information you get.

Retirement Needs Analysis

Most experts feel you need at least 75 percent of your pre-retirement income to maintain the same lifestyle after you retire. This percentage is called the wage replacement ratio (WRR).

Social Security benefits make up the foundation of one's retirement needs, but most people find they need much more than their Social Security checks. If you don't have adequate retirement savings, you might have to think about delaying retirement, or working part-time after you retire.

Plan on paying off as many of your debts and mortgages as possible between now and the time that you retire. An important part of retirement planning is planning for debt reduction or elimination.

> **Go Figure**
>
> People who are 75 or older spend 26.5 percent less, on average, than those between the ages of 65 to 74. A good rule of thumb is to assume that by age 75, you'll spend 20 percent less than when you first retire.

Older retirees tend not to spend as much money as younger retirees. They normally don't have a mortgage, and they don't have expenses associated with travel and the other activities they enjoyed at a younger age. Most older people are less active, and therefore spend less money.

Many older people do, however, spend more on medical care as they age, but usually not enough to offset the steady drop in the rest of their living costs.

Some older folks spend less only because their incomes dropped when they retired. Most retirees, however, cut back spending voluntarily, and almost half of them continue adding to their savings for several years after leaving their jobs.

As an example, let's assume that you retire when you're 66, and begin living on 80 percent of what had been your working income. And, let's assume you'll live another 25 years.

By age 75, you're likely to be spending just 64 percent of your former income. If you provide for a retirement income equal to 70 percent of your working salary, you'll probably be just fine.

The investment decisions you make at this point of your life are crucial in determining your ultimate retirement savings under a participant-directed plan.

If you invested $5,000 a year in a tax-deferred account earning an 8 percent annual return, for example, you would accumulate $247,000 after 20 years. If the same investment earned 10 percent annually (about the average annual return on common stocks over the past 30 years), your account would total $315,000 after 20 years—a full 28 percent more.

Invest wisely, and save as much as you can in your retirement accounts. Take advantage of the tax deferments, and plan for a happy retirement.

The Least You Need to Know

- There are many different types of retirement savings plans, all of which fall into the basic categories of qualified and nonqualified.

- Pension plan has become a generic term used to describe different types of retirement plans, but it really is a particular type of agreement between an employer and employee.

- Many employees love 401(k) plans, but if you've got a different type of plan you shouldn't assume that you're missing out.

- It's important to understand the terms and conditions of your retirement plan so that you can maximize the benefits it offers.

- Planning ahead for retirement by reducing debt can stretch the money you'll have after you stop working.

Chapter 21

Investing Outside of Work

In This Chapter

- ◆ Getting a handle on the stock market
- ◆ Buying and selling stock
- ◆ Understanding the bond market
- ◆ Looking at mutual funds
- ◆ The exciting world of IRAs

At any age, but especially when you're in your 40s or 50s, retirement planning should be your first priority. If your employer-sponsored retirement accounts are where they should be, however, and your payments are all under control, you might be thinking about some other types of investments. After all, retirement is expensive, and, to be assured that you have the money you need, you may need some good investments outside of your at-work plans.

Investing, as you probably know, encompasses a variety of opportunities and vehicles. It's as simple as putting money in a savings account at 2 percent interest, or as complex as the commodities market.

This chapter looks at investing in terms of stocks and bonds, with some information about mutual funds thrown in, as well. If you're a seasoned investor with a portfolio the size of the Manhattan phone book, you might just want to skim over the information included here as a basic review. If you're new to the world of stocks and bonds, you'll want to pay careful attention.

The Stock Market

We frequently hear people talking about the stock market. When the market was great in the late 1990s, everybody wanted to talk about the market and how well their investments were doing. People quit their jobs to become day traders, those steel-nerved folks who watch the market carefully, buying and selling stock in hopes of hitting it big and making tons of money. More people invested in the market than ever before, fueling the economy and keeping stockbrokers extremely busy.

In these days of market plunges, however, many investors aren't quite so anxious to talk about their stocks. Folks are still day trading, but many of them have given up the dream and gone back to "real" jobs. Stockbrokers are still busy, but these days a lot of that business entails reassuring clients.

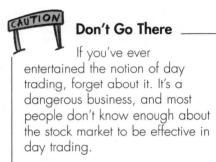

Don't Go There

If you've ever entertained the notion of day trading, forget about it. It's a dangerous business, and most people don't know enough about the stock market to be effective in day trading.

So just what is this thing called the stock market, and how does it work? Why does it rise dramatically one day, only to take a plunge the next?

The stock market is a generic term that encompasses the trading of securities. The security can be a bond or a stock, and it's traded on an exchange. There are three major exchanges in the United States.

Formed in 1792, the New York Stock Exchange (NYSE) is the largest organized stock exchange in this country. Companies must meet certain requirements in order to be listed on the NYSE, so not all stocks are traded there.

If you want to buy a stock, your broker will relay your wish, either by telephone or the Internet, to a member of his firm who's on the floor of the NYSE. The order will then go to another broker on the floor who specializes in trading the particular stock you want to buy, and he'll make the trade for you. You can actually visit the NYSE and watch all the action.

The National Association of Securities Dealers Automated Quotation System, or NASDAQ, on the other hand, trades exclusively with computers. The trading is not conducted in a central location like the NYSE, but from different locations, via computers.

A third stock exchange, the American Stock Exchange, or AMEX, was known before 1951 as the American Curb Exchange. That's because trading was conducted on the curb of Wall and Broad streets in New York City. The AMEX does not have as stringent requirements as the NYSE, which makes it attractive to many smaller companies.

The overall performance of the stock market is evaluated in different ways. The Dow Jones Industrial Average is one measure of the market, and the one we most often hear about.

The Dow Jones Industrial Average is a composite, or group, of 30 selected stocks with a daily average. If the average price of the stocks goes up, the Dow Jones Industrial Average goes up for that day. If the average price of those 30 stocks goes down, we say the Dow Jones is down. Trading depends on many factors, and the stock market can have major fluctuations in its averages. The 30 stocks change infrequently, decided upon by a group of members of the New Stock Exchange. Mergers between large firms (like Mobil and Exxon becoming Mobil Exxon) require the addition of a new company onto the Industrial Average. Cisco was added in early 2000.

> ### Go Figure
>
> When the stock market experiences an upward trend, we call it a bull market. When the trend is continuously downward, it's a bear market.

Knowing What and When to Buy

Stocks represent ownership, or equity, in a public corporation. When you buy the stock of a particular company, you're actually buying a tiny piece of the business. If the company prospers, you as a stockholder share in its profits (frequently in the form of dividends) and benefit from any rise in the market value of its stock. Conversely, if the company runs into problems, the value of your investment could decline.

Because their prices tend to fluctuate suddenly and sometimes sharply, stocks are considered more risky than bonds or cash investments. Over time, however, stocks have offered the highest returns of the three asset classes—as well as the best hedge against inflation.

So how do you know what stocks to buy, and when you should buy them?

Unless you're a real daredevil with lots of money to play around with, it's a good idea to invest your money in industries and companies that are stable, with good earning histories. Sure, you might be tempted to buy a few stocks in a sexy, new firm that's just starting up, or sink some of your money in a hot, new growth industry, and that's fine. The majority of your money, however, should go to buy stock that is tried and true.

There may be opportunity for increased profits in more risky stocks, but you should look for those that have reasonable price-to-earnings ratios. Price-to-earnings (P/E) ratios determine how the market is pricing a company's stock, and can help you to get an idea of the strength of a company.

Some investors target growth industries and only buy stock from companies within those industries.

> ### Don't Go There _____
>
> Don't be persuaded to jump on the bandwagon and invest all, or most of your money in one area—technology stocks come to mind. It's never a good idea to put all your eggs into one basket, regardless of how good the basket looks at the time.

Some examples of growth industries at the present time include the following:

- Home healthcare services
- Computer and data processing services
- Residential care
- Water supply and sanitary services
- Management and public relations

While it's fine to invest some of your money in companies in these industries, it's not a good idea to rely only on growth industries.

There is risk involved whenever you buy stock, but some stock involves less risk than others. The risk of the stock you own going up and down in value because the entire stock market goes up and down is called systematic risk. Chances are, if the entire stock market drops by 10 percent, the stocks you own will decrease in value, as well. And the same is true if the overall market value increases. You can minimize the effects of systematic risk by investing in other forms of securities, such as bonds.

Unsystematic risk is that which affects only a particular business or industry. The good news is that diversifying your portfolio can minimize unsystematic risk. That means that you have a variety of investments in different types of companies and industries. If one sector of the stock market experiences a major downturn, you'll still have stocks in other areas to offset your losses.

So when you're looking for companies in which to invest, make sure you mix them up. Your portfolio should include a mixture of some of the many kinds of stock. Blue-chip stock, for instance, is that of the tried and true companies such as IBM and General Motors. Companies experiencing unusual growth issue growth stocks. Emerging market stocks are those in new markets, in the United States and around the world.

You can find out a lot about companies in whose stock you're interested by checking out their financial statements in their annual reports. You also should look at some of the company's ratios, including price to earnings (P/E), earnings per share (EPS), return on investment (ROI), and return on equity (ROE). Pay special attention to a company's profitability and how much debt it has.

Investors have been trying since investing began to time when they buy, trade, and sell stock. Even experienced investors, however, get hung up when they try to time the market. Ideally, you want to buy stock when the price is low, and sell it when the price is high.

Realistically, however, you should buy when you (and your financial advisor, if you have one) feel the time is right. Trying to time the market might be interesting, but it rarely pays off. The best time to buy stock is after you've explored your options, researched the companies, and decided that the stock is right for you.

Knowing When to Sell Stock

Anyone who's got money in the stock market these days has been through some trying times lately. After the longest period ever of sustained gains, the market is behaving as moodily as a teenaged girl with no date for the dance.

It's tempting, at times like these, to unload your stocks and put your money back into your savings account. You shouldn't, however, be in a hurry to sell stock that you feel is not performing as well as it should. Give it some time to see if it's going to bounce back. If the entire market is in a slump, chances are that your stocks will be slumping along with it.

The one piece of advice a financial advisor will give when the market dips is to not panic. In some ways, investors are like poker players. Even when the game isn't going the way they'd like it to, they've got to sit tight, stay cool, and hang on to their cards (or stocks).

> **Go Figure**
>
> Trading stock occurs when you execute a buy or sell order, either with a broker or online, and the broker sends a message to the New York Stock Exchange for execution of the trade.

That's not to say, however, that there is never a reason to sell stocks. If you have stocks that have increased in value, and you want or need money for a good reason, then selling the stock is a reasonable thing to do.

If the stock you own turns out to be a big loser, it also makes sense to get rid of it. Be sure, though, that the stock really is bad, not just stock that's not doing well at the moment. There are investor services that can tell you how your stocks are doing, and why, or you can check out a periodical such as *Investors Business Daily*. Two investor services you can access on the Internet are Moody's Investor Service at www.moodys.com, and the Value Line's Investment Survey at www.valueline.com.

If you think the price of your stock is as high as it's going to go, it's a good idea to sell it before the price begins to drop. Predicting if your stock has hit its peak requires that you conduct fundamental analysis. Fundamental analysis is a system that evaluates a company's overall condition, based on various criteria that measure the health of the company.

You shouldn't sell stock simply because you're bored and want something that's more exciting. Nor should you sell because you're nervous about the overall condition of the stock market. Unless you're only months away from retirement and are going to need the money you have invested, hang in there, and trust that better days are ahead.

If you do sell stock, you'll need to consider the capital gains or losses that you may incur. Naturally, we all hope to sell our stock for more than we paid for it. If you hold an investment for less than one year, however, you may pay big taxes on your profits. Gains or losses from an investment of less than one year are considered short term. Short-term gains and losses are netted against each other, and short-term gains are taxed at your regular tax rate. If you're in the 28-percent tax bracket, you'll have to pay 28 percent on your gains. As you can see, short-term gains are expensive.

If you hold an investment for more than a year, the gain or loss is considered long-term. Long-term gains and losses are netted against each other, too, but the tax on them isn't quite as hefty as with short-term gains. If you're in a 15 percent tax bracket, net long-term capital gains are taxed at 10 percent. If you're in the 28 percent or greater bracket, your capital gains are taxed at 20 percent. This tax advantage makes it desirable to hold assets for more than a year, particularly if you're in a higher tax bracket.

The Bond Market

Just so you don't think that stocks are the only game in town, let's have a quick look at the bond market.

Bonds are the most common lending instruments traded on a securities market. A lending instrument is when you loan your money with the understanding that you'll get it back—with interest—after a specified time. The bond issuer promises to pay the investor a specific amount of interest for a period of time, and to repay the principal at maturity.

If a company issues a $10,000 bond that will pay 6.5 percent interest and is due on June 15, 2004, and you invest in that bond, what you're actually doing is lending the company $10,000 until June 15, 2004. Meanwhile, the company has promised to pay you 6.5 percent, or $650 each year, on your $10,000.

An important characteristic of bonds to keep in mind is that if the interest rate drops, the value of your bond increases. If the interest rate rises, the value of your bond drops.

How Are Bonds Different?

Bonds are basically different than stocks because they're lending investments rather than owning investments. If bonds are purchased prudently from secure firms or municipalities, bonds that are held to maturity are far less risky than owning a stock.

Go Figure
When the value of bond increases, it's called a premium bond. When the value decreases, it's called a discounted bond.

They're also different in that, while stocks represent ownership in a company, bonds are issued by the U.S. Treasury, U.S. government agencies, corporations, and state or local governments.

You normally can sell stock anytime you want. If you buy bonds, however, you might have to wait until the maturity date if you don't want to risk losing money.

Not all bonds are created equal. Government bonds are considered to be safer than corporate bonds because they're backed by government guarantee. Corporate bonds, on the other hand, are issued by corporations and traditionally pay more interest than government bonds.

High-yield bonds, also known as junk bonds, are issued primarily by corporations, and considered to be riskier than standard bonds, but they pay more. Municipal bonds are those issued by state, local, or county governments; hospitals; and colleges. The interest you earn on these types of bonds is not subject to federal income tax. Depending on where you live, it may not be subject to state or local taxes, either.

If your portfolio contains only stocks, you should consider buying some bonds for the purpose of diversification. Bond returns tend to fluctuate less sharply than stock returns, and bonds could help to reduce your portfolio's overall volatility.

Are Bonds Safer?

Bonds usually are safer investments than stocks. You should know, however, that there have been companies that were unable to repay their bonds at maturity. That's called credit risk, and it does happen. Some other risks associated with bonds are …

- If you need your money back before the agreed-upon time period, you may have to sell the bond for less than you paid for it.

- The market value of your bonds could decline due to rising interest rates. Remember that, in general, bond prices fall when interest rates rise—and rise when interest rates fall.

- During periods of falling interest rates, corporate and municipal bond issuers may prepay, or call, their loans before maturity in order to reissue the loans at a lower rate. You, as the lender, must then reinvest this prepaid principal sooner than you had anticipated—and possibly at a lower interest rate. This is known as call risk.

- You could lose money if a bond issuer defaults—that is, fails to make timely payments of principal and interest. That's called credit risk, and it also could occur if a bond's credit rating is reduced.

- The interest income you earn from a bond investment remains the same over the life of the bond, but the value of that income could be eroded by inflation. That's inflation risk.

- The credit quality or market value of your bonds could suffer in response to an event such as a merger, leveraged buyout, or other corporate restructuring. This is known as event risk.

Having said all that, it's hard to imagine that bonds are considered a safer investment than stocks, but it's true. Remember that government bonds are backed by a U.S. government guarantee, which makes them particularly safe. And some bonds issued by states and municipalities are usually tax free, which makes them particularly attractive to many investors.

When you begin to invest in individual bonds, decide which risk is greatest to you, and work with your financial advisor to find the best choice for your objectives.

Mutual Funds

Mutual funds, which pool your money with that of many other investors to buy stocks, bonds, and other securities, often take a back seat to stocks and bonds when folks start thinking about investing.

They happen, however, to be a very important investment vehicle. Mutual funds can be compared to pies. If the value of the mutual fund goes down, the pie—including your piece of it—gets smaller. If the value increases, the pie gets bigger. Some benefits of mutual funds are:

- **Diversification.** Some mutual funds contain just a handful of securities, while others can have thousands of separate issues. This broad exposure helps reduce risk, although it doesn't completely eliminate it.

- **Professional management.** An experienced manager makes sure the fund's investments remain consistent with its investment objective, whether that's to track a market index, or use extensive research and market forecasts to actively select securities.

- **Liquidity.** You can sell your mutual funds whenever you want. It's easy, and there is no penalty for early withdrawal (although there may be a redemption fee, depending on the fund). A redemption fee is charged by the mutual fund company to reimburse it for the internal fee paid to your advisor or broker when you purchased the mutual fund. This can be expensive, but usually declines as the years progress.

- **Convenience.** Most mutual funds allow you to buy and sell shares, change distribution options, and obtain information by telephone, by mail, or online.

We love mutual funds, and think they're great investments. They are not, however, perfect. Some disadvantages include:

- **No guarantees.** Your stock or bond fund investment, unlike a bank deposit, could fall in value. And, while a money market fund seeks a stable share price, its yield fluctuates, unlike a certificate of deposit. In addition, mutual funds are not insured or guaranteed by an agency of the U.S. government. Investors tell me they like their mutual fund better than stocks when they are invested in a stock mutual fund. They do own stock!

◆ **Potentially high costs.** Some mutual funds carry steep sales commissions, redemption fees, and operating expenses.

◆ **Diversification.** Diversification is good, but if you're too spread out, you limit your chances of scoring big if a single security goes through the roof.

There are four categories of mutual funds:

◆ **Money market funds** are those in which the value of your original investment doesn't change. They are similar to savings accounts, but with higher yields and some other advantages, including check writing privileges.

Money Morsel

If you're investing in mutual funds, be sure to coordinate the securities they include with what you already have in your retirement accounts. You don't want to lean too much in any one direction, so make sure you have a good balance.

◆ **Bond funds** are mutual funds that invest in bonds.

◆ **Stock funds** are mutual funds that invest in stocks.

◆ **Balanced funds** are funds that invest almost equally in stocks and bonds.

Mutual funds are a good investment tool for investors who don't want to be involved in the investment process, or who can't afford to hire a money manager.

IRAs, Roth IRAs, and SEP IRAs

An individual retirement account, or IRA, is a tax-deferred account, which means you don't pay any taxes on it until you withdraw from the fund. Your investment earnings compound tax-free for as long as they're invested. This enables your account to grow faster than it would if the money was subject to annual taxes on income and capital gains.

In some cases, your contribution to an IRA is also tax deductible. This applies if you're not an active participant in an employer-sponsored plan—such as a 401(k)—or if your modified adjusted gross income is below a certain threshold. For 2001, the threshold is $33,000 for single filers, and $53,000 for joint filers. Partial deductions are allowed on incomes up to $43,000 for single filers and $63,000 for joint filers (in 2001). These figures are going up each year until 2008.

Money Morsel

If your contributions to a traditional IRA aren't tax deductible, you should consider looking around for another type of investment, possibly a Roth IRA.

IRAs used to be the darling of investment vehicles. Folks couldn't get enough of them until the late 1980s, when lawmakers ruined the fun by imposing all kinds of restrictions on IRAs.

Still, many people contribute to IRAs as a means of retirement savings. Anyone under age 70½ who has earned income from wages or a salary may contribute to a traditional IRA. You may make annual contributions of up to $2,000, or 100 percent of your earned income, whichever is less. These limits will increase in stages until you're able to contribute $5,000 per year in 2008 and after.

A married couple with only one spouse working outside the home may currently contribute a total of $4,000 into separate IRAs, provided the "wage-earning spouse" has at least $4,000 in earned income. Neither spouse's IRA may receive more than $2,000 annually.

Contributions for a given year must be made no later than the tax-filing deadline for that tax year. For example, you may make your 2001 contribution any time between January 1, 2001, and April 15, 2002.

A problem with IRAs is that, if you withdraw money before you turn 59½, you have to pay income tax on the money, plus a 10 percent penalty tax. There are certain conditions that allow you to withdraw money from your IRA without penalty, such as if you need it to pay for medical expenses, you become disabled, or you purchase your first house.

While your money remains tax free for as long as it remains in the IRA account, your assets aren't shielded from taxes forever. When you withdraw money, you'll have to pay ordinary income tax on your investment earnings. The long period of tax deferral that occurs while your money is invested, however, makes the taxes you have to pay when you withdraw your money easier to take.

In addition, people who are 50 years or older will be permitted, beginning in 2002, to make special "catch-up" contributions to their IRAs. If you're over 50, you'll be able to toss in $500 more until 2006, when the amount jumps to $1,000 more.

Roth IRAs

Roth IRAs are fairly new—and they're interesting investment tools. They're exciting for investors because, if held for the required time period, the funds you take out are tax-free. Funds you put in a Roth IRA are not tax deductible, but the withdrawals are tax-exempt, and you don't have to wait until you're 59½ to get them, nor do you have to begin taking the money from the Roth IRA at 70½.

In addition to being beneficial during retirement, Roth IRA income is a boon to those who might inherit it. One of the biggest drawbacks to traditional IRAs, annuities, and qualified retirement plans is that at death, the accumulated deferred income tax is taxable to the beneficiary.

Until recently, a nonspouse beneficiary had to take a large tax liability within five years of receiving the money. If you inherited $200,000 from your father's IRA, for instance, you could pay taxes on the entire amount during the year your dad died, or you could pay tax on approximately $40,000 every year afterward for five years.

The tax law changed in 2001, however, and now, if there is a proper beneficiary designation, the deferral can continue for the lifetime of the beneficiary, based on life expectancy.

The beneficiary will need to take minimum distributions over his lifetime, but he can control the amount he receives, along with the accompanying taxes.

A single person with an adjusted gross income of not more than $100,000, or a married couple that files jointly and has an income of $150,000 or less, can each contribute up to $2,000 of earned income each year to a Roth IRA.

You also can contribute up to $2,000 to a Roth IRA of a nonworking spouse (or a spouse with low earnings), but total contributions to an individual's traditional and Roth IRAs must not exceed $2,000 in any tax year. As with traditional IRAs, however, your allowed contribution to a Roth IRA will increase to $5,000 a year by 2008.

Because your contributions to a Roth IRA are after-tax dollars, you can withdraw your contributions at any time, without paying any taxes or penalties. If you withdraw *earnings* from an account that is less than 5 years old, however, you may pay ordinary income tax, plus an additional penalty tax of 10 percent.

As with a traditional IRA, there are exceptions to the rule, and instances in which you would not be penalized for withdrawing from an account that's less than five years old.

As stated above, one of the major benefits of a Roth IRA is that you are not required to take minimum distributions after age 70½. If you do not need income from your Roth IRA, you can let your money continue to grow tax-free. Your beneficiary, however, must take required minimum distributions.

You can convert your traditional IRA to a Roth IRA if you file a single or joint tax return reporting an adjusted gross income of $100,000 or less for the tax year of the conversion. Keep in mind, however, that you'll owe taxes (but no penalty) on the conversion.

SEP IRAs

A Simplified Employee Pension—Individual Retirement Account (SEP-IRA) is a plan that allows owners of small businesses and people who are self-employed to set aside money for retirement through tax-deferred investment accounts. A SEP-IRA is funded solely by employer contributions (which are tax-deductible as a business expense). The SEP-IRA really is an employer-sponsored plan, but we included it in this section in order to keep it with the other IRA information.

The owner of a small business can contribute up to $30,000, or 15 percent of each employee's compensation to the employee's SEP-IRA account. The amount of the contribution can vary from year to year, and a contribution is not necessary every year. It's not difficult to set up a SEP-IRA, but there are rules and restrictions that apply.

Employees cannot contribute to a SEP-IRA themselves, but they're immediately vested once an account has been opened in their name, and can withdraw their employer's contributions at any time. A penalty may apply if funds are taken prematurely.

If you're self-employed, a SEP-IRA can be a real bonus. Under the Economic Growth and Tax Relief Reconciliation Act of 2001, you can base your annual contribution on income up to $200,000.

As you can see, investment opportunities are many, but you've got to do your homework in order to make good decisions about where to put your money.

The Least You Need to Know

- ◆ The stock market is a generic term that encompasses the trading of securities.
- ◆ It's important to be able to identify good companies from which to buy stock, and to know when it's time to sell your stock.
- ◆ Stocks are an owning investment, while bonds are a loaning investment.
- ◆ Bonds are generally considered to be a safer investment than stocks.
- ◆ Mutual funds are popular investments that pool your money with that of many others to buy a variety of securities.
- ◆ IRAs offer tax advantages and are a blessing for people who don't have employer-sponsored retirement accounts.

Chapter 22

Investing Lump Sums

In This Chapter

- ◆ Understanding the challenges of investing lump sums
- ◆ Striking a balance with your income tax
- ◆ Putting severance pay to work for you
- ◆ Stock options, settlements, and inheritances
- ◆ Using dollar-cost averaging to reduce risk and increase your wealth
- ◆ Knowing enough to ask for advice
- ◆ What to do with retirement lump sums?

Saving and investing money normally is done in a systematic manner, a little bit at a time. You contribute some of every paycheck to your 401(k). A bit more goes into your daughter's college fund. Still another piece goes toward your emergency fund. Little by little, you build up the accounts.

There's a good chance, however, that at one point of your life or another, you'll receive a significant amount of money—all at once. It could be an inheritance, a tax refund, a bonus, or severance pay. However you get it, a lump sum of money can be a challenge.

What do you do with it? You could take your family to Disney World, or you and your spouse to a romantic, secluded island. You could do that remodeling you've been putting off, or finally buy yourself that little boat you've always wanted.

Or you could invest the money. Granted, that doesn't sound like nearly as much fun as the other options, but it's a smart move.

The very best thing you can do with a lump sum, regardless of where it comes from, is to pay off high-interest debt (that means credit cards). Investing money at 10 percent is great, but it doesn't make sense to do that if you're paying 18 percent on $10,000 worth of credit card debt. Pay that first, and then consider your options.

Tax Refunds

While it seems that most of us middle-aged folks end up owing taxes in April instead of looking forward to refunds, there may be circumstances under which you'll receive a tax refund.

If you're getting substantial tax refunds, it's because you're having too much withheld from your paycheck. You may be able to cut your withholding rate and increase your take-home pay, allowing you to invest the money throughout the year.

If you got a tax refund this year of $3,600, and you're paid every two weeks, you received $138 less per pay period than you should have. That's money you could have invested in an interest-bearing account, or used to help out with the bills.

Having said all that, if you do get a tax refund, you'll need to decide what to do with it.

Go Figure
George W. saw to it that we all got a lump sum recently in the form of immediate tax relief. Most Americans who pay federal income tax received between $300 and $600 in 2001, courtesy of the U.S. government.

The best thing, obviously, if you don't have credit card or other high-interest debt, is to invest the money. You could add it to a college fund, or buy some stock in what you hope will be the next Microsoft. Saving is better than spending, although the government and retailers count on us spending those tax refund checks as a means of jump-starting the economy.

If you just can't sink the entire check into savings, let's at least reach a compromise. Invest part of it, then spend the rest. And have fun.

Severance Pay

We spent a good bit of Part 4, "Life Changes," discussing job layoffs and downsizing, so we won't get into it here in much detail. Just remember that no one is ever really safe from the possibility of losing his or her job. And, keep in mind that losing a job can be extremely difficult, both financially and emotionally.

If your employer does hand you a pink slip; however, hope and pray that there's a check along with it. Severance pay can ease the pain of losing a job because it gives you some financial security until you can find other employment.

Being suddenly without a paycheck is a scary situation. Having some money, up front, to tide you over can help make life a lot less scary.

Money Morsel

If your company doesn't offer you any severance pay, ask for some. You've already been fired, what can it hurt? Some employers would offer something in hopes of eliminating any possibility of a lawsuit.

Many companies offer a severance package of a week's pay for each year of service, plus unused vacation, sick, and personal time. It's often presented as a lump sum.

If you receive a severance package, think carefully about what you'll do with it. If you're not confident that you'll soon find another job, and you don't have much emergency money put aside, chances are you'll need to dig into your severance in order to keep paying your bills. Unemployment compensation helps, but it doesn't pay you the full amount that you had been earning. If you've got a lot of bills or other expenses, keep your severance pay accessible in case you need it.

To keep the money available, you can open a designated savings account at the bank. Don't add the money to an existing account; it's better to keep it separate. Or you could open a money market fund with a mutual fund company. Although the rate on money market funds has been low recently, they do have some decent earning potential, certainly higher than your savings account and they keep your money accessible.

If you find, however, that between your unemployment pay and other sources of income, you don't need the severance money, you've got a nice opportunity. You probably should still keep the money available until you begin a new job and resume getting a paycheck. Once you're back at work, however, you could use the severance pay to wipe out a car bill, reduce your mortgage, or have the roof fixed. Once you've done those things, invest any money left over in a college or retirement fund.

Bonuses

Bonuses can be a once-in-a-career bonanza, or an annual event for employees. One-time bonuses aren't too common, but, if you get a big check (or even not-so-big) that's a once in a lifetime situation, enjoy it. And don't forget to follow the recommendations noted throughout this chapter.

Usually, employees who receive bonuses get them every year as a supplement to their compensation (pay). A bonus might be based on the performance of the employee, the company, or a combination. Regardless of how the bonus is determined, it normally arrives every year, usually around the same time.

Some employers pay out bonuses during the holiday season, hoping to generate good cheer and employee loyalty. Bonuses can be based on a percentage of pay, or represent a fixed pay period (i.e., two weeks' pay), so that the funds received by the employees are proportional to their salary.

Some companies offer bonuses only at the corporate level, and base them on whether or not the firm and its employees have reached pre-determined goals.

If you're anticipating an annual bonus, remember that it's only anticipated until you've actually got it. Don't ever spend money before you have it, anticipating being able to pay it back. Employers are not obligated to give bonuses, and you could be sorely disappointed—not to mention financially strapped—if you spend a bonus that never comes.

If you do get a bonus, and you don't have high-interest debt to pay, consider putting it in your emergency fund. If you don't have an emergency fund, use the money to get one started. Everyone should have such a fund as a buffer in case of job loss, disability, divorce, or so forth.

Don't Go There

It's always tempting to spend a lump sum outright, especially one that you weren't expecting to have. Resist the temptation, however, unless it's on something you really need. Once the money is gone, it's gone.

Go Figure

Financial planners estimate that 55 percent of Americans don't have an emergency fund.

Many people, even those in their 40s and 50s, still live pretty much from paycheck to paycheck, with little money left over after meeting all the expenses. Even a major car repair can send them into debt, and a period of unemployment due to illness or disability can be devastating. If you don't have dental coverage and have ever needed a couple of crowns or a root canal, you know how expensive taking care of your teeth can be.

Most experts recommend that you have an emergency fund of at least three months' income, and preferably up to six months' income. A bonus would be a great way to supplement your emergency fund, or to get one started if you haven't already. If you've already got a sufficient emergency fund established, bonus money can be saved or invested.

Just as a point, many people, us included, use the words "save" and "invest" interchangeably. While saving money in a bank account technically is investing it, there's really a difference between saving and investing.

Saving money is storing it safely away (not under your mattress, please!) for short-term needs, or for a specific purpose such as your daughter's wedding or your parent's fiftieth wedding anniversary party. Investing, on the other hand, is a longer-term process that involves risk.

A bonus is, indeed, just that. It's extra money, and often unplanned. Using it wisely to start or supplement an emergency fund is a great investment in your future.

Stock Options

Stock options used to be primarily given to the big shots within a company, but more and more businesses these days are offering stock options to nonmanagement types as a means of attracting, retaining, rewarding, or providing incentive to employees.

An employee stock option allows you to buy shares of stock in the company for which you work at a specified price, and over a period of time. Normally, you're required to hold the stock for a certain amount of time.

Let's say you've landed a job with Mapquest, the Internet site that gives you directions from one location to another and provides other information and services. You're offered Mapquest stock at $1 a share until August 2002. When August comes, the stock is valued at $25 a share. If you exercise your stock option, the difference between the $1 and $25, less taxes, is yours.

Be aware, however, that the alternative can happen. Some friends own option shares of K-Mart at $22 per share, set to expire in August 2002. Unless K-Mart is doing significantly better by next year, these friends will be stuck with bad stock. K-Mart stock is currently valued at about $9.50 per share—making that option one you don't want to exercise.

You normally are required to keep the stock options for a specified holding period. If the value of the stock increases during that holding period, you should purchase the options shares and take the gain.

The gain may be considered current income, or capital gain income, depending on whether you held the option shares for more than a year.

Stock options can be tricky, and it's a good idea to get some advice from a financial consultant if your options are significant. If you get a lump sum when you exercise your stock options, an advisor can tell you how to best reinvest the money.

Settlements

If you find yourself in possession of a lump sum of money due to settlement on a lawsuit or a contract, your first order of business should be to evaluate your needs.

Many people have settled lawsuits from which they received compensation for injury that occurred in an accident. Thrilled to have the money, they go out and buy a new car or some other expensive item or items. Too late, they realize that they don't have enough money to cover ongoing, uninsured medical expenses.

Go Figure

Research shows that people who make at least $15,000 a year generally are happier than those who make less than that. It also reveals, however, that those who make $75,000 or more a year are no happier than those who make $25,000. So if you've got a lump sum heading your way, enjoy it, but don't expect it to solve all your problems and make you a happy person if you aren't happy already.

Lawyers for the defendant in a settlement case sometimes will request that a settlement be paid in monthly payouts (via an annuity) to the claimants in a lawsuit. The annuity settlement provides a guaranteed income for the injured party for a set period of time, or perhaps even for life. This eliminates the need for the claimants to handle a lot of money all at once.

But more frequently, settlements, lottery winnings, and so forth are awarded in lump sums. This requires the receivers to find an investment manager, and plan an asset allocation to provide income and assure there will be money for future needs.

Dealing with a lump sum of money is difficult. You need to make a lot of decisions, and you'll probably need a lot of help.

If you get a lump sum of money, be sure to allocate your assets. Decide how much you want to spend on stocks, or bonds, or whatever. Then, look into getting the most from your money by *dollar cost averaging* your investments.

Huh? Dollar cost averaging means that you invest equal amounts of money at regular intervals—usually each month.

Adding It Up

Dollar cost averaging is based on the belief that the market, or a particular stock, will rise in price over the long term, and that it's neither worthwhile, nor possible, to identify intermediate highs and lows.

Because you're always investing the same amount, you can buy more investments when the price is low, and fewer shares when the price is high. As a result, the average dollar amount you pay per share is always lower than the average market price per share during the time you're investing.

And, because your investments are made over a period of time, you can plan to buy big when the price is low, and slow down your spending when the price is high. As a result, the average market price per investment during the time you are investing should be more constant than if you go in all at one time.

Dollar-cost averaging is an easy, controlled way to build a significant investment portfolio. If you get a lump sum of money, and you're not a seasoned investor, it may be the way for you to go. Dollar-cost averaging has proven to reduce risk and to help build investments over time.

Inheritances

Sooner or later, we all experience the loss of a loved one. And, while many people think it would be simply fabulous to inherit a million dollars from some long-lost aunt who they didn't know or love, the truth is, receiving an inheritance is normally a very bittersweet experience.

Sure, who couldn't use $25,000, or $100,000, or half a million, or five million dollars? When it comes at the cost of losing a parent, or a spouse, or a best friend, however, the money is not—at least for a while—a happy addition to your life.

Most people desire to leave something behind for their children and/or grandchildren. Perhaps it's a natural tendency to want to continue to provide for those you love—even after death. That's why clients spend hours with lawyers and financial planners, working to keep as much of their estates as possible in the hands of their families, and out of the hands of the government.

If you receive an inheritance, you'll need to realize that it's very different from a bonus, for instance. An inheritance is a gift. It's not earned, in any way. This gift, hopefully, can provide some substantial security in your life.

> **Go Figure**
>
> Fully 20 percent of people 50 years or older who were surveyed said that an inheritance—or a lack of one—had caused hard feelings among members of their families.

We strongly recommend that you invest the entire inheritance, then use the income that the funds generate for the extras in life. Financial advisors call this the "not using principal" strategy. You invest the principal, and use the income you get from it for trips, toward a car, a bigger home, or whatever.

If you inherit $100,000, and invest it so you're getting a five percent return, you'll have $5,000 more per year than you did before you got the inheritance. If you receive more, your additional income will be more.

If you spend the money you get as inheritance, it's gone. Many people have inherited $100,000 or $200,000 and, thinking they were wealthy because it was more money than they ever had before, went on wild shopping sprees that quickly left them broke.

If you get a large sum of money, be sure to contact a financial advisor. You should never attempt to invest large sums on your own if you're inexperienced.

Retirement Lump Sum Payouts

Whether you are changing jobs or are lucky enough to retire early, there will be several opportunities during your lifetime when you are presented with making decisions concerning a lump sum retirement payout. This might occur when you change jobs, and hopefully, you'll roll the money over into an IRA or into your new employer's 401(k) plan at work. Deciding whether to open an IRA or roll the funds into your new employer's 401(k) was previously discussed in Chapter 20, "Investing at Work."

This roll-over will continue the tax deferred growth of the funds, as well as guaranteeing you won't have a penalty and income tax liability on the withdrawal until you actually retire.

So when we talk about lump sum payouts, we're actually talking about the requirement or ability to take all your retirement funds from your employer's plan when you actually retire. Although this might be a little premature for a discussion with people in their 40s and 50s, many people have the goal to retire at age 55. Maybe you're one of the lucky ones who can do this.

Of course, you don't want to take all the funds out of a retirement plan creating a horrendous tax liability. If you are required to or you want to take out the funds from the retirement plan, roll-over all the funds into an IRA held at your local bank or with a brokerage firm, then you can start to withdraw the funds needed to retire.

The rollover must be made from the company's plan directly to the new account. If you don't have a "trustee to trustee" transfer, your employer is required to withhold 20 percent in taxes. This money is held by the IRS until you file your return in April and is considered a distribution. Ouch! The withholding and withdrawals can easily be avoided by rolling over the funds directly to the new investment firm.

Once you've rolled the funds into a new account, you can set up monthly withdrawals or keep it building until you are ready to begin distributions at 59½ or later. The withdrawals depend on whether you have enough money on which to live without using the retirement funds.

When your retirement account was managed within your employer's plan, your employer was watching the funds and making certain the fund choices were good. Once you leave their plan, the choices are yours and the problems begin.

First, are you going to handle investing the money yourself within a family of funds, a brokerage account, or are you going to find a financial advisor who will guide you through the process. It's frustrating to see persons with $230,000 in retirement money hook up with a commission financial adviser who gets paid 5 percent of the value of the retirement account (that's over $10,000) just to guide you into investing your funds within an annuity or mutual fund family.

So as we'll discuss in the next chapter, look for a financial adviser who gets paid on an hourly basis to help you find a good place to invest your money.

There are pros and cons to investing in an annuity, but qualified retirement money should not go into an IRA annuity. IRAs are already sheltered from tax liability until withdrawn (the funds are sheltered from tax analogous to being sheltered by an umbrella). Annuities are also sheltered, but it's like putting an umbrella over an umbrella and as you can only imagine, the internal fees of the IRA annuity are higher than just a mutual fund IRA.

An annuity is a contract between an insurance company and an individual that will provide periodic payments to the individual, or to a designated beneficiary, in return for an investment. Usually, the annuity agrees to provide payments to the purchaser (known as the annuitant) beginning at some future date. An IRA annuity is somewhat different because it must follow the IRA payout rules rather than the annuity rules. So if you have a lump sum payout, set up an IRA not an IRA annuity.

We've all been taught since we've been kids that you can't withdraw from an IRA until you are 59½. Well, as usual, the IRA has exceptions to their rules. So if you retire at 55, and want to use your retirement funds, you can withdraw money from an IRA within a very limited set of rules. The IRS requires that you take a fixed periodic payment for at least 5 years or until you are 59½, whichever comes later.

That sounds like Greek, so we'll give you some examples to clarify the rules. This is a very obscure and little known rule and it's important for people who are forced to retire early or want to retire early. No one wants to pay more tax than they have to and no one wants to pay a 10 percent penalty on retirement money withdrawn before they are 59½.

If you retire at 57 and set up a monthly payout for five years, you won't be able to change your payout until after age 62 since you need to take the fixed payment for 5 years. But if you retire at 52, you'll need to continue the fixed payment for 7½ years until your 59½ to guarantee you aren't penalized for the withdrawals. Of course, the funds are taxed, but not penalized.

The monthly payout is calculated based on your life expectancy, similar to a minimum required distribution, so visit with a CPA before you use this interesting option.

Also remember when you rollover funds, that the total can be divided into separate accounts and the funds used differently. If you want to set up fixed payments, know they cannot be changed without creating a tax nightmare. Not once during the entire time period can you change the payout, so if you need more money, you'll be penalized for all the years you've been taking withdrawals. Thus, it's best to have another fund, either with other retirement money or preferably with nonretirement money from which to purchase a car or other needs.

The following are things to remember with a lump sum payout:

◆ Roll-over, don't withdraw your lump sum payout to prevent possible penalties, and certainly income taxation on the funds.

◆ Use a "trustee to trustee" transfer of funds to prevent income tax withholding. This continues deferral on the funds until withdrawn.

◆ Withdrawals before age 59½ can be accomplished without a 10 percent penalty, but within strict guidelines.

◆ Review whether to stay with the same investment firm as your employer is using, or look for a fee only financial advisor to guide you where to move your money.

◆ The total retirement fund can be rolled into various retirement accounts, to be used differently.

◆ An IRA annuity has greater internal costs than just an IRA or just annuity.

The Least You Need to Know

◆ Knowing how to invest lump sums can be challenging, even to experienced investors.

◆ The best thing to do with a lump sum of money, if you have high-interest debt, is to use the money to get rid of the debt.

◆ If you're getting big tax refunds, you're having too much withheld from your paycheck, and you should adjust your withholdings.

◆ Severance pay that's not needed for regular expenses is a perfect means for starting or adding to an emergency fund.

◆ Never depend on a bonus or spend it in advance, even if you've always received it in the past.

◆ Understanding stock options can be challenging, but they sometimes can result in significant financial gain.

◆ Settlements, inheritances, and other lump sums can be invested using a dollar-cost averaging method, which reduces risk.

Chapter 23

Finding a Good Financial Advisor

In This Chapter

- ◆ Making your money work for you
- ◆ Understanding different types of advisors
- ◆ Knowing who to hire
- ◆ How financial advisors earn their money
- ◆ Watching out for bad apples

At this time of life, when we're looking ahead to retirement while perhaps still juggling college costs, mortgage payments, and other major expenses, our financial situations can get a little complicated.

We may be looking to get more heavily involved in the stock market, or to get rid of some major debt. Basically, we're all wondering how to make whatever money we have work the hardest for us that it possibly can.

You've read a lot of information in previous chapters of this book about stretching your dollars, coping with major expenses, and investing, both in and out of work. All that information, however, can sometimes seem extremely complicated and overwhelming.

If that's the case, it may be time to consider hiring a financial advisor, which is the focus of this chapter.

Why You Should Have an Advisor

Finances are important, to be sure, and when they're your finances, it's even more important that you handle them wisely.

If you have a major financial setback when you're in your 20s, it's just that—a setback. Let's say that some 22-year-old gets out of college and lands himself a great, high-paying job. Fueled by the enthusiasm and shortsightedness that often accompanies youth, he goes out and buys a great house. Four bedrooms, oversized garage, Jacuzzi in the master bath ... you get the picture. He also buys himself a flashy little sports car and develops expensive tastes in wine and women.

He soon finds a woman who loves him—and his lifestyle—and they get married. They take a fabulous honeymoon to some tropical islands you and I never even heard of, and return to live happily ever after.

Six months later, however (you know what's coming, right?), our friend loses his job. He looks around and realizes that he's in trouble—serious trouble. There goes the house, the sports car, and the Cabernet. You can decide about the wife. He might even have to declare bankruptcy and start over.

The point, of course, is that at age 22 or 23, he has an opportunity to start over. At age 45, 50, or 55, a major setback turns into a financial crisis that may be impossible to overcome.

Don't Go There

There's a ton of information on the Internet about personal finances, investing, and so forth. Unless you're really financially savvy, however, don't depend on what you read on the Internet as your sole source of information. Some of the advice that's out there is good, and some is awful.

Most people have more assets at this stage of life than they did in their 20s and 30s. Knowing how to best manage those assets is very important, but not something with which most folks are really familiar.

The most important reason why you should have a good financial advisor, however, is to help you to prepare for retirement. No one wants to be a burden on his or her family in old age, and most of us hope to have enough money to really enjoy life.

Some people don't ever consult a financial advisor because they think they can manage their money on their own—and maybe they can. If you're like most of us, however, you probably can benefit from some professional help.

When you hire a financial advisor, it should not mean that you relinquish any and all responsibility for your money over to that person.

It's still your money, and it's vitally important that you stay on top of what's going on with your finances. A financial advisor is there to assist you—to help you get the most from your money. That doesn't mean that you don't need to be involved. Always read over the statements that you get, and feel free to ask any questions you have concerning your accounts. You and your financial advisor should work as a team to make you as financially successful as possible.

> **Don't Go There**
>
> Don't ever assume that you're sailing on smooth financial waters just because you've hired a financial advisor. Mistakes happen. If you don't keep an eye on your statements and take time to understand what's going on with your money, you risk missing those mistakes and losing some of your hard-earned savings.

If you agree that hiring a financial advisor probably makes sense for you, read on. There are various types of advisors, some of whom may be way more qualified than others.

Not All Financial Advisors Are Equal

When you start looking for a financial advisor, you're likely to come across categories such as the following:

- ◆ Financial consultants
- ◆ Financial planners
- ◆ Money managers
- ◆ Personal financial specialists

So who's a mid-lifer to hire? In order to choose the type of advisor who will be able to do the best job for you, it's important to understand what each of those categories of financial advisors entails. Let's have a look.

Financial Planners

Financial planners can be anyone who offers financial advice or services. Many people use the terms financial planner and financial advisor interchangeably.

A financial planner, as the term implies, will help you come up with a financial plan. And she may or may not implement the plan, depending on your agreement. Some people prefer to execute their financial plans on their own, while others like to work closely with an advisor.

If you hire a financial planner, make sure you're familiar with her credentials. Qualifications can vary widely within this category of financial advisor, with some advisors having far more expertise and experience than others. The first question you should ask is whether or not the financial advisor is certified.

Certified Financial Planners

A certified financial planner, or CFP, has earned the Certified Financial Planning credential, which is a national certification. This is accomplished by completing a home-study course and passing a cumulative, 10-hour exam.

In order to qualify for certification, a person must have worked for three years in a financial area, such as banking, planning, or investments.

Once certified, CFPs are charged with keeping up with what's happening within the financial industry, and must take 30 hours of continuing education courses every two years. They also must promise to adhere to a prescribed code of ethics.

Money Morsel

A certified financial planner (CFP) is, by any other name, still certified. CFPs might be called financial planners, financial consultants, or financial advisors. The important thing is that they're all certified.

Financial Consultants

A financial consultant provides an overview of financial information and options in order to help you choose the products that will best meet your financial needs.

He may, for instance, describe to you in detail the advantages and disadvantages of different kinds of IRAs, or how much money you'll need in order to invest in a particular fund. He generally will not produce a financial plan for you, only offer information and advice.

CPAs and Personal Finance Specialists

Many people have a financial advisor, and a separate certified public accountant (CPA). There's an increasing trend, however, for folks to depend on their CPAs for financial help and advice.

If you want to use your CPA as your financial advisor, that's fine. CPAs typically keep up-to-date on what's happening within the industry because they're responsible for knowing about laws and regulations that change all the time. And your CPA, especially if you've had the same one for a long time, is very familiar with your financial situation. Check though, to see if she has been designated by the American Institute of Certified Public

Accountants as a personal financial specialist (PFS). Your accountant certainly should be willing to share her credentials with her clients, or, you can check with the American Institute of Certified Public Accountants by calling 212-596-6200. The fax number is 212-596-6213, and you can access the institute online at www.aicpa.org.

In order to receive the PFS certification, a CPA must have three years of financial planning experience, and pass a six-hour test.

> **Money Morsel**
>
> Many people prefer to use the same person as both their CPA and financial advisor because it allows them to deal with only one person. And people tend to use the same accountants for long periods of time, which allows them to develop a relationship with their CPAs.

Insurance Agents

You might not tend to think of an insurance agent as a financial advisor, but some agents specialize in financial planning.

Those who do, may (although they're not required to) have a Chartered Life Underwriter (CLU) or a Charter Financial Consultant (ChFC) designation. Some may have both.

These are designations by the American College in Bryn Mawr, Pennsylvania. Agents must successfully complete a 10-course program in order to receive a CLU or ChFC designation, and must complete continuing education courses in order to remain certified.

Money Managers

Typically, people that have a lot of money are those who employ money managers. Money managers will, after reviewing your overall financial situation, handle your funds, make trades on your behalf, and buy and sell stocks and bonds for you.

They consider all aspects of your finances, including factors such as your risk tolerance and personal goals.

Finding an Advisor Who's Right for You

As you can see, there are many types of financial advisors. It's important to understand that not all are alike, and to review each one's qualifications carefully. So what type do you check out first? A CPA? Insurance agent? Financial consultant? Money manager?

Think carefully about what you want, and expect, a financial advisor to do. If you're into the big bucks and you want a professional who will get your money to where it needs to be, when it needs to be there, perhaps you should consider a money manager.

Money Morsel

We've all heard the stories about unscrupulous financial advisors who scam or steal money from clients. While that behavior is not limited to professionals in the financial field, it's worth your time to be aware that it does occur, and to keep a close watch on your investments and funds.

Don't Go There

Some financial advisors are far more conservative than others. If you're a very low-risk investor, don't match yourself with an advisor who can't see his way past anything but tech stocks. You and he definitely will not be a match made in heaven.

If you're fairly adept at handling your own finances, but would like someone around to answer questions and dispense advice from time to time, a CPA or financial consultant may be a wise choice.

Whatever category of advisor you choose from, your most important job is to make sure the person you consider has great qualifications. Talk to friends, relatives, and co-workers to find out who they use, and whether or not they're satisfied customers.

After you've identified some potential advisors, contact them and arrange for get-acquainted meetings. You don't need to, or even should, provide every detail concerning your finances during this meeting. Instead, you should be concentrating on getting a feeling for each person's general views and philosophies on investments, an overview of his qualifications, and a feeling for whether or not you'd be comfortable working with him.

Some questions you should ask your potential financial advisor are listed as follows:

- Are you certified? Granted, there are different sorts of accreditations, but at least you know that someone who's been certified has successfully completed course work and is likely to be on top of what's happening in the industry.

- How long have you been in business? As in every field, experience counts. Having been in finances for a period of time gives an advisor the opportunity to gain perspective and develop a sense of timing for the ups and downs of the industry.

- How are you paid? Some advisors charge a flat fee, others bill you by the hour, and some work on commission. You'll find out in the next section why it's important to know how a prospective advisor charges.

- What's your background? This will get your prospective advisor to describe his education and job background, both of which you should consider before hiring.

- Can you give me some references? Always ask for references, and check them out. No one, of course, is going to give you the name of somebody who fired her as a reference, but if five people absolutely rave about the job your potential advisor has done for them, chances are that she's pretty good.

Once you've met with several financial advisors, developed a feeling for whether or not you'd like to work with each of them, and checked out all their references, choose the one (assuming the qualifications are equal) with whom you are most comfortable and feel you'll work the best.

Fees Associated with Financial Advisors

Different kinds of financial advisors have different types of fees. Some will bill you hourly or charge a flat fee, while others work on commission for products they sell. One thing for sure, though, is that financial advisors don't work for free. Let's take a look at how various types of advisors might earn their money.

Certified financial planners may charge in different ways. Some charge flat fees, while others work on commission. There's concern in the financial industry about CFPs who work for commission. Many CFPs are employed by brokerage firms, which encourage them to sell the products on which the firm will earn the highest commissions.

If that's the case, your advisor could recommend that you buy a particular mutual fund, not because he really believes that it's a great fund, but because his firm will receive a big commission on it. Make sure you ask a CRP how she earns her money. If she tells you she works on commission, be sure to have her explain exactly how she chooses the products she'll recommend that you buy.

Financial consultants generally charge either a flat or hourly fee for their services. Remember that they don't typically sell products—they allow you to do so, based on their information and advice.

Certified public accountants, both those with and without the personal financial specialist designation, normally charge an hourly fee. If a CPA or PFS starts pushing particular products, you should ask what's going on.

Insurance agents, on the other hand, generally earn their money through commissions. And money managers typically receive a percentage of the market value of their client's account as compensation for their services.

Money Morsel

Fees for financial advisors vary greatly, so be sure you find out up front what someone you're considering hiring charges. Also, be sure to ask whether you'll be billed for your initial meeting. Most professionals will schedule a get-acquainted meeting for no charge, but others will bill you.

Go Figure

A fee-only financial advisor makes her money by charging clients each time they ask for advice or information. If your advisor is fee only, ask to be billed regularly so you can keep track of exactly what it is you're paying for.

If your advisor works solely on commission, talk to him about any concerns you have in that area. If you feel that you couldn't be comfortable with that arrangement, look for someone else.

Some Things Your Advisor Should Never Do

While most financial advisors adhere to industry standards and codes of ethics, there are, as in every business, some who will try to get away with practices that are less than honest and fair.

If your advisor tells you that he's fee only, but you find out that he's been making big bucks off of the mutual funds he's been pushing on you, that's a serious infraction called *misrepresentation*. He's misrepresented himself to you about how he earns him money, and given you serious doubt about the products he's recommended.

If you suspect that your advisor may be getting commissions and he's told you he's not, or are having other kinds of problems with him, you can check to see whether there have been any complaints lodged against him in the past. All financial advisors are required to register with their state Securities Exchange Commission and fill out a form called the Uniform Application for Investment Advisor Registration.

If you are uncomfortable about something your advisor has said or done, you can contact either your state Securities Exchange Commission or the Washington, D.C., office and request a copy of your advisor's registration. The form will contain information about whether your advisor has had problems in the past, such as being sanctioned or having his license suspended.

Adding It Up

Misrepresentation occurs when a financial advisor guarantees that an investment will be successful, misinforms you about how he earns his money, or tells you that he's something or someone who he's not. If he tells you he has a degree from the Harvard Business School when he really doesn't, for instance, that's misrepresentation.

Another means of misrepresentation is when your advisor tells you to put your money in a certain investment because you're guaranteed to make 20 or 30 percent, and you end up losing most of your investment.

It's one thing for an advisor to recommend an investment and tell you he thinks you'll do well in it. He can't, shouldn't, however, guarantee an investment unless somehow he has a written guarantee.

Another practice you should be aware of is called churning and burning. This is when an advisor moves investments from one fund to another, pulling down a commission with every move.

If it seems that your advisor is trading and moving your investments more often than necessary, don't hesitate to ask why he's doing so. If he doesn't have a good response, ask to speak to his supervisor or the office manager.

Probably the biggest complaint clients have regarding their financial advisor is that they're ignored, or their wishes not carried out as expressed. If you request your financial advisor to make a particular investment on your behalf, he should do so. He may advise you that he doesn't think it's a good idea, but, if you insist, he should follow your instructions.

If your advisor doesn't do what you ask him to, or acts without your approval, it's time to look for someone else to handle your money. You should always feel free to call your advisor and request a meeting. If he's too busy to meet with you, there are plenty of other financial advisors available.

Not everyone needs a financial advisor, but most people in their 40s and 50s who have some money saved can benefit from the services of a qualified professional. Just be sure to hire the best advisor you can find, and work to establish and maintain a good relationship.

The Least You Need to Know

- ◆ A good financial advisor should be able to help you make the most of your money, regardless of how much you've got.
- ◆ There are different types of financial advisors, some of who may have better qualifications than others.
- ◆ Regardless of the type of the advisor you hire, it's important to learn all you can about his background and experience.
- ◆ It's important to ask up front how a financial advisor earns her money, because some charge flat or hourly fees, while others work on commission.
- ◆ It's good to be aware of, and keep your eye out for some unethical practices that less-than-honest financial advisors might try.

Part 6

Preparing for the Future

You know how fast time flies. Days and weeks turn into months faster than you can turn the pages of your calendar. You swear you've just got the last needles from your Christmas tree cleaned off the carpet and the holiday season is once again upon you.

The future comes fast, and you've got to be ready. Estate planning isn't just for old folks—it's for everybody. If you haven't thought about how best to distribute your assets when you die, there's no time to spare. Planning is essential, not so much for yourself, but for your family.

The last section of the book, Chapters 24 through 27, examine methods of planning for the future, and tell you straight out why it's necessary to plan, now. You'll also learn about helping your parents to deal with financial and other issues.

Chapter 24

You're Never Too Young to Plan

In This Chapter

◆ Understanding the importance of a will

◆ Deciding who will take care of your kids

◆ Protecting your family and business

◆ Considering a living will

◆ Understanding power of attorney

◆ Doing what you need to do

When we're young, we assume that we'll live forever. We're invincible. By the time we reach our 40s and 50s, however, most people have a pretty good handle on their mortality. Sure, we expect that we'll continue to live for a long time. It's just that by now, we know we won't live forever.

And, we understand by this stage of the game that life is tenuous. We've probably all known somebody about the same age who was killed in an accident, or died from cancer or another disease. Maybe you've even had a friend or relative of the same age who died suddenly of a heart attack or a stroke. It's by no means common—but it happens.

Because not one of us can ever be sure that we're going to wake up tomorrow morning to see the sun rise again, it's extremely important to plan for a future without you in it. Everyone at this age should have a will. If you haven't already made provisions for minor children, you'll need to do that. If you have a business, you need to plan how you're going to protect it if you're no longer around.

This kind of planning is extremely important, and yet many, many people don't bother to execute it. If you've been reluctant to deal with it until now, it's extremely important that you read this chapter. Nobody likes to think about dying, but, eventually, we all will. And we have a responsibility to protect those we'll leave behind by making sure they're cared for.

Don't Go There

Beware of generic wills that you can buy in office supply stores or stationary stores. Not all states accept generic documents, and these forms aren't customized, so they may not be exactly what you need.

You Do Have a Will, Don't You?

Everyone who is of legal age and has any assets at all should have a will. If you don't, and you die, the court will determine how your property gets distributed. It also will appoint somebody to take charge of closing out your estate. The person or firm appointed can charge up to 5 percent of the value of the estate, which won't come as a nice surprise to your survivors.

Most lawyers will draft a basic will for about $300, and it's an investment you simply can't afford to be without.

What It Should Include

A will does not have to be long or complicated, or filled with language that nobody can understand. It does, however, need to include certain information. Basically, a will contains a description of a person's assets, property, and belongings. And it describes how those things are to be divided after the person's death.

A will also can contain specific instructions assigning certain items to individuals, and should name an executor to handle the estate. The executor is the person who administers the estate of the person who has died.

Many people include a letter of instruction along with their will to address more personal and specific issues. Some of those issues could include the following:

◆ Special instructions for the funeral or burial

◆ Detailed lists of possessions to be passed along to various people

◆ Locations of all important documents and items

◆ Lists of all insurance policies, stocks, bank accounts, access numbers, and so forth

◆ Personal messages to family members or friends

A letter of instruction should not be kept with the actual will, but in a spot that is easily accessible in the event of your death. And make sure that your spouse or another trusted person knows that it's there. You can leave the most specific instructions possible for your funeral or burial, but if nobody finds them until three days after you've been buried, they're of no use.

Most married people name their spouse as the executor, unless there's a specific reason not to. When choosing an executor, keep in mind that it can be a time-consuming, tedious job. Don't appoint someone who will be overly burdened by the work involved.

An executor normally is responsible for seeing that the wishes of the deceased person are carried out, and for paying any owed taxes or outstanding bills. Other duties of an executor may include closing bank accounts, arranging for appraisals of assets, filing insurance claims, inventorying assets, notifying creditors, setting up checking accounts to use to pay bills, informing beneficiaries and distributing bequests, and filing final income tax returns.

When including an executor in your will, keep in mind all that is involved, and be considerate. Make sure the person you choose has both the time and ability for the job.

Making Sure It's Valid

Requirements vary from state to state regarding the validity of wills. Your lawyer will direct you in making sure that yours is valid.

A valid will must be dated, and signed by the person making the will, and at least one (usually two) witnesses. Generally, a will is a fairly straightforward document. Just make sure that you meet the basic requirements for validity to assure fewer problems for your heirs.

Deciding Where to Keep It

It's extremely important that your will is accessible in the event that it becomes necessary. While the original should be safely stashed away, it's a good idea to leave a copy of your will somewhere in your home, and for your spouse or another family member to know where it is.

The person who will be executor of your will also should have a list of your assets, and know where to find important papers regarding insurance and other legal and financial matters.

It's highly recommended that you update lists of your assets and liabilities each year. Having these on hand can make matters a lot easier for your executor if you were to die.

Many people keep their will, along with other valuables, in a safe-deposit box in their bank or credit union. Safe-deposit boxes are used to store personal property that is important or expensive, and difficult or impossible to replace. Many people use the boxes to store insurance policies, stock certificates, jewelry, birth certificates, property records, business contracts, adoption papers, inventories of household valuables, and so forth.

You have access to your safe deposit box during bank hours. Generally, two keys—one which you keep, and one that is kept at the bank—are needed to open the box. If you have your will in your safe-deposit box, make sure that a copy is available in a more accessible location, as well. And make sure that more than one family member knows the location of your safe-deposit box and where you keep your key. Many people make the mistake of sharing that information only with a spouse, never considering what would happen if both of you are killed in an accident.

Money Morsel

A convenient time to update lists of assets and liabilities is when you're gathering your income tax paperwork in late January or early February.

If the only copy of your will is in your locked safe-deposit box, and you die on Saturday, for instance, your will would be inaccessible until the bank reopened Monday morning. And some states require that safe-deposit boxes be sealed at the time of death, although a survivor normally would be able to retrieve the will before that happened.

When you write and sign your will, your lawyer may suggest or request that the original copy be stored in their office vault. The charge is free, and a great service, if friends or family know that the will is held there. Also, the attorney who prepared your will does not need to be the same lawyer who works with your executor to settle your estate. The attorney who prepares your will is your lawyer. Your executor may prefer to work with someone else.

Regardless of where you choose to keep your will, it should be in a place that's known and accessible to others.

Choosing a Guardian for Minor Children

Naming a guardian for a minor child or children is frequently the most difficult decision a person or couple must make. And yet, it's necessary, and one of the best ways to assure that your kids will be well cared for by someone you trust in the event that you, or you and your spouse, should die before they're adults.

Not naming a guardian for your children can be a disaster. There have been nightmare cases of families fighting over children, either because more than one relative wishes to raise them, or even worse, because no one wants to raise them. Children who lose their parents certainly need to be placed into a loving and stable environment, and to be financially provided for.

While the natural inclination of most people is to name a family member as guardian for your children, that's not always the smartest or best alternative. If your only brother is a bachelor who lives in Aspen so that he can spend every weekend on the ski slopes, you've got to wonder if he's going to be willing or equipped to handle kids.

If your parents are on the younger side and willing, they may be candidates, but think twice about setting your child up to lose another person she loves by placing her with elderly grandparents. They may be loving and willing, but older people sometimes lack the energy or patience necessary to raising children. Grandparents may be designated to assist the appointed guardians.

Religion is sometimes the primary basis on which a person or couple will appoint a particular person as guardian. Home environment is another. Will your children feel loved with their appointed guardians? Who do you know that will raise your children in a manner comparable to how you are raising them?

Remember that the guardian you name will raise your children. He or she, or they, if you appoint a couple, will work with the trustee of your estate to make sure your children have enough money to cover the major expenses they'll encounter, such as college tuition. Money from your estate generally will be used for support of your children, and this should be stipulated in your will.

Don't Go There

Don't even think of appointing a guardian without carefully discussing the matter with the designee. You've got to be absolutely sure the person you choose is willing and able to assume the responsibilities.

You must discuss the guardianship relationship with the people you would like to have serve in that capacity. They may not feel that they're physically able, or may have other concerns that would prohibit them from taking the job.

Some guidelines for choosing a guardian are listed as follows:

◆ **Love.** This is the most important qualification for guardianship. You want to choose someone who will love your children unconditionally, as a parent does.

◆ **Similar values and ideals.** Placing your kids into a household with wildly different values and ideals is bound to be disorienting and distressing. Try to find a situation in which they'll be raised in approximately the same manner that you were raising them.

◆ **Energy.** Raising children is difficult, and requires patience and energy. Be sure you find someone who's up to the task.

Appointing a guardian for your children is extremely emotional, and can be quite traumatic. No one likes to think about not being around to see their children reach adulthood. For their sake, however, appointing a guardian is not an option—it's a necessity.

Protecting Your Family and Your Business

You've worked for years to start and grow a business. There were long, long days, many moments of doubt, and some pretty spotty paychecks at the beginning. Now, however, your business is doing just great, and you and your family are reaping the rewards of all your hard work.

In order to protect your family and your business, you've got to plan for the serious contingencies of death and disability.

You read about disability insurance in Chapter 2, "Figuring Out Where You Are in Life," so we won't spend much time on it now. Just remember that, in the event that you become disabled, disability insurance will help to replace the salary you're not getting.

If you're the primary or sole wage earner in your household, whether you're self-employed or work for someone else, you absolutely need to have disability insurance in order to assure that your family will have the money it needs.

Money Morsel

Remember that most disability insurance policies don't cover the full amount of your salary, but kick in about 60 percent. Your emergency fund can be used to supplement the insurance payments.

If you decide that, in the event of your death, you want your business to be sold and the proceeds passed along to your family, it's important to take steps now to assure that will happen.

A person's business often is his or her greatest asset, but usually the least liquid. If you want your business to be sold, make it easier for your executor by stating realistically what the business is worth.

Keep an annual valuation of the business, and let your executor know where it is. Make sure you update the valuation yearly, and that it's a realistic estimate of what your business is worth. Knowing what the business or property is worth will make it easier for your executor to get it on the market and sold.

You also might keep a list of potential buyers for your business along with the valuation. If a competitor has ever talked about the possibility of a merger with your company, or anyone has ever expressed interest in buying it, make sure your executor knows that in order to hasten the selling process.

If you have a partner in your business, he or she should be the obvious choice for buying your share of the enterprise if you die. Indeed, your partner is the first person your executor should meet with about selling your share of the business. And, there are some steps that you and your partner can take now to assure that he'll be able to buy your share in the event of your death.

Ask your accountant or lawyer about the possibility of you and your partner getting a *buy-sell agreement*. This agreement usually occurs between partners, or closely held corporate shareholders.

The buy-sell agreement sets a price for the business, based on periodic valuations. The agreement also can require the sale of a partner's share of the business to the other partner for a specific price within a specified time. It can state, for instance, that if you die, your partner will pay $400,000 for your share of the business within six months of the time of your death.

Or the agreement may not require your partner to buy your share of the business, but might offer him the first right of refusal. That means that your partner is given the opportunity to buy your share. If he doesn't want to buy, or isn't able to financially, other arrangements must be made.

An agreement that grants first right of refusal is a good idea, and very important to your partner if there's a possibility that someone from outside might quickly want to buy your share of the business from your executor.

Adding It Up

A **buy-sell agreement** that provides first right of refusal to your business partner simply gives him or her the first chance at buying your share of the business in the event of your death. It's a good way to protect your partner, your business, and your family.

If you and your partner agree that you want the other to own the business in the event that one of you dies, but you're not sure that he'd have the funds to purchase your half, there's a solution.

Business partners can buy life insurance that names the other as the beneficiary. When one partner dies, the other gets the proceeds from the policy, which can be used to buy the deceased partner's share of the business. That way, your partner gets to keep the business, and your family gets the money from your portion of it.

If you own a business and haven't planned for what will happen to it if you die, make an appointment with your lawyer or accountant today. Protecting your business and protecting your family go hand in hand, and you want to make sure that you do both.

What About Long-Term-Care Insurance?

If you've got good life and disability insurance policies (see Chapter 2 if you need a refresher on either of those), you may want to give a thought to long-term-care insurance.

Relatively new, long-term-care insurance has sparked debate about whether or not it's necessary or a good idea for most people. While critics say it's too expensive, and that many people who buy it will get no benefit from it, proponents say that everyone should have it to avoid becoming a burden to their families.

Long-term-care insurance sometimes is called nursing home insurance, and it does provides coverage in the event that you'd need to be in a home. A comprehensive long-term-care policy, however, also should provide for services such as assisted living in a residential setting other than your own home, help with daily activities in your own home, and community programs such as adult day care.

Money Morsel

Insurance companies will tell you that one out of two people will eventually be in a nursing home. That statistic is misleading, however, because it includes those who may spend a week or two in a nursing home to get rehab after a fall or stroke. It's estimated that only four percent of elderly people actually live in nursing homes full-time.

Go Figure

The United Seniors Health Cooperative in Washington, D.C., estimates that a 55-year-old will pay between $300 and $1,500 a year for long-term-care insurance, depending on coverage. A 75-year-old just buying long-term-care insurance can expect to pay between $1,000 and $6,000 a year.

It seems strange to think about long-term-care insurance when you're only in your 40s or 50s and still very healthy. Some people, however, say that this is exactly the time that you should not only think about this insurance, but go ahead and buy it. A policy will be easier to get, and less expensive, if you buy it when you're relatively young and healthy.

Nursing homes are very expensive, there's no question about it. It can cost $4,000 a month or more to live in one, which would put a serious dent in the pocketbooks of most of us.

Whether or not you decide to buy long-term-care insurance should be a part of your overall financial planning. If you're considering it, think about these guidelines from the American Association of Retired Persons (AARP):

- Make sure you have a good reason to buy. Your goals should be to protect your assets, minimize dependence on other family members, and control where and how you receive long-term-care services.

◆ Long-term-care insurance can be expensive, particularly for older people. Learn as much as you can about long-term-care insurance and various policies, and consider your individual circumstances.

◆ Be wary of buying if paying for the premiums means lowering your standard of living or giving up other things you need.

◆ Keep in mind that you will probably be paying premiums for a number of years. Will you still be able to afford the policy if your circumstances change or if premiums increase?

◆ If you would quickly qualify for Medicaid if you needed long-term care, a long-term policy would not make sense for you. That is, you would spend your savings in a short time (within six months to a year) if you were paying out of pocket.

If your family has a history of chronic illness, such as diabetes, cardiovascular disease, or Alzheimer's, it makes more sense to consider long-term-care insurance than if all your relative have lived to be 90 in excellent health.

There are many types of long-term-care policies, so be sure to shop around. The AARP offers a great deal of information on its Web site. You can go to access information about long-term-care insurance at www.aarp.org/confacts/health/privltc.html.

Living Wills

Living wills are documents that state your wishes should you become profoundly ill, irreversibly incompetent, or need life support or heroic measures to keep you alive. A living will spells out to your doctor, the hospital, your family, and all others concerned what medical measures should, or should not be taken.

Money Morsel

Living wills and medical powers of attorney are known by different names in some states. A living will also may be known as a directive to physicians, health care declaration, declaration with respect to life-sustaining treatment, or medical directive. If you wish to draft a living will, be sure you use a form that's valid in your state.

It is intended to be used when the person can no longer communicate or make decisions on her own, and is designed to be a guide for family members and medical personnel. A living will goes into effect when a doctor has determined that death is fairly certain, or when it's been determined that a person is permanently unconscious.

Think about this. Let's say you do not have a living will. One day you're in a major car accident, and requiring life support to keep you alive. Your family—probably your spouse—will be called upon to make the agonizing decision of whether or not to continue life support.

You should have a living will in order to assure that your wishes are carried out, and to make what would be an awful situation easier for your family.

A living will must be signed in front of at least one witness, and the definition of an acceptable witness varies from state to state. Generally, a witness should be someone other than a health care provider or a family member, or anyone else who may have a financial interest in the patient's estate. Some states also require that a living will be notarized.

Many living wills include a section that releases doctors from legal liability for withholding measures that may possibly prolong life. This is to prevent family members from coming back and suing a doctor for not doing everything in his power to save your life.

Power of Attorney

Most of us in our 40s and 50s don't think about executing a *power of attorney*, but we all should. A power of attorney is simply a document that authorizes another person to act legally on your behalf, in the event that you're unable to take care of your own affairs and make your own decisions.

There also is a document called a *medical power of attorney*, which appoints someone else to make decisions concerning your medical care, other than those things that are covered in your living will.

The person who you name in a power of attorney to act legally in your behalf is called the agent, or attorney-in-fact. The second name can be a bit misleading. The agent does not have to be a lawyer. Any trusted person—your spouse, a child, other relative, or a close friend—can be your agent.

Adding It Up

A **power of attorney** authorizes another person to act legally on your behalf. A **medical power of attorney** appoints another person to make decisions concerning your medical care.

An agent would handle chores such as writing checks and investing savings in the event you were not capable of doing so yourself. He or she also could buy and sell property, and enter into contracts on your behalf. If you sign a power of attorney, it only becomes applicable if you're no longer able to handle matters yourself.

As with a living will, a power of attorney is a safeguard for you and your family. There are different types of power of attorney, so be sure you do your homework, or consult a lawyer before drafting one.

Preparing for future contingencies isn't always pleasant. It forces us to confront our mortality, and to think about end-of-life issues. Hopefully, we'll all live healthfully into our 80s and 90s. Realistically, however, some of us will not. Preparing for the possibility of disability or early death is a gift you can give to those who love you.

The Least You Need to Know

- Everyone should have a will in order to avoid having the court determine the distribution of your assets in the event of your death.

- Careful consideration and thought is necessary before you appoint a person or persons to be the guardians for your children, in the event of your death.

- If you own a business, there are steps you can take to protect it and to assure that it will be a source of income for your family.

- A living will informs family and health care providers of your wishes concerning end-of-life treatment.

- Granting power of attorney authorizes another person to act legally on your behalf.

25

Helping Aging Parents Plan

In This Chapter

- ◆ Stepping in when it's necessary
- ◆ Helping Mom and Dad with money matters
- ◆ Keeping everyone involved and up to date
- ◆ Planning for appropriate housing
- ◆ Knowing that care-giving is hard work

If you're lucky, your parent or parents are financially stable, in a comfortable living situation, and have planned well for their futures.

It's nice to be able to sit back, confident that Mom is financially comfortable, and settled nicely in the new, manageable home she moved into after Dad died. Or that Mom and Dad are planning to take some of the trips they've always wanted to, now that Dad's finally retired.

Maybe your parent or parents require help with daily tasks such as dressing and bathing, and reside in an assisted living center. Or they may still live at home, managing quite nicely in their 70s and 80s.

If your parents are independent and capable, count your blessings. Don't, however, skip over this chapter because you think it doesn't pertain to you.

As members of the sandwich generation, we all need to think about the possibility that we'll one day be called upon to assist our aging parents. As you read in Chapter 1, "So, How's Mid Life Treating You?" there are 25 million family caregivers in the United States, most of whom are women who work and have children. Caring for an aging parent can be rewarding, but it can put tremendous stress not only on the primary care giver, but on her family, as well.

In this chapter, we'll explore how you know when it's time to step in to help aging parents, and some of the tasks you might find yourself responsible for.

Knowing If Your Parents Need Help

Sometimes, the fact that your parents need your help is painfully obvious. Your dad has a stroke; Mom falls and breaks her hip. You go to visit and find that the house is a mess and there's no food in the refrigerator.

Money Morsel

If you don't live near your parents, try to establish a contact in their building or neighborhood who will keep an eye on them. Check in with the contact now and then (or more often if you're worried about your folks) just to make sure everything is okay and your parents aren't having any major problems.

Often, however, the need for help isn't as apparent. It's important to understand that many older people—perhaps including your parents—are fiercely independent. Most of our parents are of a generation that values self-sufficiency. They may deny that they need help, even when the need is clear to everyone else.

If you don't live close to your parents, you might be unaware that they could use some help. If you live in New York and they've retired to Arizona, for instance, chances are that you don't see them too often. Their situation may change significantly between your visits, and you might not ever know that they need help with household chores, managing finances, or whatever, until the situation has become very serious.

Sometimes, one parent will express concern about the other, alerting family members that there's a problem. Maybe Mom confides that she's terribly worried about Dad because he's increasingly confused and disoriented. Or Dad fears that Mom's diabetes is getting worse, but she refuses to see the doctor about it.

If that happens, be sure to take the concerns seriously, and start thinking about how you might help. Your dad is likely to have remained quiet about his concerns for a long time for fear of being "disloyal" to your mom. By the time he finally talks to you about the problem, chances are it's quite serious. If you have brothers and sisters, remember to tell them about your concerns and get their input on how you might help your parents.

The best situation is if you're able to sit down and talk frankly with your folks about their living situation. If you notice they're having trouble keeping up with writing checks and paying their bills, for instance, it would benefit everyone to discuss the problem and figure out how to solve it.

Unfortunately, real life often isn't like that. Your dad might feel ashamed to tell you that he can't figure out the bills anymore, much less deal with his income taxes. It may be next to impossible for your mother to discuss with you the problems she's having with incontinence, much less ask you to buy her Depends.

It's extremely difficult and painful, both for you and your parents, when the parent-child relationship begins to shift and change. Of course, your parents haven't been taking care of you in your adulthood, but they maintain their parental status. If you need to step in and start taking care of them, the parent-child relationship becomes distorted. Watching that relationship change is hard.

Money Morsel

If you have sisters and brothers, be sure to inform them of any problems your parents are having. Nobody likes to feel left out of a family situation, and, they may be valuable resources for help.

As difficult as it may be to alter your relationship with your parent or parents, there are situations in which you'll have no choice. If any of the following circumstances apply to your folks, you're going to need to step in and make some changes:

- Their living situation is not safe. Dad has fallen four times—that you know of. Mom has burned the bottom of every pan she has because she can't remember to turn off the stove. Dad walked to the corner store for some groceries and couldn't find his way back home.

- One parent is causing too much strain on the other. Mom has started sitting up for most of the night to make sure that Dad doesn't wander out of the house. Or Mom's breathing condition makes it necessary for Dad to wait on her hand and foot, and he's clearly at the end of his rope.

- The situation is causing too much stress for you or other family members. You've been stopping by your mother's house four times a day since her last fall, helping her with small chores and cooking her dinner every night. On weekends, you clean her house and keep her company. You're absolutely exhausted with trying to keep up with all those responsibilities in addition to work and your own home and family. Your husband and kids are complaining that they never see you, and you've completely lost touch with all your friends.

- Circumstances are clearly out of control. You visit for the first time in four months and are shocked to see that the house is filthy and smells terrible. Or you try to call your folks and find out their phone service has been shut down because they didn't pay the bill, and their electricity is due to be discontinued, as well. Or you learn they

Money Morsel

If you need to step in to help your parents, be sure you do so in a manner that will protect their dignity. No one likes to be told they're not capable of keeping up with their responsibilities. Think carefully about what you'll say and how you'll act.

haven't been to the grocery store for three weeks because it's too difficult for them to get there and get the groceries back home.

If any of these scenarios sound too familiar, it's probably time to get your parents some help. As difficult as it might be, you need to address the problem, and help them to find a solution. It might be as simple as setting aside one night a month to help them write out checks and organize papers. Or it may be as difficult as having to start looking for a nursing home for Mom or Dad.

Assessing Their Financial Situation

Finances are one of the areas in which elderly people most often need assistance. If you need to help your parents with their finances, you'll first need to understand where they stand. The only way that you'll really be able to know what they have, what they need, and what their options are, financially, is to assess their situation.

Is there enough money, for instance, if one of them should require home health care or have to go to a nursing home? Do they have the resources necessary to pay for their regular medications? If they pay rent or have a mortgage, how do those payments affect the balance of their available money? Will they have to sell their home in order to meet their expenses?

You might be pleasantly surprised and find out that your parents have made good investments over the years and accumulated some serious assets. Or you might be dismayed to learn that they have very little, and the future is looking rather bleak. Either way, however, it's better to know than not to know.

If your parents don't have a good handle on their finances, you may have to pull everything together for them. You'd need to figure out their net worth, just as you learned in Chapter 5, "Getting It All Together," to do for yourself.

Don't Go There

Don't forget to check on Mom's credit card bills. If she's wracking up debt on her cards, your first job is to help her get them paid off and convince her to go cash only.

Once you've got an idea of their net worth, calculate their current monthly income, including pensions, Social Security payments, income from a property, and income from securities or retirement accounts.

Then, add up their current monthly expenses. These would include mortgage or rent, utilities, maintenance costs on the home, grocery bills, medical costs, entertainment, transportation, insurance premiums, clothing, travel, and so forth. This will allow you to figure out if your parents are meeting their expenses with their current income, or if they're having to dip into their savings in order to pay their bills and other expenses. Knowing this can help you to get a better picture of their overall financial situation.

Talking Things Through

Once you've got a general picture of Mom and Dad's financial situation, you should sit down and have a frank conversation concerning their future. This assures that you all have the same understanding of the situation, and opens the door for figuring out how to improve their financial condition or solve any problems that may be occurring.

Remember, though, that this conversation may be very difficult for your parents; attitudes about money have changed greatly in the past 20 or 30 years. Talking about money used to be practically taboo, unless you were speaking with a banker, insurance agent, or car salesman. Money was a private matter, and not discussed in general conversation.

Your parents probably didn't include you in any financial discussions or decisions as you were growing up, and it may be difficult for them to do so now. Revealing the details of their finances to you may signify to them a beginning of a loss of independence. This could make them resistant to sharing financial information. You'll need to be sensitive to these, and any other feelings and attitudes that your parents might have that are associated with money.

If their situation isn't great, you may need to help them figure out how they might trim their expenses or find some additional sources of income. You might even help them to set up a budget, so that they'll know exactly where their money is going, and how much they can afford to spend.

Money Morsel

Some parents simply will not discuss their finances with their children. If that's the case with your folks, don't insist or try to force them to share information with you. You'll only make them uncomfortable and resentful, and perhaps suspicious toward you. Do, however, suggest that they confer with a financial planner or lawyer, and offer to help them find a qualified person.

If any area of their expenses seems out of balance, be sure to take a close look at what's going on. If the utility bills seem to be overly costly, for instance, check out Mom's appliances. Old, nonenergy-efficient refrigerators, freezers, and other appliances can cause huge drains on electricity and increase utility bills substantially. If this is the case, consider exchanging the appliance for a different one, possibly a used one.

Medical bills are another potential drain on your parents' finances. If Mom needs eight different prescription drugs for various ailments, the cost of those medicines could be wreaking havoc with her budget. If this is the case, consider talking to her doctor about the possibility of less expensive medicines, or see if there's a generic brand. Generic drugs can cost 50 percent less than brand name ones, and they all must be approved as equivalent by the Food and Drug Administration. The cost of prescription drugs rose by 17.4 percent in 2000, despite an overall inflation rate of less than 2 percent.

If you're worried about your parents' capability to handle their own financial affairs, you might want to suggest that they consider appointing an agent in a durable power of attorney. Explain to them that signing a power of attorney doesn't mean they relinquish all control of their finances. They're still in charge, but the person they appoint as their agent will help them and take care of the day-to-day chores such as paying the bills, sorting out the insurance statements, and making bank deposits.

If they've been having a difficult time keeping up with financial matters, they may welcome the offer for help. If they're willing to appoint an agent, be sure to let them decide on their own whom that person should be. Do, however, point out that it should be someone who lives fairly close by, and who has time and is willing to perform the necessary duties.

And, be sure to keep siblings informed, and include them in any decisions you make concerning Mom and Dad's finances. Nothing is likely to breed resentment as quickly as the notion that you're meddling in your parents' financial matters and keeping it a secret from your siblings.

Deciding Together Where They'll Live

Housing is another important, and potentially difficult area in which your parents might require your assistance. Ideally, Mom and Dad will be able to live safely and comfortably in their own house for their entire lives. Some people are fortunate enough to have that happen.

> **Go Figure**
>
> It's estimated that about 1.5 million people over the age of 85 live on their own, and that number will double in the next 20 years. And researchers say that by 2020, there will be 15.2 million people who are 65 or older living by themselves.

Chances are, however, that one or both parent may someday need to move.

This could occur for many reasons. Perhaps the family home your folks have lived in for the past 40 years is simply too large and requires too much upkeep. Or one parent might die and the other moves in order to be closer to a son or daughter. Maybe Dad is tired of cleaning and cooking for himself and decides to move to an apartment building designed for elderly folks that includes meals and a cleaning service. Or Mom may need to go into assisted living because she can no longer take care of her own needs.

If your parent or parents are thinking about moving, you can assist them by letting them know what options are available. Older people have many more housing options these days than they used to, and some of them are really interesting. Let's take a quick look at some of what's available.

ECHO Housing

ECHO homes (it stands for Elder Cottage Housing Opportunity) are fairly new, but they're gaining in popularity. They're modular homes that you move onto your property for as long as necessary, and remove them when they're no longer needed. Usually about the size of a large garage, a typical ECHO home includes a living room, kitchen, eating area, bathroom, and one or two bedrooms. Because they're designed especially for older people, they are wheelchair accessible, energy efficient, and all on one level. They typically cost about $25,000. Be sure to check with the municipality in which you live to make sure this type of housing is permitted. You can find out more about ECHO housing on the Senior Resource's Web site at www.seniorresouce.com/hecho.htm.

Money Morsel

Be aware that there are many services available to help aging people be able to stay in their own homes. Most communities have programs that provide home helpers, meal-delivery, drop-in visitors, transportation services, and senior centers. Contact your local Area Agency on Aging to see what's available in your community.

Adult or Retirement Communities

These vary greatly in scope, and offer different services and amenities. Typically, retirement communities are clusters of homes on small lots. Outside maintenance usually is provided, and there normally are common areas for residents to share. Some communities include a lake or pond for fishing, a golf course, tennis courts, shuffleboard courts, horseshoe pits, and so forth. There often are planned activities, such as bingo or card games, day or overnight trips, entertainment, and educational programs. Your parent would either buy or rent the house, and would pay a monthly or quarterly fee for services such as grass cutting, snow removal, and outside painting. If your parents are considering moving to a retirement community, be sure they shop around before committing themselves. There are huge differences from community to community, and, while many are very nice, others are less desirable. The cost of retirement communities varies greatly depending on location, the type of homes, services provided, and whether your parent would buy or rent. Some retirement communities offer lots for sale, and allow you to build a house of your choice.

Continuing Care Communities

Continuing care communities are those that offer independent living, assisted living, and skilled care, all on the same campus. They're usually large, often upscale complexes, sometimes sprawling over miles of land. The basic concept of a continuing care retirement community is as follows. Mom and Dad pay an entrance fee that gets them a house or an apartment.

Mom and Dad live on their own until something happens that means one of them can't live independently anymore. Let's say that Mom has a stroke. When she returns from the hospital, she and Dad find that she can't take care of herself, and it's too much for Dad to handle. At that point, Mom gets moved to the assisted living section of the community, while Dad remains in the apartment. Dad can go visit Mom every day, and has peace of mind knowing that she's getting the care she needs. If Mom gets well enough to take care of herself again, she moves back in with Dad. If she continues to need assistance, she stays where she is. And, if she encounters another health problem that makes her unable to do anything for herself, she'll be moved to the skilled care section of the facility, which is really a nursing home.

Continuing care communities are expensive places to live. Entrance fees can range from $30,000 to $300,000 or more, depending on the type of dwellings offered. And, monthly fees can vary from $500 to $3,500, depending on services.

Senior Apartments

Senior apartments can be built and run privately, although many are constructed and maintained by the Department of Housing and Urban Development (HUD). HUD housing is intended for low-income seniors, and is subsidized by the government. The eligibility for this type of housing varies from state to state, so you'll need to inquire with your local housing authority if you want to see if your parent qualifies. Because this type of housing is built exclusively for seniors and uses federal money, it must be fully handicap-accessible. Most senior apartments have dining rooms where residents may eat, although many include individual kitchens. Some community agencies offer services on-site at senior apartments, and many senior apartments have their own bus or van to transport residents to the doctor, grocery store, or so forth.

Assisted Living

Assisted living is a level of care that's somewhere between independent living and nursing home care. It varies greatly because every person in an assisted living facility may have different levels of need. Geriatric specialists say that people in assisted living generally need help with activities of daily living, such as dressing, bathing, eating, and using the bathroom. Assisted living also provides, or provides help with, tasks such as using a telephone, taking medicine, cooking, managing finances, using transportation, and so forth. Most provide three meals a day, with residents eating together in a dining room. Many offer transportation to doctor appointments, shopping, and other locations; activities and recreation; and housekeeping and laundry services. Assisted living facilities are not nursing homes. While some facilities accept high-need residents, most do not take people who suffer from dementia or who are incontinent.

Money Morsel

Anticipating an increased need for assisted living, the Marriott hotel chain has entered the assisted living arena with its Brighton Gardens communities. These are upscale assisted living facilities that cater to the needs of elderly persons.

Nursing Homes

No one likes to think about sending a parent to a nursing home, but there sometimes is just no choice. If Mom has Alzheimer's disease or anther type of dementia, is incontinent, can't move, or is just too sick for you to care for and no longer qualifies for assisted living, she may need the skilled care of a nursing home staff. Most nursing homes provide 24-hour nursing care, on-call physicians, personal care, meals and nutritional monitoring, laundry, activities, therapy, rehabilitation services, and counseling. Patients with different needs normally are placed in different sections of the building. Alzheimer's patients, for instance, may live in a separate wing. People who are in the nursing home temporarily for rehabilitation services after a stroke or illness may be housed in a certain area. All nursing homes have to be licensed, and they're inspected by state and federal agencies. There are a lot of issues—financial, practical, and emotional—involved with placing a loved one in a nursing home. Some resources to help you are listed in Appendix B, "Resources."

Senior citizens are coming up with some innovative housing solutions on their own. Some are taking on a roommate, or arranging for house sharing situations. Allow your parents to be creative when assessing their living arrangements.

Sorting It All Out

Helping your parents with financial issues, housing arrangements, health care, and other topics relating to aging can be extremely difficult. You'll need to be patient, caring, and understanding.

It's important to understand that everyone has a different capacity for care-giving. Some people are naturals, while others have to work harder to be helpful and available.

If you're about to start helping your parent or parents to deal with finances, housing, or other issues, be sure to talk to your own family about how they may be impacted. If you'll be spending a lot of time helping an aging parent, you'll likely need to make some adjustments in your own life.

Be as helpful as you can to aging parents, but allow them to continue making their own decisions and to remain independent for as long as possible. Be respectful, and remember that, regardless of how much assistance they require, they're still your parents.

The Least You Need to Know

- If it's very clear that your parents need help, it's your responsibility to step in and provide assistance, even if they're resistant.
- Before you can help a parent or parents with their financial matters, you'll need to get a clear understanding of their situation.
- Once you understand your parents' financial position, sit down and discuss the situation, and look at how you might address any problems or issues.
- Help your parents to make decisions concerning living arrangements by letting them know all the options available.
- Remember that care giving requires patience, understanding, and great empathy.

Estate Planning 101

In This Chapter

- ◆ Understanding what an estate plan does and why you need one
- ◆ Thinking carefully about your executor
- ◆ Controlling assets with trusts and gifting
- ◆ The perils of dying without a planned estate
- ◆ Knowing the top 10 mistakes of estate planning

If you think that estate planning is only for elderly people who have lots of property and money, it's time that we clear up a major misconception. Estate planning, which is simply the process of planning for the transfer of your property, is not only for elderly folks—or for rich ones.

A person's estate is simply his or her property and possessions, regardless of how much, or how little. Perhaps you have a home, a business, stocks, bonds, or money in the bank. All of those assets, and others, make up your estate. An estate can be worth $5,000, $500,000, or $5 million.

In this chapter, we'll take a look at how you go about planning for your estate in the manner that will provide the greatest benefit to your family. Good estate planning can ensure that more of your assets get passed along to your heirs, and fewer to the government, attorneys, or needless expenses.

The Purpose of an Estate Plan

Many people in their 40s and 50s feel that they're too young to think about estate planning. Realistically, however, we all know that things happen. People die in accidents. Others get incurable diseases and don't live into old age. Because life is uncertain, it's best to plan ahead.

Estate planning helps to assure that your assets will be distributed in the manner you would like. It also can help to reduce the amount of tax your heirs will have to pay, and to keep certain assets out of the public court proceedings called the "probate process." Not only people with lots of assets benefit from estate planning, although it may be more important in order to protect those assets.

Why Everyone Should Have One

Having a good estate plan in place can give you great peace of mind. It also will help your family to manage your finances and proceed in an orderly fashion if you were to die.

When a person dies, whatever property he owned is transferred to another person or persons. Basically, there are three methods of property transfer.

Operation of Law

This type of transfer occurs with property that is owned jointly, such as in the case of a husband and wife. If you and your spouse own property that is held jointly with the right of survivorship, the property automatically passes to the surviving spouse when one of you dies. The law directs who will own the property at death. This law applies to any assets that are held jointly, not just property in the sense of land or a home.

Adding It Up

There also is a form of ownership that occurs among a husband and wife. It's called **tenants in the entirety,** and is similar to the joint tenants with the right of survivorship form of ownership. Tenants in the entirety, however, is exclusively held between spouses.

Joint property is very common in families, and a frequent way that property is transferred. A particular kind of joint ownership is known as tenants in common. The tenants in common law allows property to be passed to someone other than the person with whom the property is jointly owned. Let's say that you own a share of a vacation home with your three brothers and sisters. Tenants in common allows you to stipulate in your will that, when you die, your share of the vacation home will be passed along to your children—not automatically transferred to your siblings, with whom you own the house. If you're married, the property most likely would be passed along to your spouse, and then to your children.

Contract of Law

This method distributes property through a beneficiary designation. A beneficiary designation is simply a document that states who should receive a person's property at the time of death. Contract of Law is the method by which IRAs, pensions, life insurance policies, and trusts are distributed at the time of the death of their owner. Transfer is made to the designee, without any worry of the decedent's will or joint property.

Probate

Probate is the process of verifying a will, and is conducted in public court. The court gives authorization to an executor to gather assets, pay death taxes and expenses, and then transfer property to the beneficiaries of the will, as directed. If a person dies without a will (but you'd never let that happen to you, right?) a judge will appoint an executor.

During probate, everyone who has a stake in the will of the person who has died is contacted and informed that the process has begun. Stakeholders include heirs, beneficiaries, and creditors. The estate of the deceased person is inventoried and appraised, and then everyone who is due money from the estate is paid. Whatever is left over is then distributed to the heirs.

Probate can be a long and expensive process, sometimes costing thousands and thousands of dollars in legal fees. Knowing how to keep some of your assets from passing through probate through smart estate planning can save both time and money.

> **Go Figure**
>
> The name of the local government office that handles probate varies from county to county. It could be called probate court, probate office, surrogate's office, or register of wills.

Regardless of how your property is transferred after your death, it is imperative that you have a will. Drafting a will is the most important aspect of estate planning. It specifies distribution of all property not transferred by operation of law or contract, and spells out your specific wishes and requests. If you don't have a will, have one drafted immediately.

Choosing an Executor

Choosing an executor for your estate is a decision that should not be made lightly. The executor (or executrix, if a woman) will be named in your will, and is responsible for administering your estate. Many lawyers will recommend naming an executor and an alternate executor, in case the executor dies or becomes incapacitated before your death.

We briefly discussed the duties of an executor or executrix in Chapter 24, but you should understand that administering an estate can be a lengthy and time-consuming job. The duties of an executor include the following:

- Identifying and listing all debt
- Notifying creditors that they need to file claims for payment
- Filing claims with insurance companies
- Inventorying all assets
- Arranging for appraisals of assets
- Closing bank and investment accounts of the decedent
- Setting up a checking account to use to pay bills
- Gathering and then distributing all assets according to the decedent's wishes
- Filing final income tax returns
- Filing the state and federal death tax returns, if applicable

The executor of your will should be a person you trust, who is capable of, and willing to undertake the tasks involved. Be sure you ask whomever you choose if they're willing to be your executor before you name that person in your will.

Methods of Controlling Assets

Even in death, you can't avoid taxes. The so-called "death tax,"—the money the government grabs out of your estate after you die, is a hot topic these days, and currently in the process of being revised.

Basically, if you had died in 2001, before the death tax revisions, your estate would have been taxed if it was valued at $675,000 or more. That number will jump to $1 million in 2002, $2 million in 2003, $3 million in 2004, and $3.5 million in 2009. That is, all money within an estate over those amounts will be taxed.

Go Figure
The federal tax rate is based on the value of the estate, ranging from 37 to 50 percent. The top tax bracket, however, is set to drop to 45 percent in 2009.

If your estate is valued at less than $675,000 (in 2001), no federal taxes would apply, but it still may be subject to state death taxes.

In order to avoid taxes, people with sizable estates plan to remove assets from their estate, thereby reducing the value of their property. Two primary methods of shrinking an estate are through trusting and gifting.

Trusts

Many people set up trusts in order to manage their assets while they're living, and to transfer those assets at the time of their death. Trusts allow you to transfer ownership of property or money to a person who is designated to manage and distribute the assets according to your instructions, for the benefit of another.

Some trusts may provide significant tax advantages, while others are for the benefit of persons unable to handle their affairs. Other trusts provide income for a spouse or beneficiary who is not included among your heirs.

The person who establishes the trust is called the "grantor." The person who manages the trust is known as the "trustee," and the people who eventually receive money or other assets from a trust are called "beneficiaries."

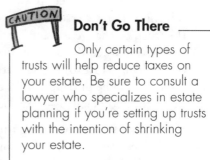

Don't Go There

Only certain types of trusts will help reduce taxes on your estate. Be sure to consult a lawyer who specializes in estate planning if you're setting up trusts with the intention of shrinking your estate.

Trusts also are necessary if you have minor children. You can specify in your will that any money left to children who are under a certain age, be placed in a trust for their benefit until they reach the age stated. You appoint a trustee, who will see that the money is properly invested and available for the child if necessary. When the child reaches the age stated in the document, the trust is dissolved and the child receives the remaining assets. In most cases, income tax on the money earned by the trust is taken out of the trust until the child reaches the age stated in the document. At that time, the child usually has to pay income tax.

There are many varieties of trusts, but all fall under two basic flavors: revocable and irrevocable. Revocable means changeable, irrevocable means it's beyond your control—it's not changeable. Within each category are various types of trusts. Let's have a look at some common kinds of trusts.

Testamentary Trust

This type of trust is laid out in a person's will and established after his death. Until a person dies, the document can be changed, since the will can be changed at any time. However, once you die, the trust becomes irrevocable. The testator keeps control of the assets included in the trust during his lifetime, and can stipulate when beneficiaries should receive their money or property from the trust.

Testamentary trusts can help to reduce estate taxes at a second party's death (usually a spouse). Testamentary trusts can be funded directly with assets that come from a beneficiary designation, such as proceeds of a life insurance policy that names the trust as its beneficiary. Or it can be funded through assets that are subject to probate.

Revocable Living Trust

This type of trust is set up while the grantor is still living, and allows the grantor to keep full control of the assets. The grantor also has the ability to revoke or amend the terms of the trust, or change the appointed trustee, while living. A revocable living trust becomes irrevocable when the grantor dies or becomes incapacitated. Many people consider a revocable living trust to be a substitute for a will, because the trust also can instruct how assets should be distributed. It's extremely difficult, however, for a trust to include everything covered in a will—it can be done but it takes a great deal of planning.

If you have a revocable living trust, you should still have a will. A revocable living trust can reduce the cost of settling an estate, and also the amount of time it takes. Funds held in a trust can be distributed much sooner than assets in an estate. A trust can also protect privacy because assets included in the trust don't have to pass through probate, which is a court proceeding in which a person's estate is settled. As stated earlier in this chapter, all creditors are paid off during probate, and heirs receive their shares of the estate after everything is settled. Waiting isn't usually necessary with a trust—distribution can occur when the trustee feels comfortable making distribution. And, while wills can be contested, trusts very rarely are contested.

Go Figure
A will is a public document, available for inspection at your local courthouse when it goes into probate. Anyone who happens to be interested can make a trip downtown, obtain a copy of your will, and read all the details—juicy, or not.

A revocable trust can be funded or unfunded at death. If unfunded, the document is held (like your will) in a safe place, and then used when assets are paid to it. If the trust is funded prior to your death, you re-register assets from your name into the name of the trust. Shares of stock for example, are re-registered from belonging to Daniel Smith, to belonging to the Daniel Smith Trust, with Daniel Smith and Susan Jones as trustees. If you fund a trust prior to death, all assets held in the trust bypass probate.

Irrevocable Trust

Usually established and used by people with a great deal of assets, irrevocable trusts, as the name implies, can't be amended or destroyed. Once the trust is set up, it remains in place, giving the grantor no opportunity to change his mind.

Irrevocable trusts are used primarily to reduce estate taxes, though they are also used to protect property for minor heirs. Irrevocable trusts also can be set up to provide income for a beneficiary, and then to divert the income to another place when the beneficiary dies.

Property that is turned over to an irrevocable trust, if set up properly, is no longer considered part of the estate of the person who turned it over. It still may be subject to other taxes, such as gift or capital gains, but those traditionally have been far lower than estate taxes. As with a revocable living trust, assets included in an irrevocable trust do not have to pass through probate.

There are various types of irrevocable trusts, the most common of which is the irrevocable life insurance trust. In that case, the trust "owns" a large life insurance policy, from which proceeds are paid directly into the trust at the time of the death of the grantor. Other irrevocable trusts include residuary trusts and marital trusts.

> **Money Morsel**
>
> Assets that are in your control at the time of death generally are subject to federal estate taxes. Those not in your control, such as in a irrevocable trust, are not subject to federal tax because they're not considered as part of your property.

There are many types of trusts, all with different rules and benefits. Consult a financial planner or lawyer who specializes in estate planning for more information, or check out some of the resources listed in Appendix B.

Gifting

Another means of shrinking an estate to reduce taxes is through gifting. Most of us aren't in a position where we'd benefit from handing out gifts of $10,000 in order to avoid taxes. If your parents' estate is large enough that they're looking for ways to reduce it, however, you may want to suggest gifting.

An individual can give $10,000 per year to as many people as he or she wants, with no one paying death or income taxes on any of it. Wealthy people often use gifting to reduce the size of their estates. It's effective because there is no limit to the number of people to whom you can give money.

> **Money Morsel**
>
> Tax-free gifts in addition to a $10,000 gift may be made if the money is paid directly to an institution for medical costs or education. Gift money sent directly to a college to be applied toward tuition, for instance, would not be subject to gift tax, even if the college student already had received $10,000 in the same year.

There is a catch to gifting, as you might have imagined. The total of any gifts given over $10,000 per year are subtracted from the amount at which estate taxes kick in (called the exemption amount). That means, if you—or perhaps your parent—gives away $100,000 in gifts, your estate (or Dad's) will be taxed at anything over $910,000 instead of the usual $1,000,000. And gifts of more than $10,000 are subject to a federal gift tax that mirrors the estate tax. This gift tax, however, isn't due until the amount of all gifting is greater than the federal estate exemption amount.

Gifting has been an estate planning tools for generations. It will be interesting to see what impact the ongoing estate tax revisions may have on gifting.

Dying Without an Estate Plan

Even if your estate is simple and straightforward, you need to have an estate plan, the most important part of which is your will. If you never set up a trust or make a gift, that's okay. If you fail to draft a will and die without one, however, that's another story.

Until the World Trade Center catastrophe, few of us thought about the probability of dying without a will. An untimely death can occur anytime, so be prepared by getting a will!

Every state has laws concerning how your property will be distributed if you die without a will. They're called laws of intestate succession. They are, in fact, actually the state's way of writing a will for you, if you neglected to do it yourself. Although the laws strive to distribute property fairly—such as equal division among children—they can only do so much.

A law of intestate succession can't know, for instance, that you and your cousin have always been closer than any other two people on earth, and you really wanted her to have your house, which she loves.

When somebody dies without a will, all community property generally is passed to the spouse. Property owned separately gets divided between the spouse and children. If there is no spouse or children, the property usually passes to the next closest relative. If property is passed to minor children, it's generally placed by the court in a blocked bank account or guardianship account, and is not available to the children without a court order until they've reached majority, usually 18. And, a court order normally is awarded only in an emergency situation, not so that the money is available for the daily upkeep of the child.

These laws also don't make provision for leaving property to your church or a charity, as many people like to do. In short, dying without having your estate planning complete (especially your will), is not a good idea. If you are ever in a situation of having a loved one die without a will, you should seek legal advice.

Ten Most Common Estate Planning Errors

Actually, there are 11 most common estate planning errors. The first, and worst, mistake is to have no plan at all. The other 10 mistakes, according to financial experts, are listed as follows:

1. **Improper use of jointly held property.** Owning everything jointly makes the provisions of one's will ineffective. Property held jointly with the right of survivorship is left outright to the survivor. Frequently, an inequitable amount of property goes to a joint tenant because he or she receives the property directly, and the decedent's will divides the assets transferred by probate to the remaining heirs on a percentage basis, such as thirds. Since the will only covers probate property, an equalization of all of your assets need not be made.

2. **Improperly arranged life insurance.** If the primary beneficiary of your life insurance policy is deceased, and you never named a secondary beneficiary, your family can be in for big problems. If your children are minors, and you haven't designated a trust to hold the life insurance proceeds until they reach a certain age, your insurance proceeds are subject to claims in the estate, and will pass through the estate.

3. **Lack of liquidity.** Not having enough ready cash available to cover death taxes and other final expenses is a major concern for many people.

4. **Choosing the wrong executor.** Often, an executor hasn't got the time to devote to the often long and drawn-out process of estate administration. Or, how do you know that your executor will be fair and knowledgeable, and not display a conflict of interest?

5. **Will errors.** Too many wills do not get updated. People tend to draft wills when they get married or divorced, or when they have their children. The will often remains neglected for years after that. An incorrect will can pass property to an incorrect heir.

6. **Leaving everything to your spouse.** There can be serious tax consequences if you pass all your property to your spouse, and then he or she passes it along to your children. Leaving everything to a spouse isn't always the best way to proceed.

7. **Improper disposition of assets.** This is when your assets get passed along to the wrong person. A 20-year-old, for instance might receive a larger amount of money than he or she is capable of handling. Inequitable distributions due to incorrect beneficiary designations is a major error.

8. **Failure to stabilize and maximize.** It's very important that you know, and record, the value of your business interest, and have an agreement in place that makes provisions for the business if you die. It's also important to make sure you've got primary and secondary beneficiary designations on all contracts—from pensions plans to tax-deferred annuities. IRAs and other retirement vehicles often are a family's largest

asset beside their home, yet they don't plan the accurate disposition to maximize death tax and income liabilities.

9. **Lack of adequate records.** Where are your assets located? Do you have an updated list of the names and numbers of your closest advisors? An executor needs access to last year's tax returns, the locations of all your bank accounts, information about insurance policies, and so forth. Make sure you record all relevant information and have it in an accessible location.

10. **Not having a master plan.** You can learn everything you can about estate planning, but if you don't have a well-thought-out master plan, you'll still be at square one. Be sure to take the time once a year to quantify in dollar terms your financial needs and objectives, and chart a plan for reaching your goal in the most efficient and effective way.

Having a clear and intelligent estate plan can help to put your mind at ease about the future, and assure that your heirs will get maximum benefits from what you leave behind. Estate planning is a useful tool, not something to be avoided or ignored.

The Least You Need to Know

- A well-thought-out estate plan can help you to reduce taxes and make sure that your property is distributed the way you want it to be.

- Estate plans are not just for people who own a lot of property or have a lot of money, and they are not just for elderly people.

- You should choose an executor for your estate carefully, giving thought to the time and effort that will be required.

- Setting up trusts and gifting money are common methods of reducing the value of an estate.

- Dying without a will means that your property will be distributed according to state law, not your wishes.

- There are common errors that many people make when planning their estates.

Chapter 27

Seeing Into Your Crystal Ball

In This Chapter

- ◆ Looking at what may lie ahead
- ◆ Considering your future plans
- ◆ Understanding some myths about aging
- ◆ Planning financially to make your dreams come true
- ◆ Knowing how to age with style

Our world is in a tumultuous time, at present, due to the September 11, 2001, terrorist attacks in our country and the resulting chaos. Many of us are feeling decidedly and understandably uncertain about the future, and what it may hold for us and those we love.

Of course, even before the attacks, none of us would have been able to predict what the future holds. And most of us wouldn't want to. Would you really want to know, for instance, at what age you'll die, or if you'll outlive your spouse? Isn't it enough to know that there are both joys and hardships ahead, and try to prepare ourselves to deal with both as well as we can?

We can plan as carefully and thoroughly as we wish, but we really have very limited control over our lives.

Maybe you've been planning since you were in your 40s to retire when you reached 62, only to have illness force you to leave the workplace in your late

50s. Or on a happier note, you may win $5 million in the lottery when you're 52 and decide to add an extra 10 years onto your retirement.

Just because we can't know what will happen to us in the future doesn't mean we should not be optimistic, and plan to live long and happily. And we can, and should, do everything possible to assure that will happen.

In this—the last chapter of the book—we'll dare to look ahead and try to predict what our futures might hold. Knowing that our predictions are subject to change, due to circumstances beyond our control, we'll move bravely ahead and have a look at the years to come.

What Lies Ahead for You and Your Family?

Hopefully, your life will move ahead as you've hoped and planned for it, staying pretty much on course. With good living and a dose of luck, we'll live to watch our children grow up, and have many years with our grandchildren, great-grandchildren, and—who knows—great-great-grandchildren.

The average life expectancy is at 76.7 for men and 79.5 for women, and expected to continue rising. Treatments for our most serious diseases are improving rapidly and dramatically, and we're learning more and more about the best ways to take care of ourselves. We should expect to live for many years, and as a result, we must make sure we're prepared for many more years.

When you look into the future for you and your family, what do you see? Big, fancy weddings for sons and daughters? A trip to South America, and then a tour of Europe for you and your spouse? Maybe you've always wanted to move to the country when you retire, and raise horses. Or to start your own consulting business. Perhaps you see yourself going back to college, or as a caregiver for your grandkids, or running a dog training school.

Maybe you've assured your children that you'll help them financially when they buy their first homes, or you've decided that you'll set up funds for each of your grandchildren to give them a head start on their college savings.

You may have decided that you're not the type to fully retire, and are busy looking for part-time or flex-time opportunities. Maybe you own and run a business, and have no plans of even slowing down as you reach your 60s and 70s.

> **Go Figure**
>
> A national poll by *The Los Angeles Times* revealed recently that three out of four respondents feel younger than their actual ages. Those in their 70s and 80s say they feel like they're in their 60s, and those in their 60s say they feel like they're in their early 50s.

All of these hopes and plans require different levels of financial planning. Big, fancy weddings require big dollars, as do college funds for four, five, or six grandchildren. It's great to want to help out your kids and grandkids. Just be certain to make sure your own financial situation is where it needs to be before you start passing out money.

And, even if you're planning on keeping every cent you have for yourself, make sure that your priorities are in place. That is, be sure that your retirement savings are adequate to fund the tour of Europe. You sure don't want to end up broke when you're in your 80s, sitting in a bare, cold room, with nothing but a 20-year-old photo album of your European tour.

Planning Things You Want to Do

One of the best things about getting older is that you probably have more options than you did earlier in life. Let's face it. When you're a kid, your options are pretty limited. Kids don't have a lot of clout, and they pretty much have to do what their parents or guardians tell them to do.

Teenagers, while financially better off than any time in history, still have limited options. They have to go to school, which takes up most of their time. And, many of them have to work in order to buy all the stuff that advertisers and marketers tell them they need to have.

Teens end up having overflowing closets, and maybe their own cars, but they still have to deal with a limited number of choices.

Most college-age kids are either working, in school, or both, giving them little time to discover all of what else life offers. And young adults just getting started in life generally have to work pretty hard to get themselves established.

Options remain limited for those who have children in their 20s and 30s. Raising kids, along with all the other responsibilities of adulthood, takes a lot of time, energy, and money, leaving little of those resources left over.

> **Go Figure**
>
> Teenagers are estimated to have collectively spent about 155 billion dollars in 2000. That's an increase of more than 50 percent since 5 years earlier. With the average 17-year-old spending more than $100 a week, it's not hard to figure out why teens are such hot marketing targets, is it?

Once the kids get to college, you're probably still working, plus spending a good deal of time worrying about tuition bills, the cost of textbooks, and whether or not Tommy's learned to use the washing machine or if he's remembering to set his alarm clock on the mornings he has classes.

Once the kids are out of college, though—maybe even out of the house—your life begins to slow down a bit. It might seem strange for a while to be able to actually read the entire newspaper before you leave for work, or to join a friend for dinner on a Tuesday night.

There are no more PTA meetings, or swim meets to eat up every Saturday afternoon between November and March. You no longer spend a couple of hours every day in your car, hoping you'll be able to pick up Janie from dance class before Stephen has to be at soccer practice.

And, once your kids are moved out and supporting themselves, your financial burden is likely to be considerably lighter than in past years. No more tuition payments. No more car insurance for teenagers. No more low-rise jeans at $35 a pair, or $49 soccer shoes, or piano lessons at $25 an hour.

Money Morsel

Instead of being nostalgic about time that's passed, practice reveling in your newfound freedom and independence that comes once kids have moved out and started their own lives.

So go ahead and plan for those things you want to do. Delight in your options, and make the most of everything life has to offer. Take up fly-fishing. See New York City for the first time—or the hundredth. Go to a Broadway show, and dinner afterward. Buy a mountain bike and find some good trails. Finally play a round of golf at Pebble Beach. Drive along Big Sur. Drive across the country. Ride a mule into the Grand Canyon. Visit New England in the fall when the leaves are at their peak colors.

Helen Keller is quoted as saying, "Life is either a daring adventure or nothing." Hopefully, you have the resources—time, daring, energy, and finances—to take advantage of your options and make your life fun and meaningful.

Some Misconceptions About Aging

We all know that elderly folks are those who sit around in rocking chairs all day, either puffing on a pipe or keeping busy with some knitting. They go to bed early, are always cold, and keep a constant watch on their digestive systems by eating only bland, dependable foods such as oatmeal and well-cooked meats and vegetables. Wrong!

The definition of elderly—much like that of middle age—depends on where it comes from. Lately, though, we've seen this breakdown of age:

◆ Young-old is defined as 55 (yikes!) or older

◆ Old is defined as 65 or older

◆ Elderly is everyone over 75

Can't say for you, but 55 doesn't sound anywhere close to old to us, and at 75, we don't think you're ready to head to the rocking chair for good.

In fact, the current generation of older folks, those in their 60s, 70s, and into their 80s, are redefining the way society looks at, and thinks about aging. Many people are vibrant and active well into their 80s and beyond.

> **Go Figure**
>
> A nationwide poll showed that 25 percent of retired people said they stopped working too soon.

A book getting a lot of attention lately is *Successful Aging*, by John W. Rowe, M.D., and Robert L. Kahn, Ph.D. The book reports on the findings of a major scientific study of aging in America by the John D. and Catherine T. MacArthur Foundation. The study, as reported in the book, reveals six prevalent myths regarding older people.

These myths, which our society has bought into for years, are as follows:

- Most elderly people are sick.
- Elderly people don't pull their own weight in society.
- Elderly people are set in their ways (you can't teach an old dog new tricks).
- Elderly people aren't mentally or physically sharp and alert.
- Ailments caused by poor lifestyle choices, such as smoking, can't be improved upon or undone.
- Physical aging is primarily predetermined by genetics.

If you're tempted to go along with these assumptions concerning elderly folks, you'd better think again. The study revealed that most older people are, indeed, not sick at all, but generally healthy. Nearly 90 percent of those between 65 and 74 who participated in the study reported no disability whatsoever.

And the study showed, most elderly people more than pull their own weight in society. One-third work for pay, and another third are busy volunteering in churches, hospitals, and charities. Most elderly people report that, to varying degrees, they help out family members, friends, and neighbors.

Scientists are increasingly convinced, the study reports, that only about 30 percent of physical aging can be blamed on genes. The rest is due to lifestyle and environment. The good news, however, is that we're learning that problems caused by poor lifestyle choices, such as smoking or years of eating fatty foods, can be slowed down or even reversed when positive changes in habits occur.

While some elderly people might be resistant to change, there are many actually looking for new experiences. Older folks are using the Internet for shopping, keeping in touch with family members, and learning about all sorts of topics. They're attending college classes, taking art lessons, and scheduling trips to Prague, Alaska, and Scandinavia.

And as far as physical and mental sharpness goes, plenty of elderly people are still running their own businesses, running in road races, and running for office in various organizations and groups.

As we age, isn't it nice to know that aging isn't something to be feared or dreaded? Getting older is a blessing, when you consider the alternative, and we must be sure not to let myths and misconceptions cloud how we view our futures.

Making Sure You Can Afford Your Dreams

If you've got dreams, you've got to have the means to fund them.

Whether your dreams include a vacation home, a brand-new home, or being able to leave a substantial legacy for your children, you must be sure that your financial situation can ensure them.

If you're not sure whether you're where you should be, financially, schedule yourself an appointment with a financial advisor. Have him or her review all aspects of your finances with you, and listen carefully to the advice he or she dispenses.

It's a good idea, at this point in your life, to prioritize your future plans. Consider all of the necessities first, and then add on your wants and wishes. Remember that experts say many people run into trouble during retirement because they underestimate the number of years they'll spend there. If you're planning to retire when you're 65, don't assume that you'll only reach the average life expectancy of 76.7 or 79.5.

We all know lots of folks—probably some in your own family—who are well into their 80s or even 90s. You shouldn't assume that you'll die at the same ages that your parents or grandparents did.

If you haven't adequately saved for retirement at this point, don't give up because you think it's too late. Saving only $45 a week between the time you're 40 and 65 will add up to $50,000 if you average a nine percent rate of return. Take a minute to think of how you could save $45 a week. How hard could it be? Forty-five dollars is one or two meals a week in a restaurant. It's the blouse on sale in the department store that you like, but really don't need. It's that overnight getaway you were thinking about taking, or the fancy wheel covers for your car, or those fabulous new fingernails the technician was talking about.

And if you need to start saving more seriously than $45 a week, think about going credit free. Studies show that more and more Americans are loading up their credit cards while saving less and less. If you have trouble keeping your credit card in your wallet when you go shopping, leave it at home.

Decide that you'll only use cash unless it's a real emergency (a good sale in the Ralph Lauren department doesn't count as an emergency), and stick to your plan. If you must, use a debit card, which is just like using cash. For some reason, though, many people find it more difficult to part with actual money than they do to hand over a credit card for a purchase.

> ### Go Figure
>
> America's love affair with credit is reflected in both minor and major purchases. The average down payment on new vehicles has decreased from 25 percent in 1992 to just 7 percent in 2001.

Other methods of boosting your retirement account could include the following:

◆ **Postpone a major purchase, such as a car.** Sure, you've been thinking about buying a new car for two years now, and there are some terrific buys these days down on the Acura lot. Just because your car is now five years old and pushing the 60,000-mile mark, however, doesn't mean it's a smart idea for you to run out and buy a new one. There's no rule that says Americans shall only keep the same car for four, or five, or six years. Find a good mechanic and hang on to the vehicle you've got.

◆ **Trade in your large vehicle for a smaller one.** A two-, three-, or four-person family, unless there are special circumstances, simply doesn't need a Suburban or an Expedition. The SUV-craze has cost Americans millions and millions of dollars in gas and insurance costs, not to mention the initial prices of these huge vehicles. If you're driving an SUV or a very large car for no good reason, consider trading it in on a smaller one. You'll save money, and have a lot easier time in tight parking spaces, as well.

◆ **Take a good look at your job.** If you're badly underpaid in your job, consider looking for another one. Just because you're in your 40s or 50s doesn't mean that you're tied to a job. Many people stay in jobs they don't like or that don't pay as well as they should, simply because they're comfortable and reluctant to make a change. That's not a good idea for either your career or your retirement savings account.

◆ **Stop supplementing your kids' incomes.** If your kids are on their own and working, don't be tempted to continue handing over cash like they were still teenagers. Your primary financial responsibility at this point is to get your retirement account up to speed, not to be sure your 25-year-old can get that great new Jetta she's been longing for.

◆ **Downsize your living space.** If your kids are in college or moved out of the house, maybe it's time to think about boosting your retirement account by moving to a smaller house or apartment. It's a fact that one or two people require less space than four or five people. Just be sure, if you decide to downsize, that you really end up saving money. If your goal is to pump up your retirement accounts, don't be sucked into buying a place that's smaller, but actually more expensive than your current house or apartment.

When consulting with a financial advisor, be sure to share your hopes and plans for the future. It's important that an advisor understands your goals in order to be able to help you figure out how to fund them.

Aging with Style

If you take care of yourself—physically, financially, and emotionally—you stand a good chance of aging well. Assume that you'll live to be 90 or 95. Plan financially for 90 or 95. And, make sure that you have enough interests and things going on in your life so that you'll still be having a great time at 90 or 95.

There's no question that people who remain active, busy, and engaged in life and with the people around them are happier as they age. There are countless opportunities for older people. The question is, to what extent will you take advantage of them?

People who remain active and willing to take on new tasks and experiences as they age are those who age with style. They remain interested in what's going on around them. They remain committed to ideals, organizations, and people. They remain caring, loving, and mentally alert.

Start now to assure that you'll be a person who ages with style. Pay attention to your health—physical, spiritual, and emotional. Plan for healthy finances, and then put your faith in something larger than yourself and stop worrying. Have a great future.

The Least You Need to Know

- Regardless of what we think lies ahead for us, we must be prepared for unexpected twists and turns.

- Take advantage of the options you may have in mid life, and plan to do what you may not have been able to previously.

- New studies support what we should have known all along; that elderly people can, and most do, remain healthy, active, and involved.

- If you're not prepared financially for retirement, consider taking some big steps now to get you on the right path.

- Remember to stay connected, stay involved, and have fun as you age.

Glossary

401(k)   A retirement plan into which an employee can contribute a portion of his or her salary (usually before taxes). Contributions can grow tax-deferred until they are withdrawn upon retirement.

adjustable life insurance   A hybrid whole life insurance product where you don't pay as large an initial premium as with a whole life product. The death benefit is dependent on the amount of premiums paid over the life of the policy.

adjustable-rate mortgage   A mortgage set up with an interest rate that can change at specific intervals, as determined under the initial contract.

adjusted gross income (AGI)   Your gross income less certain allowed business-related deductions. These deductions include alimony payments, contributions to a Keogh retirement plan, and, in some cases, contributions to an IRA.

ADRs (American Depository Receipts)   Trust receipts for shares of a foreign company purchased and held by a foreign branch of the bank. The ADRs are legal claims against the equity interest that the bank holds. ADRs are an excellent alternative to direct investing in foreign companies.

aggressive growth fund   A type of mutual fund that has a primary investment objective of seeking capital gains. It is understood that the potential for above-average returns in such an investment is countered by above-average risks.

American Stock Exchange (AMEX)   At one time, AMEX was the second largest stock exchange in the U.S. AMEX has recently been merged with NASDAQ. Currently, the two exchanges still operate independently.

amortization   Reducing the principal of a loan by making regular payments.

amortization schedule   A schedule of regular payments with which to repay a loan. The schedule indicates to the borrower the amount of each payment that is principal, that which is interest, and that which is the remaining balance of the loan.

analysis   *See* fundamental analysis.

annual dividend   A share of a company's net profits that are distributed by the company to a class of its stockholders each year. The dividend is paid in a fixed amount for each share of stock held. Although most companies make quarterly payments in cash, dividends also may be made in other forms of property, such as stock. Dividends must be approved by the company's directors before each payment is made.

annual fee   The amount a cardholder pays to a credit card company for the right to hold a particular credit card.

annual report   A source of operating data on a company published annually by most publicly held firms. Also known as a shareholder's report.

annuity   A stream of equal payments, as to a retiree, that occur at predetermined intervals (for example, monthly or annually). The payments may continue for a fixed period or for a contingent period, such as the recipient's lifetime. Annuities are most often associated with insurance companies and retirement programs.

ask price   The lowest price at which a given security is offered for sale.

asset allocation   The process of determining the assignment of investment funds to broad categories of assets. For example, you (or your broker) decide what percentage of your stock should be in technology investments.

at the market   Refers to a security transaction that occurs at whatever price the broker can get for you at the time of the trade. You either buy or sell a stock at a set price, or you give an order to buy the security at whatever price the security happens to be when the order is placed.

baby boomer   A common term used to define individuals born between 1946 and 1964.

balanced mutual fund   A mutual fund whose primary objective is to buy a combination of stocks and bonds. These middle-of-the-road funds balance their portfolios to achieve both moderate income and moderate capital growth. These funds tend to be less volatile than stock-only funds. Balanced funds tend, on average, to be invested as 45 percent bonds and 55 percent stocks.

bear market   An extended period of general price decline in the stock market as a whole.

beneficiary   The person who is named to receive the proceeds from an investment vehicle, trust, or contract. A beneficiary can be an individual, a company, or an organization.

beta (B)   A mathematical measure of the risk on a portfolio or a given stock compared with rates of return on the market as a whole. A beta of less than one is less volatile than the general market. A beta above one is more volatile than the market.

bid price   The highest price offered to purchase a given security.

blackout period   The period of time between when the surviving spouse's Social Security benefits cease after the children are grown until they receive Social Security benefits (the earliest date would be age 60).

blue chip investment   A high-quality investment involving a lower-than-average risk. Blue chip investment is generally used to refer to securities of companies having a long history of sustained earnings and dividend payments.

blue chip stock   This is the common phrase for stock of well-established companies that historically pay dividends in good years and bad. Some examples of blue chip stocks are General Motors, Exxon, and IBM.

bond   A debt instrument. The issuer promises to pay the investor a specified amount of interest for a period of time and to repay the principal at maturity.

bond fund   A mutual fund that invests in bonds and passes current income to its shareholders, with capital gains as a secondary objective. Some bond funds purchase long-term securities providing a relatively high current yield, but varying substantially in price with changes in interest rates. Other funds choose short-term securities having lower yields, but fluctuating little in value.

broker   A person who earns a commission or fee for acting as an agent in making contracts or sales.

budget   A schedule of income and expenses commonly broken into monthly intervals and typically covering a one-year period.

bull market   An extended period of generally rising prices in the market as a whole.

business risk   The degree of uncertainty associated with a company's earnings and its ability to pay interest, dividends, and other returns owed investors.

C corporations   C corporations get a double whammy when it comes to paying federal income tax. The corporation has to pay a tax on its earned profit, and the people who get salaries or corporate dividends have to pay again.

capital expenses   Expenses spent to improve property.

capital gain   Profits from the sale of an investment or asset. Tax on this gain is usually due when the asset is sold.

capital gains exclusion   An exclusion to the practice of taxing capital gains that applies to the sale of real estate.

capitalization   The sum of a corporation's long-term debt, stock, and retained earnings—also called invested capital.

cash flow   Shows the ability of a company to meet its day-to-day operating expenses and satisfy its short-term obligations as they come due. It's a measure of how well they can pay their bills, and it's important for an investor to know this information.

cash-value life insurance   In this insurance, part of the premium is used to provide death benefits, and the remainder is available to earn interest. Cash-value life insurance is a protection plan and a savings plan that charges significantly higher premiums than term insurance.

certificate of deposit (CD)   A receipt for a deposit of funds in a financial institution that permits the holder to receive the deposit plus interest at maturity.

certified financial planner (CFP)   A professional financial planner who has completed a series of correspondence courses and passed a 10-hour examination in subject areas such as insurance, securities, and taxes. The designation is awarded by the College for Financial Planning in Denver, Colorado.

certified public accountant (CPA)   An accountant who has met certain state requirements as to age, education, experience, residence, and accounting knowledge. Accountants must pass an extensive series of examinations before becoming CPAs.

chartered financial consultant (ChFC)   A professional financial planner who has completed a series of 10 courses and examinations in subject areas such as economics, insurance, investments, and tax shelters. The designation is awarded by the American College of Bryn Mawr, Pennsylvania.

churning and burning   To trade securities very actively in a brokerage account in order to increase brokerage commissions rather than customer profits. Brokers may be tempted to churn accounts because their income is directly related to the volume of trading undertaken by the customers. Churning is illegal and unethical.

closed-ended fund   A type of mutual fund in which only a limited number of shares can be sold.

collateral   Assets pledged as security for a loan. If a borrower defaults on the terms of a loan, the collateral may be sold, with the proceeds used to satisfy any remaining obligations.

High-quality collateral reduces risk to the lender and results in a lower rate of interest on the loan.

commercial bank   Financial institutions, either chartered by the federal or state government that take deposits, loan money, and provide other services to individuals or corporations.

commission   The sum or percentage allowed to a broker (agent) for his services.

common stock   Shares of ownership of a company; a class of capital stock that has no preference to dividends or any other distributions.

compound interest   Interest paid on interest from previous periods in addition to principal. Essentially, compounding involves adding interest to principal and any previous interest in order to calculate interest in the next period. Compound interest may be figured daily, monthly, quarterly, or annually.

consumer price index (CPI)   A measure of the relative cost of living compared with a base year (currently 1967). The CPI can be a misleading indicator of inflationary impact on a given person because it is constructed according to the spending of an urban family of four. It is used as a measure of inflation.

consumer prices   Consumer price indicators are changes in prices for a fixed market basket of about 360 goods and services. The changes are used as a measure of inflation.

corporate bond   A bond issued by a corporation as opposed to a bond issued by the U.S. Treasury or a municipality.

corporation   Formed into an association and endowed by law with the rights and liabilities of an individual.

credit history   The record of an individual's past events that pertain to credit previously given or applied for.

credit unions   Alternatives to commercial banks, credit unions are nonprofit organizations that provide many of the same services as banks. Generally, credit unions can offer better rates on loans and savings because they don't pay federal taxes.

customer service representative (CSR)   A front-line bank employee who opens checking and savings accounts, certificates of deposit, and so forth. They know the products their financial institutions provide.

cyclical stock   Common stock of a firm whose earnings are heavily influenced by cyclical changes in general economic activity. As investors anticipate changes in profits, cyclical stocks often reach their high and low levels before the respective highs and lows in the economy.

debit card   A plastic card used for purchasing goods and services or obtaining cash advanced in which payment is made from existing funds in a bank account.

deductible   The amount the insured must pay before an insurance company pays a claim.

deduction   An expenditure permitted to be used in order to reduce an individual's income tax liability.

default   Failure to live up to the terms of a contract or to meet financial obligations. Generally, the term is used to indicate the inability of a homeowner to pay interest or principal on a debt when it is due.

defensive stock   A stock that tends to resist general stock market declines and whose price will remain stable or even prosper when economic activity is tapering.

defensive stock annual report   A source of operating data on a company published annually by most publicly held firms. Also known as a shareholder's report.

defined benefit plan   A qualified retirement plan that specifies the benefits received, rather than contributions into the plan, usually expressed as a percentage of pre-retirement compensation and number of years of service. The responsibility for the benefit is on the company, not the employee.

defined contribution plan   A qualified retirement plan that specifies the annual contributions to the plan, usually expressed as a percentage of the employee's salary. Contributions can be made by the employer, the employee, or both.

depreciation   The systematic write-off of the basis of a tangible asset over the asset's estimated useful life. Depreciation is intended to reflect the wear, tear, and obsolescence of the asset.

disability   The lack of competent power, strength, or physical or mental ability.

disability insurance   Insurance intended to cover loss of income due to a disability.

discount broker   A broker that charges a lower commission than a full-service broker. In exchange, the service is less than with a full-service broker.

discounted bond   A bond in which the current market value of the bond is less than the face or par value of the bond that will be received at maturity.

discretionary expenses   Expenses that are incurred for nonessentials; money spent as a person chooses.

disposition charges   Expenses charged to a lessee for selling the vehicle or property leased at the end of the lease.

diversification   The acquisition of a group of assets in which returns on the assets are not directly related over time. Proper investment diversification, requiring a sufficient number of different assets, is intended to minimize risk associated with investing.

dividend   A share of a company's net profits distributed by the company to a class of its stockholders. The dividend is paid in a fixed amount for each share of stock held. Dividends are usually fixed in preferred stock; dividends from common stock vary as the company's performance shifts.

dividend reinvestment plan (DRIP)   Stockholders may automatically reinvest dividend payments in additional shares of the company's stock. Instead of receiving the normal dividend checks, participating stockholders will receive quarterly notification of shares purchased and shares held in their accounts. Dividend reinvestment is normally an inexpensive way of purchasing additional shares of stock because the fees are low or are completely absorbed by the company. In addition, some companies offer stock at a discount from the existing market price. Normally, these dividends are fully taxable as income even though no cash is received by the stockholder.

dollar cost averaging   Investment of an equal amount of money at regular intervals, usually each month. This process results in the purchase of extra shares during market downturns and fewer shares during market upturns. Dollar cost averaging is based on the belief that the market of a particular stock will rise in price over the long term and that it is not worthwhile (or even possible) to identify immediate highs and lows.

Dow Jones Industrial Average (DJIA)   One of the measures of the stock market that includes averages for utilities, industrial, and transportation stocks, as well as the composite averages. *See also* index.

down payment   Funds the purchaser puts down when property is sold. Remaining funds for purchase are borrowed.

durable power of attorney   A legal transfer of authority enabling one party to conduct the business of another while they are disabled or incompetent.

dwelling coverage   The part of your homeowner's insurance that covers the structure in which you live.

dwelling insurance   *See* renter's insurance.

earned income   Salary, wages, and self-employment income derived as compensation for services rendered. Unearned income includes the return you receive from investments.

elimination period   The number of days that must pass before the insured can receive benefits. The longer the period, the lower the premium that is charged.

emergency fund A source of money put away to be used in case of illness, job loss, disability, or other circumstances. Experts recommend having between three and six months' salary in an emergency fund.

emerging growth fund The common stock of a relatively young firm operating in an industry with very good growth prospects. Although this kind of stock offers unusually large returns, it is very risky because the expected growth may not occur, or the firm may be swallowed by the competition.

emerging market stock The term which broadly categorizes countries in the midst of developing their financial markets and economic infrastructures.

employer identification number (EIN) A nine-digit number assigned to corporations, partnerships, estates, trusts, and other entities for tax filing and reporting purposes.

enrolled agent A designation given by the IRS. They are licensed and can represent clients in front of the IRS in the event of an audit. Enrolled agents generally have more training than tax preparers, and they're required to participate in continuing education. As a group, they charge more than tax preparers.

equity The value of ownership in property or securities. The equity in your home is the difference between the current market value of the home and the amount still owed on the mortgage.

ERISA Employee Retirement Income Security Act of 1974. Federal legislation that sets the guidelines for employer retirement plans.

escrow The holding of assets (for example: securities, cash, a collection) by a third party, which delivers the assets to the grantee or promisee on the fulfillment of some condition. Some parts of mortgage payments are held in escrow to cover expenses owed, such as property taxes and insurance.

executor (executrix) A person named in a will who is appointed to administer the decedent's estate.

fair market value The price at which a buyer and a seller willingly consummate a trade; the prevailing price of a security or property.

Fannie Mae A security issued by the Federal National Mortgage Association (FNMA) that is backed by insured and conventional mortgages. Monthly returns to holders of Fannie Maes consist of interest and principal payments made by the homeowners on their mortgages.

Federal Home Mortgage Association (FHMA) A privately owned profit-seeking corporation that adds liquidity to the mortgage market by purchasing loans from lenders. It finances the purchases by issuing its own bonds or by selling mortgages it already owns to financial institutions.

finance charges   Interest expenses incurred from lending or leasing.

financial advisor   A professional who guides individuals to arrange and coordinate their financial affairs.

financial consultant   Someone who provides an overview of financial information and options, in order for you to choose products and services from which you will benefit.

financial planner   A person who counsels individuals and corporations with respect to evaluating financial status, identifying goals, and determining ways in which the goals can be met.

financial planning   The process of defining and setting goals to achieve financial security.

fixed-interest rate loan   A loan that has a set rate throughout the period of the loan. Payments are usually set at a specified, equal payment throughout the loan.

fixed-rate mortgage   A mortgage in which the annual interest charged does not vary throughout the period of the loan.

foreclosure   When a lender claims a property on which the loan has been defaulted.

Freddie Mac   A security issued by the Federal Home Loan Mortgage Corporation that is secured by pools of conventional home mortgages. Holders of Freddie Macs receive a share of interest and principal payments by the homeowners.

full-service broker   Normally works for a major brokerage firm. She receives commissions on the trades an individual makes, or she gets a fee based on the value of funds within an account.

fundamental analysis   The process of comparing the fundamental properties of an investment.

gap insurance   Insurance purchased to pay the difference between the value your auto insurance will pay if a leased vehicles is stolen or totaled and the amount required to terminate the lease.

global fund   A mutual fund that includes at least 25 percent foreign securities in its portfolio. The value of the fund depends on the health of foreign economies and exchange rate movements. A global fund permits an investor to diversify internationally.

GNP (gross national product)   The market value of all goods and services produced by a country over the period of a year.

good-till-cancelled order   A limit order that remains outstanding until it is executed or cancelled. Also called an open order.

Government National Mortgage Association (GNMA)   A government-owned corporation that acquires, packages, and resells mortgages and mortgage-purchased commitments in the form of mortgage-backed securities.

government obligations   A debt that is backed by the full taxing power of the U.S. government. Direct obligations include Treasury bills, Treasury bonds, and U.S. savings bonds. These investments are generally considered to be of the very highest quality.

government securities   Bonds, bills, or notes sold by the federal government to raise money.

grantor   The person who establishes a trust. Also known as the trustor.

gross income   All income except those specifically exempted by the Internal Revenue Code.

group insurance   Insurance offered only to members as a group, such as employees, often for only as long as they remain members of the group.

growth fund   An investment company whose major objective is long-term capital growth. Growth funds offer substantial potential gains over time but vary significantly in price, depending on general economic conditions.

growth stock   The stock of a firm that is expected to have above-average increases in revenues and earnings. These firms normally retain most earnings for reinvestment and therefore pay small dividends. The stocks, often selling at relatively high price-earnings ratios, are subject to wide swings in price. Object of investment is capital appreciation and long-term capital growth.

guaranteed renewable   An insurance provision that guarantees that the policy can't be canceled if you get sick.

guaranteed replacement cost provision   An insurance provision that promises to pay the total cost to replace property upon loss or damage.

hardship withdrawals   A special provision of the 401(k) plan that permits an employee to withdraw funds from his or her account while still working for the firm. The provisions for withdrawal set up the withdrawal limitations, and the withdrawn funds are taxed and may be subject to a penalty.

high-yield/junk bond   A high-risk, high-yield debt security issued by corporations or municipalities that are of lower quality. Junk bonds have a greater risk of default than higher-rated bonds. These securities are most appropriate for risk-oriented investors. They usually pay a higher interest rate than higher-rated bonds.

home equity loan   A loan in which property is used as collateral. Usually a second mortgage on a property.

homeowner's insurance   Insurance obtained by a property owner to protect the property and contents. It also provides liability coverage for accidents that occur on the property.

HOPE (Higher Opportunities for Performance in Education) Credit   A tax credit permitted for qualified tuition and related expenses for a student's *first two* years of college. The student must attend postsecondary courses at least half-time. The credit is 100 percent of the first $1,000 of qualified expenses paid during the year plus 50 percent of the next $2,000, for a maximum of $3,000.

hybrid fund   A mutual fund that has characteristics of several types of securities. An example would be a convertible bond, which is a bond that has a conversion feature that permits the investor to convert the security into a specified number of shares of common stock of the company.

income fund   An investment company, the main objective of which is to achieve current income for its owners. Thus, it tends to select securities such as bonds, preferred stocks, and common stocks that pay relatively high current returns.

income stocks   A stock with a relatively high dividend yield. The stock's issuer is typically a firm having stable earnings and dividends and operating in a mature industry. The price of an income stock is heavily influenced by changes in interest rates.

index   The measurement of the current price behavior of a representative group of stocks in relation to a base value set at an earlier point in time. The best-known indexes are the Dow Jones Industrial Average and Standard & Poor's 500 Index.

index fund   A mutual fund that keeps a portfolio of securities designed to match the performance of the market as a whole. The market is represented by an index, such as the Standard & Poor's 500. An index fund has low administrative expenses; it appeals to investors who believe it is difficult or impossible for investment managers to beat the market.

individual retirement account (IRA)   A retirement savings plan in which you can contribute up to $2,000 per year. Funds can grow tax-deferred until they are withdrawn at retirement. Contributions may or may not be tax-deductible depending on income level and participation in other retirement plans.

inflation   A general increase in the price level of goods and services.

inflation rider   Additional insurance coverage that is purchased to provide that the underlying policy coverage increases with inflation.

initial public offering (IPO)   A company's first sale of stock to the public. Securities offered in an IPO are often, but not always, those of young, small companies seeking outside equity capital and a public market for their stock. Investors purchasing stock in IPOs generally assume very large risks for the possibility of large gains.

insurance   A mechanism that permits individual to reduce risk by sharing in the losses associated with the occurrence of certain events.

insurance bond   An insurance policy guaranteeing that funds will be retained as pledged.

intangible personal property   Property that attains its value from what it represents, not from what it's worth. An example is a stock certificate.

interest   The cost for the use of borrowed money.

interest-sensitive stock   A stock that tends to move in the opposite direction of interest rates. Interest-sensitive stocks include nearly all preferred stocks and the common stocks of industries such as electric utilities, banks, and insurance companies. A common stock may be interest-sensitive because its dividend is relatively fixed (as with an electric utility) or because the firm raises a large portion of its funds through borrowing (as with a savings and loan).

international fund   A mutual fund that invests only outside the country in which it is located.

international stock   This is stock of companies located outside the United States.

investing   When you buy something with the expectation of making a profit.

investment   The process of purchasing securities or property for which stability of value and level of expected returns are somewhat predictable.

investment return   The return achieved on an investment, including current income and any change in value during an investor's holding period; also known as total return.

IPO (initial public offering)   The stock offering of a company when it goes public. *See also* initial public offering.

irrevocable trust   Usually set up and used by people with many assets, irrevocable trusts can't be amended or destroyed. Once set up, the trust remains in place and can't be changed. Used primarily to reduce estate taxes, they are also used to protect property for heirs who can't handle their money due to age (a minor) or being a spendthrift.

itemized deduction   An expenditure permitted to be used to reduce an individual's income-tax liability.

Keogh   A federally approved retirement program that permits self-employed people to set money aside for savings up to $30,000 (or up to 25 percent of their income). All contributions and income earned by the account are tax-deferred until withdrawals are made during retirement.

large-cap stocks   Stocks in companies with over $10 billion in capitalization, the largest companies.

leading indicator   A statistic indicating that the economy is pointing in a direction opposite of where the economy currently is.

lease   A contract under which someone obtains the use of an object, such as a vehicle or property, for a specified time and a specified amount of money.

lending instrument   A debt instrument; companies borrow money from investors and agree to pay a stated rate of interest over a specified period of time, at the end of which the original sum will be repaid.

leverage   Measures different types of financing for firms and indicates the amount of debt being used to support the resources and operations of the company.

leverage ratios   These are the amount of debt being used to support the company, and the ability of the firm to service its debt. Debt-equity ratio measures the amount of financial leverage being utilized by a company.

Lifetime Learning Credit   A tax credit for expenses that don't qualify for the HOPE credit. The Lifetime Learning Credit is available for any school year for courses to acquire or improve job skills. The credit may be for undergraduate, graduate, or professional degree courses.

limit order   An order to buy at a specified price (or lower) or sell at (or above) a specified price.

liquidity   The ability to quickly convert assets into cash without significant loss.

liquidity ratios   These are current ratios and net working capital. You measure the ability of the company to meet its day-to-day operating expenses and satisfy short-term obligations as they come due.

living will   Also called medical directives, a document that states your wishes should you become profoundly ill, irreversibly incompetent, and need life support or heroic measures to keep you alive.

long-term capital gains   Profits from the sale of investments that you've held for more than a year. Long-term capital gains are taxed at either 10 or 20 percent, depending on your income tax bracket. Investors in the 15 percent bracket pay only a 10 percent tax on their capital gains, while all others pay a 20 percent tax on their long-term capital gains.

long-term stock   Stock that you keep for more than a year before selling.

marginal tax bracket   The percentage of extra income received that must be paid in taxes, or the proportional amount of taxes paid on a given income or the given dollar value of an asset. If the tax is calculated on the basis of total income, it is the average tax rate. If the tax is calculated only on the extra units of income, the rate is the marginal tax rate.

market measures   *See* common stock.

market order   An order to buy or sell stock at the best price available at the time the order is placed with the broker.

market timing   Buying and selling stock, in part or in whole, depending on when an investor feels it's advantageous to get in and out of the stock market.

market value   The prevailing market price of a security or property; an indication of how the market as a whole has assessed the security's or the property's worth.

maturity   The termination of the period that an obligation has to run (bonds); mortgages have a date of maturity, when they are due to be repaid in full.

medical directive (living will)   A legal document directing the implementation or withholding of medical procedures while a person is unconscious and terminally ill.

mid-cap stocks   Stocks in companies with $1 billion to $10 billion capitalization.

middle age   The period between the ages of 40 and 60. Note that there are many definitions of middle age; this one pertains to financial middle age.

misrepresentation   To represent a financial product incorrectly, improperly, or falsely.

money manager   A person who is paid a fee to supervise the investment decisions of others. The term is usually used for management of individual portfolios as compared to institutional funds. *See also* portfolio manager.

money market accounts   Accounts held in banks, on which you receive interest.

money market fund   A mutual fund that sells shares of ownership and uses the proceeds to purchase short-term, high-quality securities such as treasury bills, negotiable certificates of deposit, and commercial paper. Income earned by shareholders is received in the form of additional shares of stock in the fund (normally priced at $1 each). Although no fees are generally charged to purchase or redeem shares in a money market fund, an annual management charge is levied by the fund's advisors. This investment pays a return that varies with short-term interest rates. It is relatively liquid and safe, but yields and features vary.

money purchase plan   A qualified employer retirement plan in which each employee has an individual account. The employer must make annual contributions to each employee's account. The amount of contribution is determined by a pre-set formula, based on a fixed percentage or a flat monetary amount.

mortgage   A conditional conveyance of property to a creditor as security for the repayment of money.

mortgage life insurance   Term insurance that will pay the outstanding balance on the insured person's home loan should he or she die.

municipal bond   The debt issue of a city, county, state, or other political entity. Interest paid by most municipal bonds is exempt from federal income taxes and often from state and local taxes. Municipal bonds with tax-exempt interest appeal mainly to investors with significant amounts of other taxable income.

municipal bond fund   A mutual fund that invests in tax-exempt securities and passes through tax-free current income to its shareholders. Some municipal bond funds purchase long-term securities providing a relatively high current yield, but varying substantially in price with changes in interest rates. Other funds choose short-term securities having lower yields but fluctuating little in value.

mutual fund   An open-ended investment company that invests its shareholders' money in a diversified group of securities of other corporations. Mutual funds are usually diversified and professionally managed.

NASDAQ (National Association of Security Dealers Automated Quotation System)   A system (exchange) providing up-to-date bid and ask prices on thousands of over-the-counter securities.

net income   The income you have after you've paid taxes and any and all other liabilities, expenses, or charges against it.

net working capital   An absolute measure of a company's liquidity.

net worth   The amount of wealth calculated by taking the total value of assets owned and subtracting all liabilities.

New York Stock Exchange (NYSE)   The largest, oldest, key organized trading exchange in the United States for stock and bond transactions, accounting for over 50 percent of the total volume of shares traded on organized exchanges.

no-load fund   A mutual fund sold without a sales charge. No-load funds sell directly to customers at net asset value with no intermediate salesperson charging a fee.

nondiversifiable risk   *See* systematic risk.

nonqualified retirement plans   Pension and profit sharing plans that do not meet ERISA requirements to be considered qualified. Usually set up for key employees, deferred compensation and stock options are types of nonqualified plans.

nontaxable income   Income specifically exempted from taxation. On federal income tax returns, interest from most municipal bonds, life insurance proceeds, gifts, and inheritances is generally nontaxable income.

odd lot   Less than 100 shares of a stock.

open order   *See* good-till-cancelled order.

open-ended fund   A mutual fund with no limit on the number of shares it can offer for sale.

operating agreement   The formal agreement designed and agreed to by members of an investment club.

Operation of Law   Transfer of property, at death, from one joint owner to the other joint owner(s) rather than via a will, trust, or beneficiary designation.

partnership   A legal relationship between two or more persons contractually associated as joint principals in a business.

pension plan   An employer-sponsored retirement plan in which a retiree receives a fixed periodic payment made in consideration of past services, injury or loss sustained, merit or poverty, and so on.

performance   The level of profit you make from a particular investment. Performance is measured for a period of time—either a quarter, half-year, or annual rate of return.

personal credit score   A score given to individuals by the three major credit firms based on their credit report and credit history. Lenders use this score to decide whether to lend to an individual and at what interest rate.

personal finance   Every aspect of one's life that deals with money.

personal income   This is the before-tax income, received in the form of wages and salaries, interest and dividends, rents, and other payments such as Social Security, unemployment, and pensions. This report helps explain trends in consumer buying habits. When personal income rises, it often means that people will increase their buying.

points   Prepaid interest paid as a fee to a mortgage lender to cover the cost of applying for the loan. One point is one percent of the loan's value.

portfolio   A group of investments assembled to meet an investment goal.

portfolio manager   A person who is paid a fee to supervise the investment decisions of others. The term is normally used in reference to the managers of large institutions, such as bank trust departments, pension funds, insurance companies, and mutual funds.

power of attorney   A legal transfer of authority. It enables one party to conduct the business of another while they are away or incompetent.

preferred stock   A security that shows ownership in a corporation and gives the holder a claim prior to the claim of common shareholders on earnings and also generally on assets in the event of liquidation. Most preferred stock issues pay a fixed dividend set at the time of issuance, stated in a dollar amount or as a percentage of par value. Because no maturity date is stipulated, these securities are priced on dividend yield and trade much like long-term corporate bonds. As a general rule, preferred stock has limited appeal for individual investors.

premium   The amount paid, in one sum or periodically, for a contract of insurance.

premium bond   A bond in which the current market value of the bond is more than the face or par value of the bond that will be received at maturity.

price/earnings ratio (P/E ratio)   A common stock analysis statistic in which the current price of a stock is divided by the current (or sometimes the projected) earnings per share of the issuing firm.

principal   The capital sum, as distinguished from interest or profit.

probate   The process of verifying a will, after death, at the courthouse. The court gives authorization to an executor (or administrator) to gather assets, pay death taxes and expenses, and then transfer property to the beneficiaries of the will as directed.

producer price index   If this index goes up, it means that producers are raising prices on the products they sell. Sometimes these increases are passed along to consumers, but depending on things like competition and the state of the general economy, they may not be.

producer prices   These indicate price changes of goods at various stages of production, from crude materials such as raw cotton to finished goods like clothing and furniture. An upward surge may mean higher consumer prices later. Watch for changes in the prices of finished goods. These don't fluctuate as widely as crude materials, which makes them a better measure of inflationary pressure.

profit sharing plan   A qualified, defined contribution plan in which an employer contributes money to employees' accounts, based on the amount of profit the company has realized that year.

profitability ratios   These measure the company's success, as based on its profit.

prospectus   A formal written document related to a new securities offering that delineates the proposed business plan or the data relevant to an existing business plan. Investors need this information to make educated decisions about whether to purchase the security. The prospectus includes financial data, a summary of the firm's business history, a list of its officers, a description of its operations, and a mention of any pending litigation. A prospectus is an abridged version of the firm's registration statement, filed with the Securities and Exchange Commission.

qualified pension or profit sharing plan   A pension or profit sharing plan sponsored by an employer that meets the ERISA requirements. Usually contributions are with pre-tax dollars.

Qualified State Tuition Plan   Investment account set up under section 529 of the IRS Tax Code that permits investing for college in a tax-deferred vehicle. One plan is know as a Prepaid Tuition Plan or Tuition Assistance Plan, the other is a 529 plan.

rate   The amount charged to borrow money.

redemption fee   A fee charged to an investor if mutual fund shares are sold before the end of a previously agreed upon time period.

refinancing   Reapplying for a new mortgage, usually to receive a lower interest rate. Refinancing is done for consolidation, lower interest rate, or additional funding.

renter's insurance   Similar to homeowner's insurance, it provides insurance protection for a resident's personal property, along with liability coverage.

residual value   The value of a vehicle when it comes off a lease; the value you need to pay to acquire the vehicle.

retail sales   These are total sales at the retail level, including everything from cars to groceries. This figure gives a rough clue to consumer attitudes, and can indicate future conditions. A long slowdown in sales can lead to cuts in production. If retail sales are dropping, an investor shouldn't rush out and buy Gap, The Limited, Sears, and so on.

return on equity (ROE)   *See* return on investment (ROI).

return on investment (ROI)   Measures the return to stockholders by relating profit to shareholders' equity.

return on total assets (ROTA)   Looks at the amount of resources by the firm to support operations. Reveals management effectiveness in generating profits from the assets it has available, and is perhaps the single most important measure of return.

reverse mortgage   An arrangement in which a lender pays the homeowner a monthly payment with the idea that the lender will be repaid after the property is sold.

rider   An addition or amendment to a document.

risk   The chance that the value or return on an investment will differ from its expected value. Business risk, financial risk, purchasing power risk, interest rate risk, market risk, default risk, and foreign currency risk are all types of risk associated with investments.

Roth IRA   New in 1998, an individual retirement account in which the funds placed into the account are nondeductible. If held more than five years, all funds withdrawn are received tax-free.

round lot   The standard unit of trading in a particular type of security. For stocks, a round lot is 100 shares or a multiple thereof, although few inactive issues trade in units of 10 shares.

S corporations   S corporations get special tax status from the Internal Revenue Service (IRS), and they don't pay tax on the corporate level. All profits and losses are passed along to members or shareholders, who have to include the income on their personal tax returns. If there's a loss, shareholders write it off on their personal taxes.

S&L *See* thrifts.

S&P 500 Standard and Poor's composite of the 500 largest companies in the United States.

sandwich generation A rapidly growing group of middle-aged people, most of them women, who are caring both for children and aging parents.

sector fund Securities or other assets that share a common interest. Sector funds permit an investor to concentrate on a specific investment segment and yet diversify investments among various issuers. Sector funds entail more risk, but offer greater potential returns than funds that diversify their portfolios.

security An investment that represents evidence of debt, ownership of a business, or the legal right to determine the intrinsic interest in a business.

SEC (Securities and Exchange Commission) A federal agency that registers securities and investment advisers. The agency is in charge of the administration of federal securities law. They regulate the organized securities exchanges and over-the-counter markets by extending disclosure requirements to outstanding securities.

SEP-IRA A retirement plan for the self-employed that permits contributions up to $30,000 per year, or 15 percent of your income, whichever is lower. Similar to an IRA, except that the contribution limits are higher.

settlement The settling of property and title on an individual or individuals; the transaction when you purchase a security or property.

shareholder One who holds or owns a share or shares of a corporation.

short-term capital gains Profits that come from the sale of investments that you've held for less than a year. Any gain made as a result of the investment is taxed at the same income tax rate as all other income of the taxpayer.

simple interest Interest paid on an initial investment only. Simple interest is calculated by multiplying the principal times the annual rate of interest times the number of years involved.

simple retirement plans A relatively new retirement plan aimed at small employers (fewer than 100 employees). Simple plans are easy and inexpensive to administer. An employer must contribute annually to a simple plan.

simplified employee pension plan (SEP) A special type of joint Keogh–individual retirement account, permitting contributions from employees and employers. The SEP was developed to give small businesses a retirement plan that is easier to establish and administer than an ordinary pension plan.

small-cap stocks   Companies which have less than $1 billion capitalization.

speculation   Taking above-average risks to achieve above-average returns, generally during a relatively short period of time. Speculation involves buying something on the basis of its potential selling price rather than on the basis of its actual value.

springing power of attorney   A document that becomes valid only when the principal is declared to be mentally incompetent.

standard deduction   The minimum deduction from income allowed a taxpayer for calculating taxable income. Individuals with few itemized deductions are the standard deduction instead of itemizing deductions.

stock   Shares of ownership in a company. These shares include common stock of various classes and any preferred stock outstanding.

stock certificate   Physical proof, issued by the corporation, that an investor owns shares in the company. Stock certificates can be certificated (in paper form that you would hold in your lockbox) or in uncertificated form (held in dividend reinvestment plans and with your broker).

stock fund   A mutual fund that limits its investments to shares of common stock. Common stock funds vary in risk, from relatively low to quite high, depending on the types of stocks in which the funds invest.

stock market   The organized securities exchange for stock and bond transactions.

stockbroker   A broker who, for a commission, buys and sells stocks (and commonly other securities) for customers.

stop-loss order   An order to sell a stock when its market price reaches or drops below a specified level; a suspended order used primarily to protect the investor against rapid declines in prices and to limit loss.

summary annual report   The report provided by your employer describes the firm's retirement plan's aggregate financial status.

summary plan description   An employer document for the firm's retirement plan that explains the basic rules and features of the plan. You should receive a copy within 90 days of becoming a participant.

survivor benefits explanation   Usually provided annually, a description of your survivor benefits available to your spouse under your retirement plan.

systematic risk   Also known as the nondiversifiable risk. The risk of a stock following the market. Systematic risk is attributable to forces that affect all investments and are therefore not unique to a given investment.

target benefit plan   An age-weighted retirement plan that's normally used by a company that wishes to have a specified sum available for an older employee (usually an owner) at the time of retirement.

target price   What you anticipate your investment will be worth at a future time. If you expect your $1,000 investment to double in five years, for example, your target price is $2,000.

tax number   *See* employer identification number (EIN).

tax preparer   An individual who prepares a tax return according to law.

tax-deductible   An expense that can be used to offset gross income when calculating your taxable gross income.

tax-deferred   Income that is earned but neither received nor taxed until a later date, when the funds are withdrawn or mature. Tax-deferred assets include those within an IRA, 401(k) plan, 403(b) plan, tax-deferred annuity, tax-deferred life insurance, EE savings bonds, and others.

tax-managed   A recent concept for specified mutual funds where the tax consequences are taken into consideration when securities within the mutual fund are sold.

taxable income   Income that is subject to taxation; adjusted income minus standard or itemized deductions and exemptions.

term insurance   Life insurance in which the insurance company pays a specified sum if the insured dies during the coverage period. Term insurance includes no savings, cash value, borrowing power, or benefits at retirement. On the basis of cost, it is the least expensive insurance available, although policy prices can vary significantly among firms.

testamentary trust   A trust that is laid out in a person's will and established after his death.

thrifts   These are financial institutions commonly known as savings and loans (S&Ls).

time-share   The deed or right to spend a specified amount of time every year at a specific place.

total return   Dividend or interest income plus any capital gains, generally considered a better measure of an investment's return than dividends or interest alone.

trading stock   This is different from investing in stock. Trading stock is when you buy and sell stock actively, with the intention of turning a profit. Investing is when you buy stock with the intention of keeping it for a significant period of time.

transaction costs   The expense of buying or selling securities.

treasury bond   Longer-term (over 10 years), interest-bearing debt of the U.S. Treasury, available through a bank or brokerage firm or directly from the Federal Reserve. Treasury Bonds are quoted and traded in thirty-seconds of a point.

treasury note   Intermediate-term (1 to 10 years), interest-bearing debt of the U.S. Treasury. Treasury notes are quoted and traded in thirty-seconds of a point.

treasury stock   Shares of a firm's stock that have been issued and then repurchased. Treasury stock is not considered in paying dividends, voting, or calculating earnings per share. It may be eventually retired or reissued.

trust   A legal document/agreement allowing the transfer of ownership of property or money to a person who is designated to manage and distribute the assets according to your instructions, for the benefit of another.

trustee   The person who manages a trust.

unemployment   Measuring the percentage of the workforce that's currently involuntarily without jobs, this is a broad indicator of economic health. Another monthly figure available is the number of payroll jobs. This may be a better indicator for spotting changes in business. A decreasing number of jobs is a sign that firms are cutting production.

universal life insurance   *See* cash value life insurance.

unrealized losses   See unrealized profits.

unsystematic risk   The portion of an investor's portfolio's risk that can be eliminated by diversification.

value stock   A stock in which the price is considered below normal using valuation measures common to the market.

variable interest rate   Interest, either paid or received (depending on whether you are borrowing or investing funds), that changes periodically, depending on the initial contract.

variable life insurance   An insurance policy, the industry's answer to the stock market boom of the 1990s. The premium dollars are invested in a variety of mutual funds, growing until needed for the internal cost of insurance. In the early years, your premium is lower than the cost of insurance. In later years, the price of insurance increases, but hopefully the investments have accumulated enough to cover the costs.

wage replacement ratio (WRR)   The ratio amount of your Social Security benefit to your pre-retirement income. Knowing this ratio provides an idea of how much other income you will need for retirement.

warranty   A statement of promise or assurance in connection with a contract or purchase.

whole life insurance   *See* cash value life insurance.

will   A legal document directing how your property is to be disposed of after death.

yield   The percentage of return on an investment; also known as return. The dividends or interest paid by a company as a percentage of the current price.

Appendix B

Resources

If this book has served to get you more interested in your personal finances than ever, there are lots of places you can go for additional information and help.

Further Reading

The bookstores, libraries, and online booksellers are loaded with books dealing with nearly every aspect of finances. Listed on the following pages are some good ones to get you started. Also listed are some good Internet sites that deal with personal finance.

Benson, Dan. *12 Stupid Mistakes People Make With Their Money: A Step-by-Step Guide to a Secure Financial Future*. W Publishing Group, 2001.

Berman, Claire, and Deborah Brody. *Caring for Yourself While Caring for Your Elderly Parents: How to Help, How to Survive*. Henry Holt and Company, 1997.

Beyer, Gerry W. *Wills, Trusts, and Estates: Examples and Explanations*. Panel Publishers, 1999.

Bove, Alexander A. *The Complete Guide to Wills, Estates, and Trusts*. Henry Holt and Company, Inc., 2000.

Brill, Marla. *Windfall! Managing Unexpected Money So It Doesn't Manage You*. Alpha Books, 2001.

Carey, Bill, Chantal Howell Carey, and Suzanne Kiffman. *How to Sell Your Home Without a Broker.* John Wiley & Sons, 2000.

Clifford, Denis, and Cora Jordan. *Plan Your Estate.* Nolo.com, 2000.

Edmunds, Gillette. *How to Retire Early and Live Well with Less Than a Million Dollars.* Adams Media Corporation, 2000.

Eilers, Terry. *How to Sell Your Home Fast, for the Highest Price, in Any Market: From a Real Estate Insider Who Knows All the Tricks.* Hyperion, 1997.

Gordon, Robert N., and Jan M. Rosen. *Wall Street Secrets for Tax-Efficient Investing: From Tax Pain to Investment Gain.* Bloomberg Press, 2001.

Heady, Robert K. *The Complete Idiot's Guide to Managing Your Money.* Alpha Books, 2001.

Holzer, Bambi, and Elaine Floyd. *Set for Life: Financial Peace for People Over 50.* John Wiley & Sons, 1999.

———. *Getting Yours: It's Not Too Late to Get the Wealth You Want.* John Wiley & Sons, 2001.

Howe, Coy R. *Money for College Made E-Z.* Made E-Z Products, Inc., 2002.

Kiplinger's Personal Finance Staff. *Retire Worry-Free.* Kiplinger's Books & Tapes, 2001.

Kiyosaki, Robert T., and Sharon L. Lechter. *Rich Dad—Poor Dad: What the Rich Teach Their Kids About Money—That the Poor and Middle Class Do Not.* Warner Books, Inc., 2000.

Koch, Edward T., and Debra DeSalvo. *The Complete Idiot's Guide to Investing Like a Pro.* Alpha Books, 1999.

Leiberman, Trudy, Comsumer Reports Books Editors. *Complete Guide to Health Services for Seniors.* Crown Publishing Group, 2000.

Madlem, Peter W. *Power Investing with Stocks.* St. Lucie Press, 2001.

Maple, Steve M. *The Complete Idiot's Guide to Wills and Estates.* Alpha Books, 1997.

Mintzer, Richard, and Kathi Mintzer. *The Everything Money Book: Learn How to Manage, Budget, Save, and Invest Your Money So There's Plenty Left Over.* Adams Media Corp., 1999.

O'Hara, Shelley, and Nancy D. Warner. *The Complete Idiot's Guide to Buying and Selling a Home, Third Edition.* Alpha Books, 2000.

Orman, Suze. *The 9 Steps to Financial Freedom: Practical and Spiritual Steps So You Can Stop Worrying.* Crown Publishing Group, 1997.

Oz, Tony. *How to Take Money from Wall Street: Learn to Profit in Bull and Bear Markets.* Goldman Brown Business Media, 2001.

Rantz, Marilyn, and Lori Popejoy. *The New Nursing Homes: A 20-Minute Way to Find Great Long-Term Care.* Fairview Press, 2001.

Reed, Terence L. *The 8 Biggest Mistake People Make with Their Finances Before and After Retirement.* Dearborn Financial Publishing, Inc., 2001.

Rhodes, Linda Colvin. *The Complete Idiot's Guide to Caring for Aging Parents.* Alpha Books, 2000.

Robbins, Michael. *Smart Guide to Planning for Retirement.* John Wiley & Sons, 1999.

Rowland, Mary. *A Commonsense Guide to Your 401(k).* Bloomberg Press, 1997.

Savage, Terry. *The Savage Truth on Money.* John Wiley & Sons, 1999.

Schwab, Charles R. *You're Fifty—Now What? Investing for the Second Half of Your Life.* Crown Publishing Group, 2000.

Stav, Julie, and Lisa Rojany Buccieri. *Fund Your Future: Winning Strategies for Managing Your Mutual Funds and 401(k).* Berkley Publishing Group, 2001.

Turkington, Carol, and Sarah Young Fisher. *Everything You Need to Know About Money and Investing: A Financial Expert Answers the 1,001 Most Frequently Asked Questions.* Prentice Hall Press, 1998.

Webb, Martha, and Sarah Parsons. *Dress Your House for Success: 5 Fast, Easy Steps to Selling Your House, Apartment, or Condo for the Highest Possible Price.* Crown Publishing Group, 1997.

Web Sites

Some Web sites that may provide useful information about financial and other topics pertinent to people in middle age:

Bankrate.com
www.bankrate.com
Contains lots of helpful information about mortgages, credit cards, banking, and so forth.

Business Week Online
www.businessweek.com
A good place to find information about various aspects of business and finance.

Collegeboard.com
www.collegeboard.com
A source with information about finding, getting into, and paying for a college.

The College Source
www.thecollegeresource.com
Gives lots of information about locating, choosing, and paying for college.

Edmunds.com
www.edmunds.com/advice/buying/articles/42966/article.html
A great source of information about buying a new or used car, with specific information about cars for teenagers.

Family Money
www.familymoney.com
A source of practical information about budgets and other topics pertaining to your money.

Federal Trade Commission
www.ftc.gov/bcp/conline/pubs/alerts/ucaralrt.htm
An FTC site with information about buying a used car for a teenager.

Genesis
www.genesis-resources.com
A source for people who have lost a loved one, with information about grief, funerals, stress, and so forth.

Internal Revenue Service
www.irs.ustreas.gov
Get information and download forms from this site.

InvestorGuide.com
www.investorguide.com
Calls itself the only investor site you'll need.

Investor's Compass
www.icompass.com
Helps locate information about stocks and mutual funds through company-specific links.

Job Search Guide
www.labor.state.ny.us/html/jssearch/handle
Covers various aspects of losing a job and finding another one.

Lawinfo.com
www.lawinfo.com
Contains information about topics such as survivor's benefits, and more.

Middle-age-spread.com
www.middle-age-spread.com
A fun site with information about health, money, relationships, and so forth; aimed at women over 40.

MoneyCentral
www.moneycentral.msn.com
A source containing good information about money-related topics, including retirement.

The Motley Fool
www.fool.com
Loaded with all types of serious financial information, presented in an user-friendly, humorous manner.

Personal Wealth
www.usatoday.com/money
A guide from *USA Today* for anyone who invests, earns, saves, or spends money.

Prudential Financial
www.prufn.com/realestate/sellingyourhome
Lots of tips and advice about selling your own home.

The Sandwich Generation
members.aol.com/sandwchgen
Contains topics relevant to those juggling the responsibilities of kids, aging parents, jobs, etc.

Small Business Administration
www.sba.gov
A great site for anyone considering starting his or her own business.

Ultimatewedding.com
www.ultimatewedding.com
Covers most aspects of wedding planning, with particular attention to paying for a wedding.

The Wall Street Journal
www.wsj.com
Contains all kinds of business news.

WeddingNet
www.weddingnet.com
Has information about who pays for weddings and related topics, along with links to other wedding sites.

Yahoo! Finance
www.quote.yahoo.com
Provides easy links to many informative financial sites.

Index

THE COMPLETE IDIOT'S GUIDE TO

Arts & Sciences | Business & Personal Finance | Computers & the Internet | Family & Home | Hobbies & Crafts | Language Reference | Health & Fitness | Personal Enrichment | Sports & Recreation | Teens

IDIOTSGUIDES.COM
Introducing a new and different Web site

Millions of people love to learn through *The Complete Idiot's Guide*® books. Discover the same pleasure online in **idiotsguides.com**–part of The Learning Network.

Idiotsguides.com is a new and different Web site, where you can:

- Explore and download more than 150 fascinating and useful mini-guides–FREE! Print out or send to a friend.

- Share your own knowledge and experience as a mini-guide contributor.

- Join discussions with authors and exchange ideas with other lifelong learners.

- Read sample chapters from a vast library of *Complete Idiot's Guide*® books.

- Find out how to become an author.

- Check out upcoming book promotions and author signings.

- Purchase books through your favorite online retailer.

Learning for Fun. Learning for Life.

IDIOTSGUIDES.COM • LEARNINGNETWORK.COM

Copyright © 2000 Pearson Education